Data Analysis with SPSS
A First Course in Applied Statistics

Second Edition

Stephen A. Sweet
Cornell University

Karen Grace-Martin
Cornell University

Boston New York San Francisco
Mexico City Montreal Toronto London Madrid Munich Paris
Hong Kong Singapore Tokyo Cape Town Sydney

Contents

Preface ix

Acknowledgements x

About the Authors x

Chapter 1 • Key Concepts in Social Science Research   1
    Overview   1
    Empiricism and Social Science Research   1
    Data   2
    Developing Research Questions   4
    Theory and Hypothesis   6
    Relationships and Causality   7
        Association   8
        Time Order   8
        Nonspuriousness   8
    Summary   9
    Key Terms   9
    References and Further Reading   10
    Exercises   11

Chapter 2 • Getting Started: Accessing, Examining, and Saving Data   19
    Overview   19
    The Layout of SPSS   19
    Types of Variables   21
        Categorical Variables   22
        Numerical Variables   22
    Defining and Saving a New Data Set   22
    Managing Data Sets: Dropping and Adding Variables   27
    Merging and Importing Files   28
    Loading and Examining an Existing File   29
    Managing Variable Names and Labels   31
    Summary   32
    Key Terms   32
    References and Further Reading   32
    Exercises   33

Chapter 3 • Univariate Analysis: Descriptive Statistics   39
    Overview   39
    Why Do Researchers Perform Univariate Analysis?   39
    Exploring Distributions of Numerical Variables   40
        Listing, Summarizing, and Sorting Observations   40
        Histograms   42
        Stem and Leaf Plots   44
        Shapes of Distributions   46
        Measures of Central Tendency   47
        Measures of Spread   50
        Box Plots   51
    Exploring Distributions of Categorical Variables   53
        Pie Charts   55
        Bar Charts   57
    Summary   58
    Key Terms   59
    References and Further Reading   59
    Exercises   61

Chapter 4 • Constructing Variables   67
    Overview   67
    Why Construct New Variables?   67
    Recoding Existing Variables   67
    Computing New Variables   71
    Recording and Running Computations Using Syntax   76
    Using Compute to Construct an Index with Syntax   78
    Summary   80
    Key Terms   80
    References and Further Reading   80
    Exercises   81

Chapter 5 • Assessing Association through Bivariate Analysis   87
    Overview   87
    Why Do We Need Significance Tests?   87
    Analyzing Bivariate Relationships Between Two Categorical Variables   90
        Cross Tabulations   91
        Bar Charts   95
    Analyzing Bivariate Relationships Between Two Numerical Variables   96
        Correlations   96
        Scatter Plots   100
    Summary   102
    Key Terms   102
    References and Further Reading   102
    Exercises   103

Chapter 6 • Comparing Group Means through Bivariate Analysis   113
    Overview   113
    One-Way Analysis of Variance   113
    Graphing the Results of an ANOVA   115
        Bar Charts   115
        Box Plots   117
    Post-hoc Tests   118
    Assumptions of ANOVA   119
        Independence Assumption   119
        Normality Assumption   120
    T tests   121
        Independent Samples T Test   121
        Paired-Samples T Test   122
    Summary   123
    Key Terms   123
    References and Further Reading   123
    Exercises   125

Chapter 7 • Multivariate Analysis with Linear Regression   131
    Overview   131
    What Are the Advantages of Multivariate Analysis?   131
    When Can I Do a Linear Regression?   132
    Linear Regression: A Bivariate Example   133
    Interpreting Linear Regression Coefficients   135
    Interpreting the R-Square Statistic   135
    Using Linear Regression Coefficients to Make Predictions   135
    Using Coefficients to Graph Bivariate Regression Lines   137
    Multiple Linear Regression   1139
        Interpreting Multiple Linear Regression Coefficients   140
        Interpreting the Adjusted R-Square Statistic   141
        Graphing a Multiple Regression   141
    Other Concerns of Linear Regression   143
        Constant Variance and Normality of Residuals   143
        Building Multivariate Models   145
            Degrees of Freedom   145
            Collinearity   145
        Dummy Variables   146
        Outliers   147
        Causality   147
    Summary   148
    Key Terms   148
    References and Further Reading   148
    Exercises   151

Chapter 8 • Multivariate Analysis with Logistic Regression   157
Overview   157
What Is Logistic Regression?   157
What Are the Advantages of Logistic Regression?   158
When Can I Do a Logistic Regression?   159
Understanding the Relationships through Probabilities   159
Logistic Regression: A Bivariate Example   160
    Interpreting Odds Ratios and Logistic Regression Coefficients   161
    Using Logistic Regression Coefficients to Make Predictions   162
    Using Coefficients to Graph a Logistic Regression Line   164
    Model Chi-Squares and Goodness of Fit   166
Multivariate Logistic Regression: An Example   166
    Using Multivariate Logistic Regression Coefficients to Make Predictions   169
    Using Multivariate Coefficients to Graph a Logistic Regression Line   170
Summary   172
Key Terms   172
References and Further Reading   172
Exercises   173

Chapter 9 • Writing a Research Report   181
Overview   181
Writing Style and Audience   181
The Structure of a Report   182
    The Title   182
    The Abstract   183
    The Introduction   185
    The Literature Review   185
    The Methods   186
    The Findings   187
    The Conclusion   188
    The References   188
Summary   189
Key Terms   189
References and Further Reading   189

Chapter 10 • Research Projects   191
Potential Research Projects   191
Research Project 1: Racism   193
Research Project 2: Suicide   194
Research Project 3: Criminality   195
Research Project 4: Welfare   196
Research Project 5: Sexual Behavior   197
Research Project 6: Education   198
Research Project 7: Your Topic   199

Appendix 1: STATES.SAV Descriptives   201

Appendix 2: GSS98.SAV File Information   209

Appendix 3: Variable Label Abbreviations   231

Permissions   232

Index   233

Preface

This book is written for anyone pursuing a career in the social sciences, as well as those needing to learn the essentials of statistical methods. We have written less about statistics than about how to take real world observations, expose these observations to statistical analysis, and understand how to systematically study social relationships. As such, this book can offer interest to students in psychology, sociology, and education, as well as those in other disciplines relying on statistical methods. We provide an active hands-on approach to learning the skills of data analysis, using the Statistical Package for the Social Sciences (SPSS) and some of the most current data on social behavior available.

We believe that statistics are best learned in *context,* as they are applied to analyzing real world observations. Our hopes are that readers will realize what we learned long ago, that statistical analysis (contrary to popular belief) can be fun. This assertion will strike many readers as surprising and counterintuitive. We think one of the reasons traditional statistics courses are not well received by most students simply stems from focusing too much on the ways statistics are *generated*, and not enough on how statistics are *interpreted*. In contrast to the methods of calculating statistics, the interpretation of statistics involves applying the appropriate statistical methods and then analyzing the results to gain an understanding of people and society.

We also believe that statistics become interesting when they are *applied*. We do not view statistics as a means of testing mathematical skills; rather, our interests concern how statistics can be used to gain understandings of the social world. Do social policies work the way they were intended? Does a social program make a difference? In what ways do different groups of people vary from one another? In this book, we try to chart effective pathways to answering these types of research questions using real data in the same manner that professional social scientists would.

To develop skills, we introduce key concepts and statistical approaches commonly used by social scientists, and then conclude chapters with hands-on exercises. These exercises draw from two data sets, rich with information concerning social behavior. One of these data sets contains hundreds of variables about social behavior in the United States, focusing on differences between states. Among other topics, these data enable analysis of education, criminality, welfare use, health care, taxation, births, mortality, and environmental well-being. The other data set contains nearly 100 variables from the 1998 General Social Survey conducted by the Roper Center for Public Opinion. These data enable analysis of variation in individual experiences and attitudes relating to education, religion, politics, sexuality, race, and taxation. These data sets are used to build analytic skills in a step by step manner, from the initial stages of forming research questions and collecting data through advanced multivariate methods and report writing. As these two large data sets offer abundant information on places and people, they open a vista of possibilities for independent research activities.

Do I Have What It Takes and What Will I Accomplish?

There is something about statistics which seems to spark fear. Computers do likewise. Put the two together and dread may result. This is unfortunate and we believe unnecessary. Some readers (possibly you?) may have a few concerns at this point. Some may be wondering if they need to know how to use a computer to get through the exercises in this book. The short answer is yes, but there is no time like the present to learn! Prior computer experience would be of help, but a basic understanding of how to navigate in a Windows environment will be sufficient to work through the exercises in this book.

Some readers may be concerned that they lack the requisite skills in statistics or math. This text is designed to help you become refined in analyzing quantitative data; therefore existing skills in statistics and math can certainly be a help. However, this book is designed to teach basic statistical inference. Therefore, no prior statistics courses and only modest mathematical capabilities are needed to perform the exercises in this text.

Finally, some readers may wonder why they should bother with this book if they do not plan to become statisticians or social science researchers. On one level, there may be direct benefits. All of us live in a world in which numbers are used to explain our experiences. Even if one becomes an artist, the ability to read statistics critically facilitates making important decisions such as where to locate one's family, what political candidates to vote for, and what drugs should be avoided. In all likelihood, SPSS will not be used to make these decisions, but skills in quantitative data analysis can contribute to making the best informed decision. At a deeper level, understanding how data are analyzed can help all readers develop a critical perspective on how to evaluate arguments based upon quantitative data. Indeed, the real aim of this book is not so much about teaching SPSS. It is to cultivate the skills needed to be a critical consumer of information and to whet the appetite for empirical inquiry.

Acknowledgments

Many people contributed to this book at various stages of its development. Scott Morgan and Kathleen O'Leary Morgan were exceedingly generous in allowing us to reproduce the data presented in their outstanding books: *State Rankings 2000, Health State Rankings 2000,* and *Crime State Rankings 2000.* The Roper Center for Public Opinion Research allowed us to select and include variables from the *1998 General Social Surveys,* data from one of the very best public opinion polls available.

The Cornell Office of Statistical Consulting offered great help. The director, Ed Frongillo, provided excellent suggestions for refining our writing, as well as offered great support for the development of this book. Karen's colleagues Francoise Vermeylen and Yun Wang bore the burden of extra consulting while she wrote.

Our friend and colleague Phyllis Moen offered support as well. With appreciation, we tried our best to incorporate her perspectives on work, family, and life course themes, concerns advanced at the Cornell Employment and Family Careers Institute (Alfred P. Sloan Foundation Grant # 99-6-23).

We owe a deep debt of gratitude to Catherine Soria, who spent many hours arranging data, proofreading, and editing, and re-editing. Also thanks to Alex Pearson and Pavel Krivitsky, who helped organize the data sets. Jeff Lasser, our editor, at Allyn and Bacon, offered excellent advice throughout the project.

Most of all, we thank Karen's husband Michael, and Stephen's wife Jai, who gave unwavering love and support and spent many hours babysitting so we could write.

About the Authors

Stephen Sweet earned his Bachelor's degree in psychology at the State University of New York at Potsdam, and a Master's and Doctoral degree in sociology from the University of

New Hampshire. In addition to working as an Assistant Professor at the State University of New York at Potsdam, he performed a variety of research activities. At the University of New Hampshire he was employed at the *Family Research Lab*, the *Institute for Disability*, and the *Institute for Policy and Social Science Research*. He also worked as a statistical consultant for the New Hampshire Department of Education. His publications include numerous articles on pedagogy, community, work, and family, as well as a book on university life, *College and Society: An Introduction to the Sociological Imagination*. Steve is currently a senior research associate and the associate director of the Cornell Employment and Family Careers Institute, a Sloan Center for the Study of Working Families. He lives in Ithaca, NY with his wife Jai and twin son and daughter, Arjun and Nisha.

Karen Grace-Martin earned a Bachelor's degree in psychology from Union College and Master's degrees in Social Psychology and Applied Statistics from the University of California, Santa Barbara, where she was a National Science Foundation Graduate Fellow. She taught introductory statistics for two years to economics, psychology, and sociology majors at Santa Barbara City College and the University of California, Santa Barbara. She is employed as a statistical consultant in the Office of Statistical Consulting at Cornell University. She lives in Ithaca, NY with her husband Michael and son Julian.

Chapter 1
Key Concepts in Social Science Research

Overview

We begin our introduction to data analysis with the major concepts social scientists use to develop research questions, understand data, and test relationships. We do not detail how to use SPSS in this chapter. Instead, we build a foundation for using SPSS in a manner consistent with the practices of professional social science. This includes adhering to empiricism, the careful consideration of causal relationships, forming testable hypotheses, and developing valid and reliable measures. All of these concerns are relevant to analyzing the data provided in this book and successfully launching an independent research project.

Empiricism and Social Science Research

Most social scientists spend their professional lives studying the human condition. Sometimes they study the occurrence of conditions or behaviors, such as the degree to which families experience poverty, the frequency of criminal behaviors, or the proportion of the population attaining educational degrees. Gathering this information over time allows researchers to identify trends and predict future patterns. In other circumstances, they test relationships—the ways in which one set of conditions or behaviors potentially affects another. For example, criminologists identify the factors that predict crime and assess the outcomes of treatment programs. Poverty researchers assess the impact of programs or policies on social relations, especially among poor people and their communities. Similarly, one of the key concerns for education researchers is identifying factors that contribute to success in attaining high school and college degrees. These efforts require rigorous methods of observation and analysis, which are, in a word, **empirical**. The doctrine of empiricism asserts that the combination of logic and observation builds understanding.

The empirical nature of scientific inquiry created the need for statistical analysis—methods for understanding and linking observations with one another. Statistics developed because scientists agreed that it was not enough to think abstractly about how the physical and social worlds operate or to take everyday beliefs as true, but to expose beliefs to systematic measurement and rigorous analysis. Statistics is one means of critically studying how well beliefs correspond to real world circumstances.

Social scientists face considerable challenges as they strive to be empiricists. They should hold a steadfast commitment to logic and observation, and not advance politics or self-interest. It is natural to want to find results that support personal beliefs or values. However, as empiricists, scientists strive to carefully report the picture of the social world that is revealed in analyses, no matter what the implications. For instance, suppose we believed that the death penalty was an effective deterrent to crime and began a series of analyses to test our beliefs. If our results concluded the opposite, we would be obligated to report it. As the sociologist Max Weber explained (Gerth and Mills 1967), social scientists are obligated to be **value neutral** in their research. Empiricists set aside their egos and politics when they begin data analysis.

Data

This book offers an introduction to social science research by applying statistical applications to the study of two data sets, one documenting the characteristics of people, the other documenting characteristics of places. We depart from traditional methods for teaching statistics by focusing less on statistical calculations and more on how to understand what statistics reveal. We try to create a context where newcomers can apply rigorous statistical methods to their own empirical studies. This research-oriented approach teaches the skills needed for data analysis in an applied fashion. Toward this end the data sets included with this book are structured to enable newcomers to immediately use statistics and put them to practical use.

One data set, the **General Social Survey (GSS98) data**, contains information on people. These data are based on telephone interviews of men and women who responded to a series of questions concerning their attitudes, behaviors, and beliefs. Questions include, among other things, demographic information such as ethnicity, income, age, and education. Other questions tap into beliefs and behaviors, such as the degree to which individuals hold prejudicial attitudes and the amount of television they watch. Because these measures were developed through years of testing and because the respondents are drawn from a nationally representative sample of households, these data are among the very best available. The other data set, the **STATES data**, contains information on states and the types of people residing there. This information includes poverty rates, alcohol sales, crime rates, and a variety of other information about life within each state. The sources of these data include the U.S. Census, National Education Association, Department of Labor, the Internal Revenue Service, and the U.S. Department of Health and Human Services. These are among the most reliable sources of information on the social condition of the nation.

These two files are **data sets**, organized collections of information. This book addresses how to approach a data set in a systematic manner and how to launch a research project involving statistical analysis. Any research project requires collecting and understanding **data**, pieces of organized information about elements in a population (a **datum** is a single piece of information). We have taken care of the first task and collected some of the best quality data available to date on people and places. In fact, these two data sets are comparable, and in many instances identical, to the types of data that professional social scientists use to study social life. They are also the types of data policy makers use to inform legislative decisions. Our hopes are that these data will also help novice researchers understand statistics and how data analysis is applied in social science research. Those already beginning to think about research projects may find it useful to skim the appendices at the end of this book, where the data sets are described in greater detail, and to see if these can provide information to correspond with existing research interests. For others, this information may help kindle ideas and spark the imagination for a wide variety of potential projects.

Data sets are structured to link cases with variables. A **case** is the individual unit being studied. Each case has one datum, or **observation**, for each variable. For the GSS98 data, each case is an individual person. In the STATES data, each case is the individual state, such as New Hampshire. **Variables** contain information about each case and are structured in a way that makes one case comparable to another. For instance, in the GSS98 data, all of the respondents were asked their age, and as a result, one could compare any one respondent's age with that of another. The STATES data have a variable indicating crime rates, and therefore states can be ranked in terms of how much crime occurs within their geographic areas. When data are collected in a systematic manner, researchers can analyze the patterns between variables. For instance, having information on crime rates and whether the death penalty exists in the fifty states allows a researcher to analyze the relationship between these variables.

Although these two data sets are available in this book, and can help expedite many research projects, there are many other sources of data available over the Internet. As researchers consider using these resources, they need to consider their strengths and weaknesses, as data quality can vary markedly. Empiricists understand that the goals in research should be to gather and construct data that are of the highest quality. It is not enough to have any data. Data should be well suited to the issues of interest. Selecting data sets and variables is challenging, as the quality of these choices will influence the acceptability of all subsequent research activities. Even with the application of the most sophisticated statistical methods, the acronym GIGO holds true: garbage in, garbage out.

When selecting variables for study, the scientist strives to find **indicators** that best capture abstract concepts. For example, studies of criminality require using some indication of the occurrence of crime. One possibility is to use data from surveys assessing victimization, asking people if they have ever been crime victims. As many crimes are never reported to the police, this indicator will likely offer different information than arrest records or police reports. Studies of educational achievement could involve examining grade point averages, graduation rates, or scores on standardized tests.

As researchers select and construct indicators, they strive to make them as reliable and valid as possible. **Reliability** refers to the degree to which an indicator is a consistent measuring device. It is no accident that carpenters use metal tape measures instead of strings and navigators use compasses instead of star gazing. Strings and stars work, but not nearly with the consistency offered by the other methods. The same concern extends to social research, and researchers strive to select consistent tools for measuring concepts such as alienation, alcohol consumption, and depression. Consider the implications of assessing educational achievement by asking students "how well do you do in school?" Unless all students use the same standards for self-assessment, the results for different students might not reflect their achievements, but rather the different standards they hold for what counts as achievement. In such circumstances the reliability of this measure becomes questionable. For this reason, SAT scores, or other standardized test scores, tend to be favored. Similarly, one could conceivably measure school funding by asking individual property owners how much they pay in school taxes. As this indicator would rely on the homeowner's memory, the degree to which this indicator provides accurate assessments would certainly be inferior to the types of data one could collect at a town clerk's office.

Validity refers to the indicator measuring what it is supposed to measure. No one uses a steel ruler to measure temperature, simply because it was never designed for that purpose. Although this concern seems straightforward enough, novice researchers sometimes select indicators that are loosely related to the abstract concept they are really interested in studying. For example, IQ scores are sometimes erroneously used to measure educational achievement. Poverty is inappropriately used as a measure of criminality. The error in both examples is confusing a preconceived relationship with the variables intended to be measured.

To recap, social science is built on an adherence to empiricism, and for many studies this requires the use of statistics. Statistics are used to measure patterns of individual variables and relationships between variables. As social scientists develop studies, they set aside their personal agendas in favor of a dispassioned analysis of data, reporting results accurately and without bias. As they develop their research projects, they select data sets that will offer the most accurate indicators for the concepts they are interested in studying, seeking variables that are reliable (consistent) and valid (appropriate).

Developing Research Questions

We suspect that anyone who was asked why teenagers drop out of school could offer a number of plausible ideas. Some likely causes are overcrowding of classes, insufficient funding for schools, a loss of respect for authority, drugs, boring textbooks, influence of gangs, racial discrimination, and so on. Everybody has theories that they use to explain patterns of social behavior. Indeed, symbolic interactionists have long argued that without constant theory making, people would have great difficulty creating meaningful social encounters (Blumer 1969). What distinguishes social science researchers from armchair theorists is the degree of formality they use in constructing their research questions and the rigor with which they expose their theories to systematic study (Sweet 2001).

The initial step in any research project is to identify the **research question**. Developing a research question involves taking an issue, often something most people take for granted, and posing it in the form of a question. Developing a research question puts a researcher on a pathway of knowledge. Questions highlight a void, or an absence of understanding. The job of scientists is to fill this void and to resolve or explain something that, until the question was raised, was left unanswered. The research question should drive social science inquiry, not the desire to establish a particular finding as "true."

Research questions are actually very liberating for the scientist. There is a very big difference between starting a study with the intent of showing, for instance, that capital punishment is beneficial to society, and starting a study with a question "Is capital punishment an effective deterrent to crime?" The first framework leads a researcher to selectively gather information to support his or her existing stance. In contrast, by making the effects of the death penalty the question, the researcher creates a condition that forces him or her to think critically about the types of information to gather and the relationships to test. As a result, the researcher becomes unencumbered from the desire to report only the information that supports a predetermined conclusion, and creates a situation where curiosity drives analysis.

Social scientists pose questions so that unexpected results can emerge and be seriously considered. "Is there racial discrimination in the education system?" is a much better way to pose a research project than "I want to show that there is discrimination in the education system." When the research project is posed as a question it assists the researchers' efforts to identify a clear analytic strategy, and to think critically about the types of information needed to test relationships. In the process of developing a research question, novice researchers (as well as seasoned scientists) often realize that their initial ideas are too broad to be managed in one study. They can then parse out their main question into manageable subquestions, and select those questions that they are most interested in immediately pursuing. For example, some interesting subquestions about discrimination in education are:

Is there an equitable representation of minority groups within the curriculum?

Is there proportionate employment of minority members in school systems?

To what extent do graduation rates vary among racial groups?

Do minority school districts receive comparable funding to those in predominantly white school districts?

As a researcher works toward developing a study, it is important to perform a **literature review** in the early phases of the project. The literature review is an overview of past research on topics relating to the research question. The best sources for literature reviews will be scholarly journals such as *The American Journal of Sociology*, *Child Development*, *Journal of Marriage and the Family*, and *Journal of Health and Social Behavior*, to name a few. Most articles in scholarly journals have a detailed description of how data were collected and offer extensive references to other related studies. These sources are available through key word searches of computer databases located in university libraries.

The literature review does three things. First, it helps the researcher appreciate the knowledge that has been gained on a subject to date. Second, the literature review informs the researcher of the methods and analyses other scholars used to answer similar research questions. Finally, it helps researchers contribute to the cumulative building of knowledge by integrating current research activities with previous literature. When researchers examine the literature and identify questions that still need to be answered or methods that have yet to be tried, they position themselves to perform new and vital work.

One of the best strategies for novice researchers is to formalize a tentative research question. This should be made into a single question, such as "to what degree does X influence Y?" or "does X lead to Y?" or "what factors contribute to Y?" Once the question is formalized (ideally in writing), the researcher should do a literature review, surveying what others have written on the subject. Although this initially may seem like adding work to the data analysis project, in the long run it will save effort and create a more meaningful and higher quality study. Remember that existing studies offer examples of ways to develop research projects, as well as highlight considerations germane to the project.

Theory and Hypothesis

Finding answers to research questions involves developing theories and hypotheses. According to traditional scientific canons, a **theory** is an unproven explanation of facts or phenomena. Theories should generate **hypotheses,** falsifiable statements concerning expected relationships. Hypotheses should be structured in anticipation that they will be supported or refuted when exposed to some type of test. They are also structured in such a way that when the test is performed, unexpected results can potentially occur and the preexisting beliefs will not necessarily be supported. In a word, hypotheses should be constructed so that they are falsifiable.

Many social scientists use the **deductive approach**, using a theory to develop a number of hypotheses to be tested before they begin their data analysis. For example, we might theorize that inequities in school funding lead minority groups to perform, on average, worse in school than white students. The theory helps us formulate some hypotheses. Some reasonable hypotheses are:

H1:   States with higher proportions of African Americans and Hispanics will have lower school funding.

H2:   States with higher levels of school funding will have higher graduation rates.

H3:   States with higher levels of school funding will have students performing better on standardized tests.

Note that each hypothesis is written so that it is testable and can be refuted. Falsifiability is important because it allows unexpected findings to emerge and our expectations to be challenged in the light of critical observation.

Another illustration can be drawn from the theory that the death penalty is effective at deterring crime. This theory produces the following testable hypotheses:

H1:   States that have the death penalty will have lower property crime rates.

H2:   States that have the death penalty will have lower murder rates.

H3:   States that have the death penalty will have fewer criminals reenter jail after being released (have lower "recidivism" rates).

It is important to acknowledge that not all scientists follow the deductive approach when analyzing data, and that some social scientists follow an **inductive approach** termed **grounded theory** (Glaser and Straus 1967). Grounded theory, like traditional deductive social research, relies upon hypotheses, indicators, and well-formed research questions. However, unlike the traditional deductive approach, tentative theories are based on data and researchers continually refine the theories to concur with analyses. The research project ends when the researcher understands the relationships in the data and develops a theory that explains these relationships. **Exploratory data analysis** is similar in intent (Hoaglin, Mosteller, and Tukey 1983). Advocates suggest that prior to running advanced statistical procedures for a critical test of a hypothesis, researchers should get involved with the data and explore relationships using highly visual depictions of relationships.

Which is better—the more traditional deductive approach or the inductive approach? One is not necessarily better, nor are they as independent as is often supposed. We think that novice researchers can benefit from using both approaches in their own data analyses. After developing a research question, the next step is to briefly explain what they think the answer will be before beginning analysis to create a rudimentary theory. Then the theory can be parsed out into testable hypotheses, made in consideration of the available data. This step-by-step process is reflective of the deductive approach. However, once the novice researcher has developed or accessed a data set, he or she can also do some exploratory work, testing relationships with a bit more freedom, exploring the data and relationships within the data set. This exploration is not the end in itself; rather, it can open the mind to different types of relationships and to theories that might explain these relationships.

Relationships and Causality

Most social science research is about **causal relationships**, how a particular set of conditions leads to predictable outcomes. Seldom will such relationships be **deterministic**, producing inevitable results. More often, social science documents **probabilistic relationships**, in which factors increase tendencies toward particular outcomes. For example, consider the conclusion that education increases income. If this were a deterministic relationship, everyone with a college degree would have higher incomes than everyone with a high school degree. This, of course, is not the case. But it *is* the case that those with college degrees *tend* to earn more than those with high school degrees.

How does one determine if a relationship is causal? Answering this question requires identifying the relationships between independent and dependent variables. **Independent variables** are hypothesized to cause changes in **dependent variables**. We have already discussed a number of hypothesized causal relationships, such as the death penalty deterring crime and school funding increasing educational success. Diagrams of these relationships would be:

Independent Variable   **Dependent Variable**

Death Penalty $\overset{-}{\longrightarrow}$ Crime

Independent Variable   **Dependent Variable**

School Funding $\overset{+}{\longrightarrow}$ Educational Success

The very same indicators can switch from being independent variables to dependent variables, depending upon the research question being addressed. For example, increased educational success could potentially lead to lower crime rates:

Independent Variable   **Dependent Variable**

Educational Success $\overset{-}{\longrightarrow}$ Crime

Understanding the differences between independent and dependent variables is crucial. To assert a causal relationship is to claim that changes in the independent variable create changes in the dependent variable. In practice, researchers should only assert that one factor causes changes in another variable when they can reasonably satisfy the following three criteria:

> 1. *Association*: there must be a relationship between the independent and dependent variables.
> 2. *Time order*: the change in the independent variable must precede the change in the dependent variable.
> 3. *Nonspuriousness*: the effect of a third unmeasured "spurious" factor does not produce the relationship between two variables.

Association

When two variables are associated with one another, both variables correspond in predictable ways. **Associations** can either be **positive** (an increase in one variable corresponds with an increase in the other) or **negative** (an increase in one variable corresponds with a decrease in the other variable). For instance, the statement "people with higher degrees tend to have higher incomes" is a statement of positive association. "People who achieve higher levels of education tend to be less prejudiced" is a statement of negative association. Note that neither statement claims a causal relationship, only that changes in the variables correspond with one another.

It is important to note that many associations are not causal. For instance red cars are in more accidents than white cars. It isn't the red cars that are causing the accidents, it is the tendency of aggressive drivers to purchase these red cars and get into accidents (see below).

Time Order

When a change in one variable causes another variable change, logically, the independent variable needs to change before the dependent variable. For instance, the statement "instituting the death penalty will decrease crime" is a statement implying time order. Making this assertion requires having measurements of criminality at two points in time, prior to the institutionalization of the death penalty and after the death penalty has been enacted. The issue of time order seems straightforward enough. However, establishing time order can be difficult because most data are only collected at one point in time. As such, asserting the existence of a causal relationship has to be done with care. Also, as time often introduces changes in other variables, even when this condition is satisfied, causality may still not be the case (see below).

Nonspuriousness

A **spurious relationship** exists when two variables appear to be causally related, but that relationship is caused by the presence of a third unmeasured variable. In spurious relationships, if the third unmeasured variable is taken into account, the relationship between the initial two variables disappears. A classic example of a spurious relationship is that of ice cream consumption causing drowning deaths. There is an association between ice cream consumption and drowning (more people drown during times when a lot of ice cream is being consumed). The time order issue can also be satisfied (increases in ice cream sales precede increases in drowning deaths). Of course the unmeasured factor in this relationship is temperature. More people swim in the summer and more ice cream is consumed in the summer. It is in fact the warm weather operating as a spurious factor, causing both variables to increase.

Spuriousness is difficult to rule out, simply because it is impossible to account for every variable that could produce the relationship. In actual practice, good research involves measuring the factors that are theoretically likely to produce a spurious relationship. For example, even though sunspots *might* have an effect on the behavior a researcher is studying, there is no theoretical reason for this assumption, so there is no need to account for it in the analysis. However, because factors such as income and education may have a profound impact on many aspects of social life, controlling for these factors in statistical analyses is generally a good idea.

The central concern we highlight here is that researchers should be careful before they conclude that they have shown causal relationships. All three of the above criteria must be satisfied. Experimental studies, in which people are randomized to two or more groups, are valuable because they ensure time order and nonspuriousness. However, because experimental studies can rarely be done, the social sciences primarily rely on observational studies. When writing and discussing findings, therefore, always be careful about using the word "cause."

Summary

Social science research hinges on the careful construction of research questions, the pursuit of the highest quality data, and the best analytic strategies. It requires researchers to think critically about their beliefs and assumptions about the ways the social world operates. This involves creating theories and distilling them into testable hypotheses. When hypotheses are constructed, data need to be gathered and organized in a manner that will enable statistical tests. Even after statistical analyses are performed, researchers have to reflect on their methodology and assess the degree to which any relationships observed can be attributed to causal processes, or if there are other potential explanations for any patterns observed in the analysis.

Key Terms

Association
Case
Causal relationship
Data
Datum
Data set
Deductive approach
Dependent variable
Deterministic relationship
Empirical
Exploratory data analysis
Grounded theory
Hypothesis
Independent variable
Indicators

Inductive approach
Literature review
Negative association
Observation
Positive association
Probabilistic relationship
Reliability
Research question
Spurious relationship
Theory
Time order
Validity
Value neutral
Variable

References and Further Reading

Babbie, Earl. 1998. *The Practice of Social Research, 8th Edition*. Boston: Wadsworth.

Blumer, Herbert. 1969. *Symbolic Interactionism: Perspective and Method*. Englewood Cliffs, New Jersey: Prentice-Hall.

Glaser, Barney and Anselm Straus. 1967. *The Discovery of Grounded Theory*. Chicago: Aldine.

Hoaglin, David, Frederick Mosteller, and John W. Tukey. 1983. *Understanding Robust and Exploratory Data Analysis*. New York: Wiley.

Neuman, W. Lawrence. 1997. *Social Research Methods: Qualitative and Quantitative Approaches*. Boston: Allyn and Bacon.

Sweet, Stephen. 2001. *College and Society: An Introduction to the Sociological Imagination*. Boston: Allyn and Bacon.

U.S. Department of Commerce. 2000. *Statistical Abstract of the United States*. Washington, DC: U.S. Government Printing Office.

Chapter 1 Exercises

Name ——————————————————————   Date ——————————

1. Identify the independent and dependent variables in the following research projects:

    A.   A study seeks to find out if listening to heavy metal music causes teenagers to become more violent than their peers who do not listen to heavy metal music.

    ————————————   ————————————

    Independent Variable   Dependent Variable

    B.   A group of researchers is interested in examining the effects of long-term poverty. They do this by studying subjects' physiological health and attachment to the workforce.

    ————————————   ————————————

    Independent Variable(s)   Dependent Variable(s)

    C.   A study finds that self-esteem increases as a consequence of receiving good grades on examinations.

    ————————————   ————————————

    Independent Variable   Dependent Variable

2. Indicators are used to measure abstract concepts. List some indicators that might prove to be reliable and valid in measuring the following concepts:

        A. Economic Prosperity   E.g., Gross National Product

_____

_____

_____

        B. Family Violence   E.g., Admissions to Battered Women's Shelters

_____

_____

_____

3. Using Appendix 1, identify the variable labels and variable names from the STATES data that might be good indicators for the following concepts:

A. Educational Attainment

_____

Variable Name   Variable Label

_____

Variable Name   Variable Label

_____

Variable Name   Variable Label

B. Health

_____

Variable Name   Variable Label

_____

Variable Name   Variable Label

_____

Variable Name   Variable Label

4. Using Appendix 2, identify the variable labels and variable names from the GSS98 data that might be good indicators for the following concepts:

A. Religious Commitment

_____   _____
Variable Name   Variable Label

B. Prejudice

_____   _____
Variable Name   Variable Label

C. Sexual Activity

_____   _____
Variable Name   Variable Label

_____   _____
Variable Name   Variable Label

5. Can you identify a potential spurious factor that may call the following findings into question? Explain.

Researchers have found a consistent relationship between schools and crime. More crimes occur in neighborhoods surrounding high schools and junior high schools than in neighborhoods far away from schools. The researchers conclude that schools cause crime and believe that this relationship may have something to do with teachers not teaching students the appropriate lessons in the classroom.

6. The U.S. Department of Justice has found that of the children killed by their parents, 55% of the murders were performed by the child's mother and 45% of the murders were performed by the child's father. A researcher uses these data to support his contention that women are more violent than men. On the basis of these data, do you find this argument compelling? Why or why not?

7. A social commentator argues that the welfare programs introduced in the mid 1960s have caused an unparalleled expansion of poverty in the United States. Based on the following data from the *Statistical Abstract of the United States 2000*, would you agree or disagree with this causal statement? Explain.

Year	Percent Below Poverty Level
1960	22%
1965	15%
1970	13%
1975	12%
1980	13%
1985	14%
1990	14%
1995	14%
1998	13%

8. Select one of the following questions:

What causes crime?
What influences educational success?
Who is most likely to be religious?
Who is most likely to be politically liberal?

A. Develop a brief theory explaining what you think is a likely explanation.

B. List a few hypotheses that might be used to test this theory.

C. Identify any variables (using the Appendixes as the end of the book) that might be used to test the theory.

_____   _____
Variable Name   Variable Label

_____   _____
Variable Name   Variable Label

_____   _____
Variable Name   Variable Label

_____   _____
Variable Name   Variable Label

Chapter 2
Getting Started: Accessing, Examining, and Saving Data

Overview

This chapter is an introduction to SPSS and the data included with this book. When you complete the exercises in this chapter, you will know how to access data sets and evaluate the indicators included with this text. We also discuss some useful strategies for making data sets accessible, including naming, labeling, and defining variables.

We suggest that you work through the chapters with the SPSS program running on your computer. As we describe the commands, try them on your computer. Feel free to explore, as mistakes are never fatal (assuming you remember to save and back up your files—always a good practice!). The chapter will conclude with some guided exercises, reviewing some of the operations outlined here.

The Layout of SPSS

When the SPSS program starts, the program automatically opens to the **SPSS Data Editor Window**. This screen looks and operates like spreadsheet programs. Because there are no data in the SPSS program when it initially starts, the grid is empty and the Data Editor Window says "Untitled." Your screen should look like Figure 2.1.

SPSS for Windows is menu driven and the program is designed to fulfill common requests easily. There are two types of menus at the top of the window. The **menu bar** contains organized paths to the most commonly requested procedures, such as opening files, performing statistical operations, and constructing graphs. As we work through the SPSS program, you will learn many of the commands in the menu bar. You can explore some of these by drawing the cursor to a command category, such as *File* (Figure 2.2) or *Analyze* (Figure 2.3). To perform any command, hold the mouse button down, move the cursor to the command you wish to perform, and release the button. SPSS will ask for the specific information it needs to perform that command. This usually includes the variables included in the analysis and the types of output to be reported.

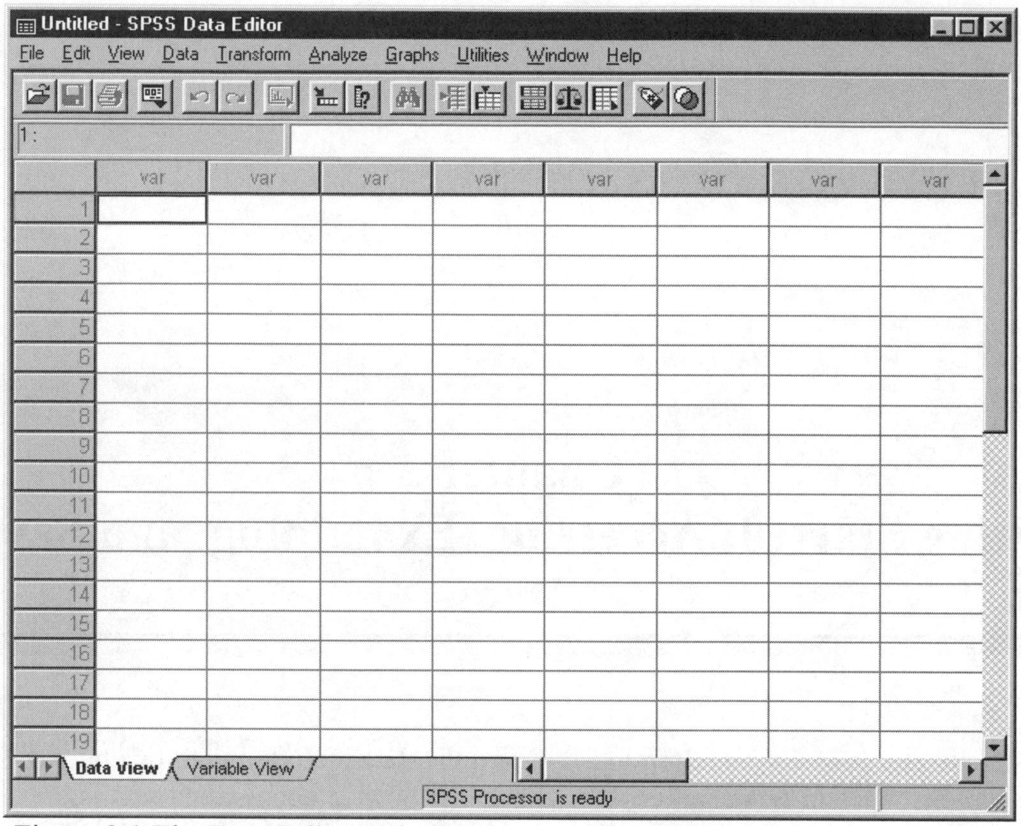

Figure 2.1 The Data Editor Window

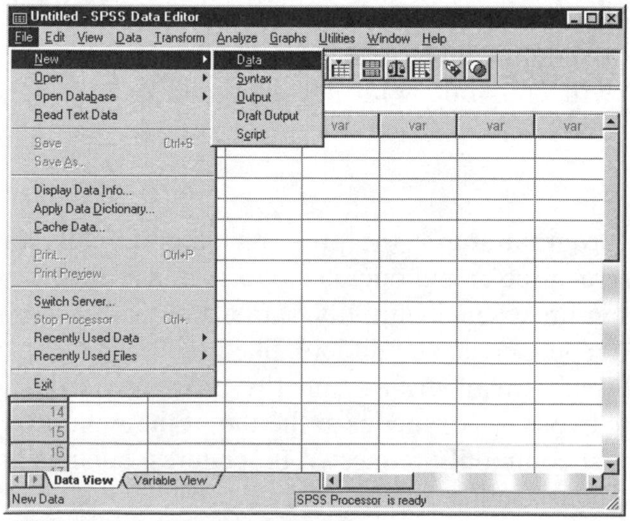

Figure 2.2 File Commands

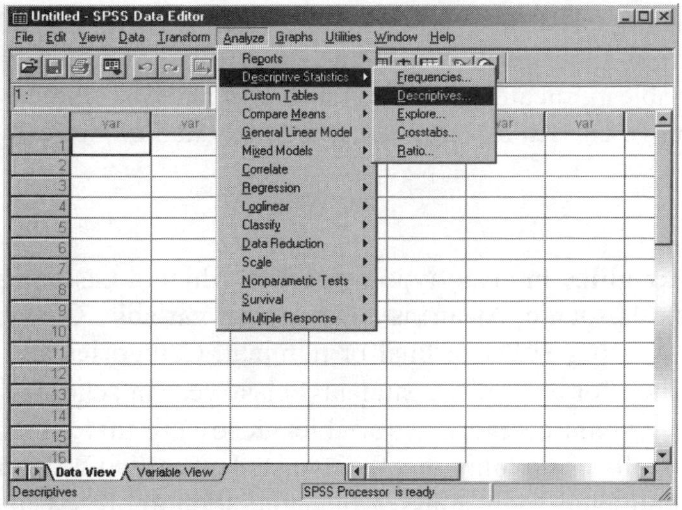

Figure 2.3 Statistics Commands

In this book, we use a shorthand method of describing how to locate specific commands. For instance, if we want you to open a new data file, you will see the following:

> *File*
> > *New*
> > > *Data*

This is a shorthand way of saying: go to the *File* command in the main menu, hold down the mouse button, move the cursor to highlight *New,* and then move the cursor to highlight *Data*. Upon releasing the mouse button, you will have told SPSS to open a new data file and SPSS will give you a window in which you can enter the pertinent information.

Beneath the menu bar is the **tool bar**. This works like the menu and it includes a number of handy devices that refine the analyses. We will not worry about using the tool bar, but as you become more familiar with the program, you will probably find yourself curious about the types of things the tool bar can do. Feel free to experiment.

Not incidentally, there is another way to run commands in SPSS called **syntax commands**. Unlike the menu driven procedures, syntax commands require a greater familiarity with the particular terminology and phrasing necessary for SPSS to perform statistical procedures. It is likely that your professor first learned to use SPSS on earlier versions of the program, which relied exclusively on these syntax commands. For complex and repetitive procedures, this is still the most efficient way to work with SPSS (in fact, this was how we constructed the data sets included in your package). However, for the purposes of the current activities, you will probably be served well by concentrating solely on the menu commands. We will introduce syntax later, as it can be helpful in advanced operations.

Types of Variables

SPSS requires formatting the data so rows in the data editor window represent cases and columns represent variables. Recall from Chapter 1 that **cases** are the units being studied, such as people, organizations, states, or countries. **Variables** are the characteristics being measured for these cases, such as age and gender for people, or per capita income and mortality rates for states. There are several variable types, each reflecting different ways of assessing and documenting information about each case. One useful way of thinking about variables is to reflect on whether variables indicate categories (such as gender or ethnicity) or numbers (such as age or income). These two classes of variables, categorical and numerical, often require different types of statistical analyses.

Categorical Variables

Categorical variables indicate typologies into which a case might fall. For example, ethnicity (White, Black, Hispanic, Asian) is a categorical variable. Categorical variables can be further distinguished as being either ordinal or nominal. Categories are considered ordinal if there is an order to them. For example, a student's class year in school—freshman, sophomore, junior, or senior, is an ordinal categorical variable. Knowing that one student is a senior and another is a sophomore tells us not only that the two students are in different class years, but also that the senior has completed more classes than the sophomore. Categorical variables are considered nominal if they do not indicate any order. A student's major is an example of a nominal categorical variable. It categorizes the student and gives information only about what a student is studying, but there is no logical order to psychology, sociology, history, or biology majors. Ethnicity is another example of a nominal variable.

Numerical Variables

Numerical variables give information indicating the quantity of a concept being measured. For example, the number of years a person has spent in school is a numerical variable, as is the number of miles a car can go on a gallon of gas. There are two types of numerical variables: count and continuous. Count variables indicate a numerical count and take on the values of whole numbers. For example, the number of classes a student is taking is a count variable. A student can take 3 or 4 classes, but cannot take 3.7 classes.

Continuous variables indicate how much of something exists and can have any value within a range. Continuous variables, therefore, are not restricted to whole numbers. For example, the number of years a student has been in school is a continuous variable. A student could have been in school 13.00 or 13.72 years. The possible values are restricted to a range – the minimum possible value is 0 if a student was just beginning school and the maximum is about 100 (if a very old person was in school his or her entire life). Note, though, that any value between 0 and 100 years is possible, including decimal values. And since decimals are possible, a continuous variable can have an infinite number of possible values (13.72 is a different value than 13.721). Miles per gallon is another example of a continuous variable.

Defining and Saving a New Data Set

With this information on the structure of data sets, we can begin to work with data in the SPSS environment. The first step is to load a data set into the statistical package. There are two ways to do this: manually entering a new data set or opening an already constructed data set.

Data entry immediately follows data collection in a research project. It is also a good way to get a feel for the structure of the SPSS program and how the system operates. In this exercise, we outline the processes involved in constructing a new data set. To illustrate the process, you will generate a data set about your family members. Your data set will contain four variables: Person, Sex, Birth Date, and Education. Each family member will constitute one case in the data set. In the event that your family is very small, you could also include friends or other relatives.

The data editor contains two spreadsheets – the **Data View** and the **Variable View** spreadsheets. The default spreadsheet is *Data View*, which displays the actual data (Figure 2.4). The rows designate the cases, and the columns designate the variables. The variable names will be at the top of each column. The *Variable View* spreadsheet contains information about each variable (Figure 2.5). Each row of the spreadsheet refers to a variable from your data set and each column contains certain information about that variable.

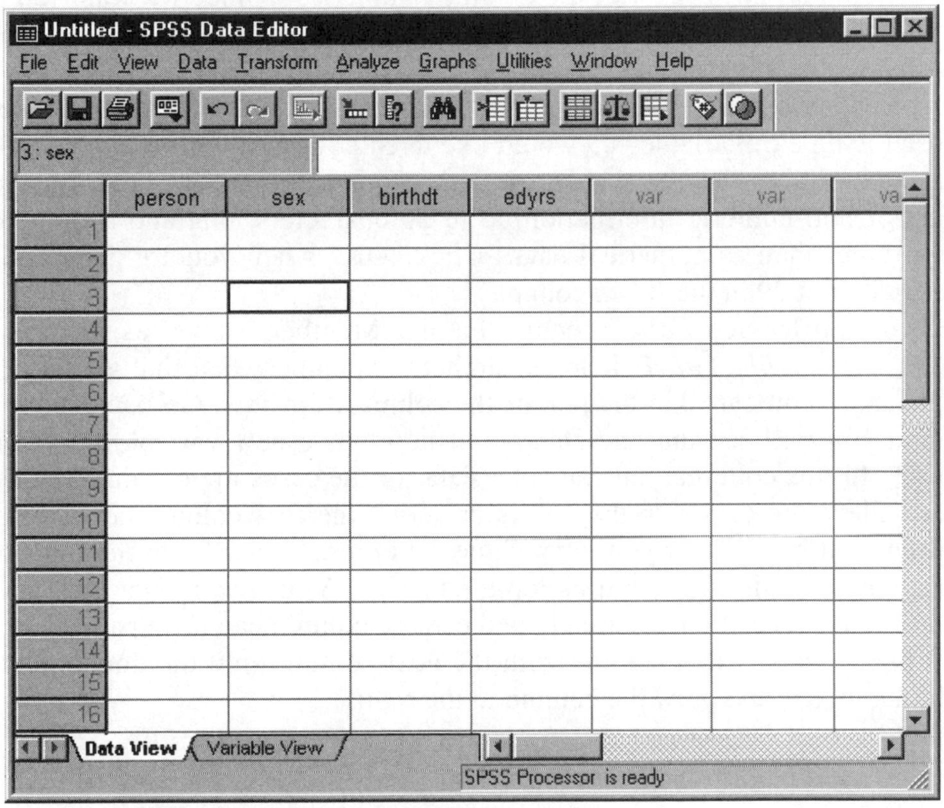

Figure 2.4 The Data View Spreadsheet

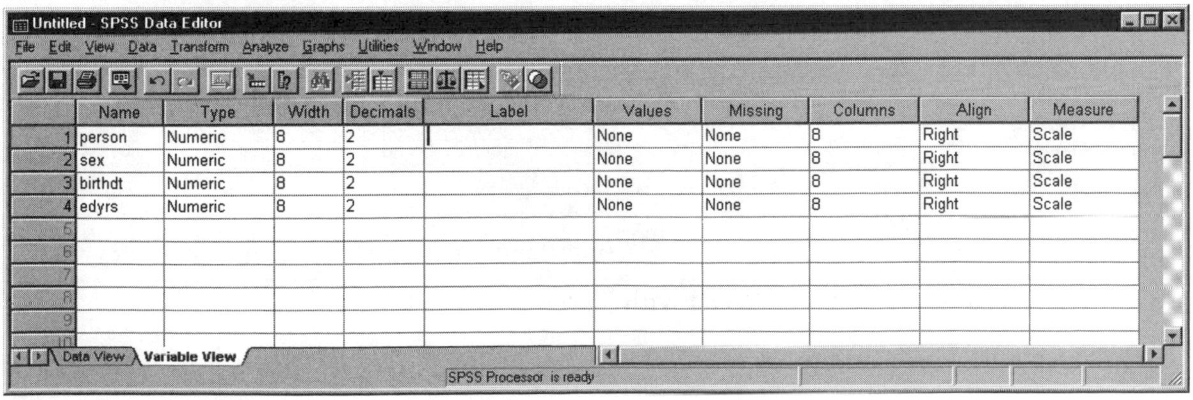

Figure 2.5 The Variable View Spreadsheet

To define the variables in your data set, enter the *Variable View* spreadsheet. There are two ways to open this spreadsheet. The first is to double click the cursor onto the top of any column of the *Data Editor* window. The second way (and the way to get back to the *Data View* when in *Variable View*) is to click on the *Variable View* tab in the lower left corner of the screen.

Once you are in *Variable View,* you can start defining variables. In the column labeled *Name,* enter "Person". A variable name is restricted to 8 letters, must contain no spaces or symbols, and must start with a letter. Press the enter key or click on the next box to move to the next column. You will notice that many boxes in the rest of the row fill in automatically with default values, some of which we will change.

The next column is *Type,* with the default "Numeric." Since we want to enter text for people's names, not numbers, we have to change the default type. If we do not, SPSS will only let us enter numbers for this variable back in the *Data View* spreadsheet. To change the default, click on the small gray box that appears next to "Numeric." A window will pop open, in which you can choose the type of variable you would like to enter. Since we want to enter text, choose "String" and enter "20" in the box for *Characters*. This informs SPSS that this variable will contain strings of non-numeric information up to 20 characters long and that the data can be treated as text rather than as numerical data. Click "OK" when you are done and notice that SPSS automatically put 20 in the *Width* column.

In the column labeled *Labels,* enter "Family Member Name" as the *Variable Label* (Figure 2.6). The **Variable Labels** help researchers remember what that abbreviated variable name really means. You can skip the rest of the columns for now. Go back to the *Data View* spreadsheet and you will see that the *Data View* now has a new variable in the first column called "Person." In this column, you can enter data for the cases in your data set, the names of your relatives. Place the cursor in the box intersecting the first column and the first row and click to highlight that box. Enter your own name, and press "Enter." In the rows below, enter your spouse's, parents', siblings', and children's names. Your *Data View* spreadsheet should look similar to Figure 2.7. If names are clipped off, the column can be expanded by placing the cursor at the intersection of this column with the next column until the double arrow appears; click and hold the mouse and draw the column to the right.

	Name	Type	Width	Decimals	Label	Values	Missing	Columns	Align	Measure
1	person	Numeric	8	2	Family member's name	None	None	8	Right	Scale
2	sex	Numeric	8	2		None	None	8	Right	Scale
3	birthdt	Numeric	8	2		None	None	8	Right	Scale
4	edyrs	Numeric	8	2		None	None	8	Right	Scale
5										
6										
7										

Figure 2.6 The Variable View Spreadsheet with Variable Label Entered

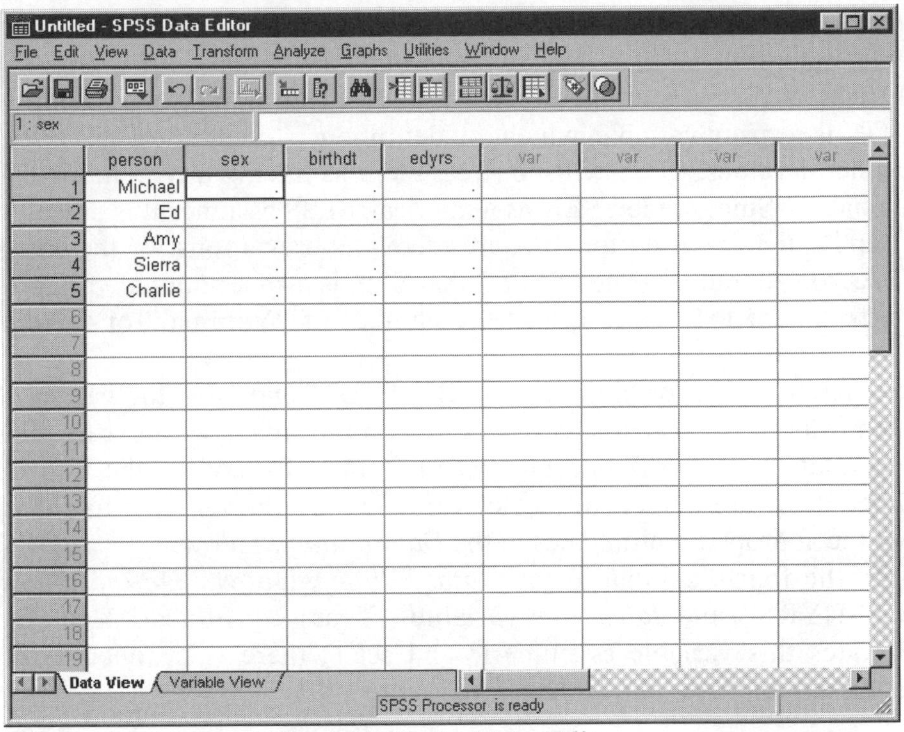

Figure 2.7 Entry of Names with the Data Editor

The other variables can be entered in a similar manner. Return to the *Variable View* spreadsheet, define the next variable as "SEX," and *label* it as "Sex of Family Member." We could make SEX a string variable, but we will keep it a numeric variable with a length of 8 characters and 2 decimal places. Represent males with the number "1" and females with the number "2." Since it would be very easy to forget which sex we defined as "1" and "2," it is extremely important to input **value labels**. As a word of warning, it is surprisingly easy to forget seemingly intuitive value labels. It takes a little more time now, but you should always enter both *Variable Labels* and *Value Labels* when defining variables.

Click on the small gray box that appears in the cell in the *Values* column and the *Value Labels* window will pop open (Figure 2.8). Within this window, enter "1" as the *Value* and "Male" as the *Value Label*, and click on *Add*. Do the same for women by entering "2" as the *Value* and "Female" as the *Value Label*. Click on *Add*. Then click on *OK*.

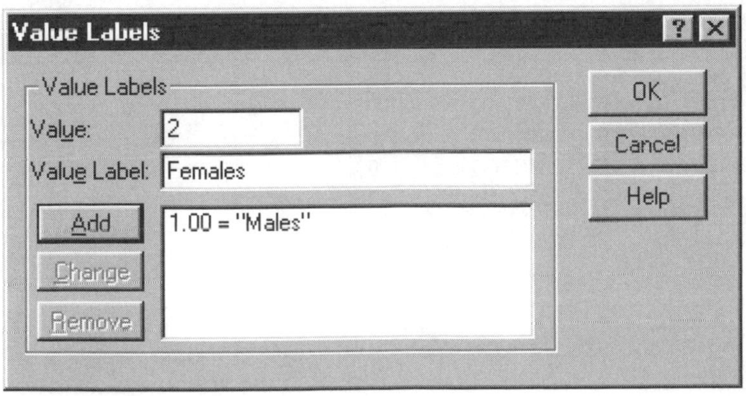

Figure 2.8 Value Labels

The column labeled *Measure* indicates the type of variable that we discussed earlier in this chapter. The default value is "Scale," which refers to a numerical variable. Notice that for the variable PERSON that you entered in the first row, the default was "Nominal." This is because PERSON is a string variable, which, by definition, is not numerical. Even if a Nominal variable has numeral values, SPSS will not treat them as having any numerical values, but as letters of the alphabet. Since we left SEX as numerical, SPSS assumes it is a Scale variable. But the numbers 1 and 2 that we used for SEX are merely abbreviations for the categories "Male" and "Female," so you should indicate to SPSS that SEX is also a nominal variable. If you click on the down arrow next to "Scale," you have choices of "Nominal" or "Ordinal." Choose "Nominal."

Define a new variable for birth date as "BIRTHDT" and *label* the variable "Birth Date." Because we want this to be treated as a date, click on the small box next to "Numeric" under *Type* and select "Date." *Date* offers a number of formats for coding the information—select mm/dd/yy. Since dates are numerical (scale) variables, we do not have to change the default *Measure*. Input the appropriate birth dates in the *Data Editor* window.

Highlight the fourth column in the *Data Editor* window. *Define* a new variable for education as "EDYRS" and *label* the variable "Years of Education." Because SPSS automatically codes this variable as numeric and scale, there is no need to do any further commands. Your variable view should look like Figure 2.9.

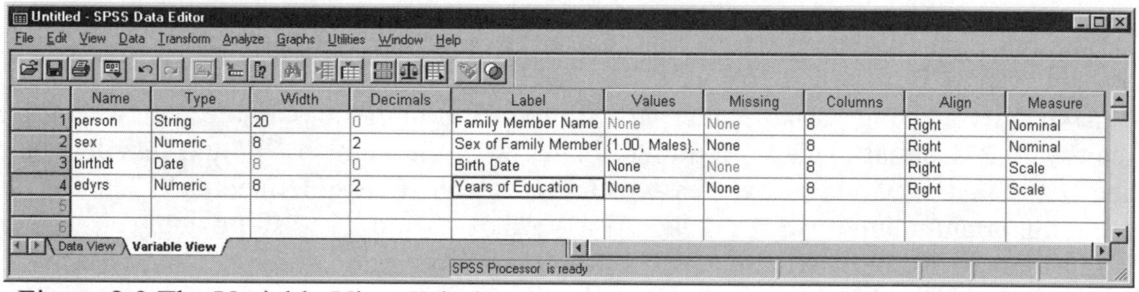

Figure 2.9 The Variable View Window

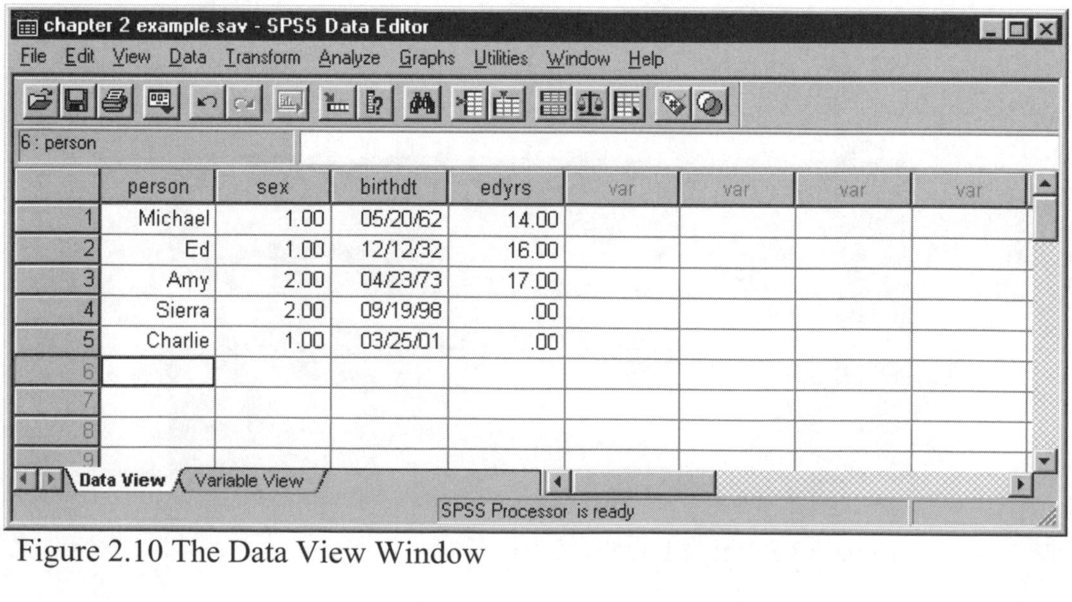

Figure 2.10 The Data View Window

You can now enter the appropriate values for each of your variables in the *Data View* spreadsheet. When you finish, your data set should look like Figure 2.10.

In some circumstances, researchers lack the necessary information to enter a value for a particular case.   For example, if you did not know your father's birth date, you should code that datum as "missing." Do this by entering a period (.) as the value.

We will work with the data you compiled here again in the future. For now, however, save your data using:

> *File*
>> *Save As*
>>> *File Name*: FAMILY.SAV
>>> *Save*

Save the data file on a disk with the name "FAMILY.SAV" We would suggest saving these data on a new disk. Congratulations, you have just defined variables, labeled variables, labeled values, and saved your data.

Managing Data Sets: Dropping and Adding Variables

Good data analysts become skilled at selecting data that are pertinent to their research questions.   There is currently so much data available that having too much can become overwhelming.   Suppose that you are interested in looking at environmental issues and are compiling a new data set from many other existing data sources.   As you compile data concerning recycling, car-pooling, etc., you come across homicide statistics.   There might be a relationship between homicide and recycling, but you have to ask yourself at this point, does this new variable have anything to do with my main research question? If it does, keep it in your data set. If it does not, there is no reason to keep it in the data because it will only take up disk space and could later cloud your thinking about what needs to be analyzed.

There are a number of ways to drop variables from the data. One way is simply to go to the top of the *Data Editor* window, highlight the column of the variable that is not desired, and use the *Edit* command:

> *Edit*
>> *Cut*

You can try this function by opening your data FAMILY.SAV and cutting the variable EDYRS. You will see this variable disappear from the *Data Editor* window. This variable can be restored by using:

> *Edit*
>> *Undo*

It is also possible to add a new variable to the data set using the command:

> *Data*
>> *Insert Variable*

Of course, once you insert a new variable, you will need to define it and enter the appropriate values in the same manner described earlier in this chapter. It is important to note that any changes in the data (such as adding or deleting variables) will be saved only if you save the data set before exiting the program. If you do not save the data, any changes will be lost. If you make substantial changes to a data set, it is prudent to save that file under a new name. As we work with data, we usually give the initial file a name such as "FAMILY.SAV." As we refine the data, adding or deleting variables, we save the new files with successive new names such as "FAMILY2.SAV," "FAMILY3.SAV," etc. One advantage of doing this is that it opens the possibility of backtracking and correcting any (inevitable) mistakes made along the way. You might develop a different system, but it is important to keep a running record of changes to your data. It is also important to never copy over the original data set unless you are absolutely sure that you want all of the changes to remain. Once a data set is copied over, the information is changed forever.

Merging and Importing Files

In some circumstances, the data you want to work with may not be in SPSS format. All of the data provided with this text are in SPSS format, which makes your work much easier. However, at some point in your career, you may find it necessary to **import** statistical information from another format, such as Lotus, Excel, dBase, or ASCII. You will find SPSS has the capability of importing an Excel file, for example, with the command:

> *File*
>> *Open*
>>> *Data*
>>>> *File name*: Filename.xls
>>>> *Files of Type*: Excel (*.xls)
>>>> *Open*

In compiling the data for your analysis, we accessed a number of different sources of data, and selected those variables that we thought would be most pertinent for the types of research projects students would be interested in, and then combined these different sources through a process called **merging**.

> *Data*
>> *Merge Files*
>>> *Add Variables*

The above command operates by combining two data sets in such a way that new variables are added on to the end of a primary file. Suppose you had a file containing your family members' social security numbers and wanted to add this information to the data set you compiled earlier. The *Add Variables* command would enable you to do this operation by merging the files according to the selected variables. You would need to first sort both files so that each family member occurs in the same order in each file using the command:

> *Data*
>> *Sort Cases*

Once each file is ordered the same, SPSS can match cases so that the appropriate information is added to each case.

It is also possible to add new cases to the data set using the *Merge Files* command. Suppose, for example, that you wanted to combine the information about your family with information about other class members' families. As long as each file has the same variables, new cases (people) can be added using:

> *Data*
> > *Merge Files*
> > > *Add Cases*

There is no immediate need for you to import or merge files. However, in the future you may want to add some variables to the data set included with this text or construct an entirely new data set from existing data. If this is the case, you will probably need to use the merge or import procedures. If you have existing data in a format that SPSS cannot import, there are good software packages available, such as DBMS/Copy, that easily translate data files from one format to another.

Loading and Examining an Existing File

As you can tell, entering data can be labor intensive and time consuming. For this reason, many professional social science researchers allot this task to companies that specialize in data entry. Thankfully, social science researchers can often use data already compiled by government agencies or by other researchers. In fact, there are a number of organizations, such as the Inter-university Consortium for Political and Social Research, that specialize in distributing data on the Internet. Your college library probably has government data in computer-ready format as well.

On the disk accompanying this text is a data set containing state level data, STATES.SAV. These data are drawn from a number of sources such as the Department of the Census and the FBI. To examine this data set, use:

> *File*
> > *Open*
> > > *Data*
> > > > *Look in:*
> > > > *File Name:* STATES.SAV
> > > > *Open*

Your computer has to search for these data in the correct place, so make sure that *Look in:* (located at the top of the window) directs your machine to search the appropriate drive.

The *Data Editor* window will fill with data from the 50 United States and the District of Columbia. Just as your family members comprised cases in the previous exercise, the states comprise cases in this data set. Your screen should look like Figure 2.11.

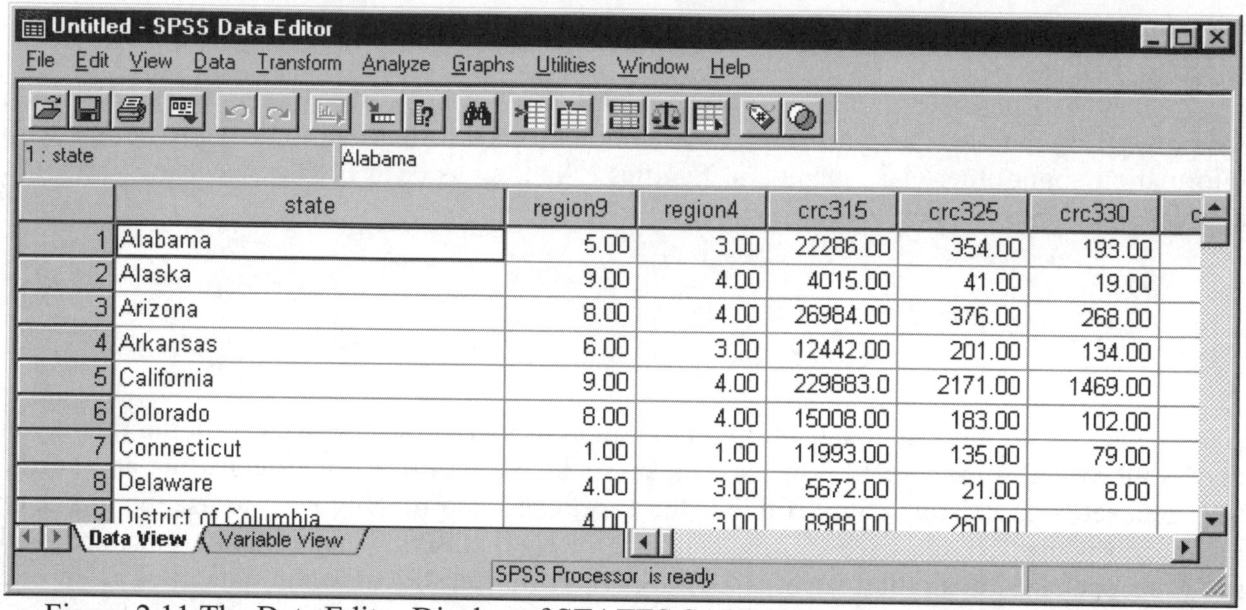

Figure 2.11 The Data Editor Display of STATES.SAV

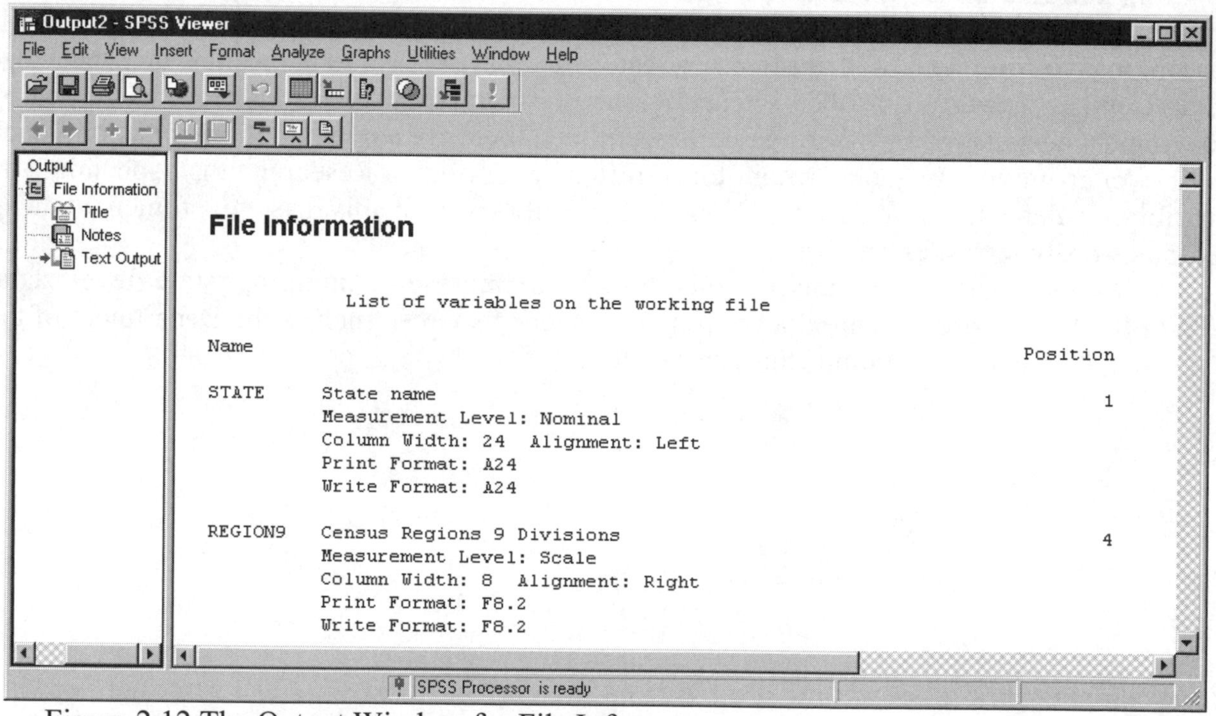

Figure 2.12 The Output Window for File Info

There are many variables in this data set, including indicators of population, educational attainment, income, and health care. Each variable is represented by a name, shown across the top row of the *Data Editor* window. One easy way to find the list of all of the variable names and variable labels is to use:

> *Utilities*
>> *File Info*

This command will display all of the variable names and labels, as well as yield information on how these variables are defined (e.g., string, numeric, or date) in the **SPSS Output Window**. Your output should look similar to Figure 2.12.

Managing Variable Names and Labels

You may have noticed that the data in the STATES data set have names that appear cumbersome. For example, why not just name variable JCC186 (Reported Juvenile Arrest Rate in 1998) JuvenileArrests? Remember, SPSS limits variable names to 8 characters or fewer. This means that almost all variables will need truncated names. Because there are so many variables relating to juvenile crime in this data set, we decided to indicate this with the initials JC (the first two letters in the name "juvenile crime"). The remaining letters and numbers indicate the source of the data. In the case of the STATES data set, all of the data have been drawn from three books:

> *Crime State Rankings 2000* (Morgan Quitno 2000)
> *Health Care State Rankings 2000* (Morgan Quitno 2000)
> *State Rankings 2000* (Morgan Quitno 2000)

The third letter in the variable name indicates the source of the data. C = *Crime State Rankings 2000*, H = *Health Care State Rankings 2000*, S = *State Rankings 2000*. The remaining numbers indicate the page of the text from which these data were drawn. Using these variable names and these texts, the data can be used to trace the data back to its original sources.

For example, variable JCC186 can be interpreted as:

> JC- Juvenile Crime
> C- *Crime State Rankings 2000*
> 186- Page 186.

To simplify searches of the data for specific subjects, below is a list of abbreviations used in the variable names in the STATES data.

Variable Name Prefixes

ar - arrests	en - environment
bi - births	fi - finance
ca - child abuse	hb - health behaviors
cr - crime	jc - juvenile crime
df - defense	le - law enforcement
di - disease	pf - physical fitness
dm - demography, population	ph - health providers
dr - drugs and alcohol	pr - prisons
dt - deaths	pv - poverty
ec - economy	sc - schooling
em - employment	

On the surface, this approach to naming variables seems cumbersome. However, it offers a few advantages: it is systematic and allows the researcher to locate the variables quickly; it groups similar concepts together alphabetically; and it enables location of the original source of the data.   After gaining experience in working with data, you will develop your own systems for naming and labeling variables.

SPSS also limits how long variable labels can be. Labels can be up to 120 characters long, but often these labels will be cut off in some of the SPSS output. We generally restrict labels to about 80 characters so that they can be fully displayed. However, this often necessitates abbreviating words in complicated or lengthy labels. In the STATES data, we have been forced to abbreviate in a number of circumstances. In most cases, the abbreviation will be apparent. Appendix 3 is a list of common abbreviations.

Summary

SPSS has the capacity to import data from other computer programs, to combine data from different sources into a single data set, and to facilitate the creation of an entirely new data set. In this chapter, you learned how to construct a data set and how to retrieve existing data. We also discussed data management and some of the skills to select appropriate data and develop systematic methods of saving and naming data sets. A well constructed data set is the foundation of all subsequent analysis, so particular attention needs to be paid to designating variable types, labeling variables clearly, and naming variables in a way so they are accessible to users.

Key Terms

Case	Ordinal variable
Categorical variable	SPSS Data Editor Window
Continuous variable	SPSS Output Window
Data view spreadsheet	Syntax commands
Count variable	Tool bar
Import	Value label
Menu bar	Variable
Merging	Variable label
Nominal variable	Variable view
Numerical variable	

References and Further Reading

Green, Samuel B., Neil J. Salkind, and Theresa M. Akey. 1999. *Using SPSS for Windows: Analyzing and Understanding Data.* Upper Saddle River, New Jersey: Prentice Hall.

Morgan, Kathleen O'Leary, Scott Morgan, and Neal Quitno. 2000. *State Rankings 2000.* Lawrence, Kansas: Morgan Quitno.

Morgan, Kathleen O'Leary, Scott Morgan, and Neal Quitno. 2000. *Crime State Rankings 2000.* Lawrence, Kansas: Morgan Quitno.

Morgan, Kathleen O'Leary, Scott Morgan, and Neal Quitno. 2000. *Health Care State Rankings. 2000.* Lawrence, Kansas: Morgan Quitno.

Chapter 2 Exercises

Name_____   Date_____

1. Create a new data set by polling 5 other people and asking the following questions:

RESPOND. What are the last four digits of your phone number?

EXER1. Do you exercise regularly? (Yes or No)

EXER2. How many hours a week would you say you exercise?

EXER3. Do you participate in team sports? (Yes or No)

EXER4. What is your favorite sport to play?

Create a new data set using these data and incorporating the following labels.

Variable Name	Label	Value Labels	Variable Type
RESPOND	Respondent Number	None	Numeric
EXER1	Exercise Regularly?	0=no 1=yes	Numeric
EXER2	Hours/Week of Exercise	None	Numeric
EXER3	Participate in Team Sports?	0=no 1=yes	Numeric
EXER4	Favorite Sport	None	String 20

Input the responses and save the data as "EXERCISE.SAV". Print *File Info* of all of the variables. Print a copy of the Data Editor window.

2. Open the data STATES.SAV. Examine the data set using the *File info* command and locate some variables that measure the following concepts. (Double click within the box of variables and scroll up or down to view all of the variables.)

A. Economic Prosperity

Variable Name   Variable Label

Variable Name   Variable Label

Variable Name   Variable Label

B. Physical Fitness

Variable Name   Variable Label

Variable Name   Variable Label

Variable Name   Variable Label

C. Educational Attainment

Variable Name   Variable Label

Variable Name   Variable Label

Variable Name   Variable Label

D. Population

Variable Name

Variable Label

Variable Name

Variable Label

Variable Name

Variable Label

E. Juvenile Delinquency

Variable Name

Variable Label

Variable Name

Variable Label

Variable Name

Variable Label

3. Your state's Department of Education hires you as a statistical consultant to help design a data set. They have already sent a survey to school superintendents, and need you to design their data set so they can begin entering information. Below is an example of a survey returned from one school district. Using the survey, answer the questions below, showing how you would design the data set.

1. Number of elementary schools: 8
2. Number of middle schools: 4
3. Number of high schools: 2
4. Average spending per pupil: $4500
5. Student/Teacher ratio: 22/1
6. High School drop-out rate: 10%
7. Does the High School offer AP classes?   Yes
8. Type of district: (circle one)   Rural (Suburban)   Urban

A. In this data set, what will be a case? _____

B. Design variable names and labels for each of the variables in the study.

Variable Name	Variable Label	Value Labels
1.		
2.		
3.		
4.		
5.		
6.		
7.		
8.		

C. Which variables are categorical?

D. Of the categorical variables, which ones are ordinal?

E. Of the categorical variables, which ones are nominal?

F. Which variables are numerical?

G. Of the numeric variables, which ones are count variables?

II. Of the numeric variables, which ones are continuous?

Chapter 3
Univariate Analysis: Descriptive Statistics

Overview

Data entry and variable creation make up the first step in data analysis. This chapter is about the second step, univariate analysis. **Univariate analysis** explores the characteristics of individual variables in isolation from all of the other variables in a data set. This chapter introduces univariate analysis, demonstrating how to understand and describe variables using graphic techniques and summary statistics. We will assess measures of central tendency and spread with descriptive statistics and examine distributions of data with tables and graphs, including pie charts, bar charts, histograms, and box plots. This chapter shows how to apply appropriate descriptive statistics and graphing techniques when analyzing data, and how to refine graphs using SPSS.

Why Do Researchers Perform Univariate Analysis?

Most social science research is interested in the relationships between variables, such as the relationships between education and crime, income and education, or religion and suicide. If this is the case, then why study variables in isolation with univariate analysis? The foremost reason is that univariate analysis is very informative. For example, to fully understand whether education affects crime requires knowing how educated people are—the percentages of the population who drop out of high school, who graduate from high school, and who go on to higher education. If crime is a concern, what are the overall crime rates? Knowing the characteristics of individual variables is essential for understanding the implications of any study.

A second reason for univariate analysis is that it enables the researcher to determine which types of bivariate and multivariate procedures can be used in more advanced analyses of data. As we show later in this book, these procedures require knowing the characteristics of individual variables, something that can only be determined through univariate analysis. Other reasons are to understand the patterns of missing data, to check for any data entry errors, and to check for unusual or impossible values.

Exploring Distributions of Numerical Variables

Throughout this chapter, we will be using the STATES and the GSS98 data to demonstrate methods for univariate analysis. We use the STATES data to show how SPSS can create statistics and graphs for numerical variables, and the GSS98 data to do the same for categorical variables. At this point, start SPSS and load the STATES data. Recall that you can do this through the menus following the commands:

> *File*
> > *Open*
> > > *Data*
> > > > *File Name:* STATES.SAV
> > > > *Open*

Our first concern is to examine distributions of numerical data. A **distribution** is an account of all of a variable's values. The most rudimentary way of describing a variable's distribution is to make a list of all the values for all the cases. Although this is a very comprehensive way of describing the data, if there are many cases, a researcher will be overwhelmed with too much information and will be unable to detect patterns. As you will see, SPSS offers a number of options that can be effectively used to understand and summarize distributions.

Listing, Summarizing, and Sorting Observations

Try this exercise. Using the STATES data, summarize the variables CRC347 (1998 Rape Rate per 100,000 people) and STATE (the 50 U.S. States and D.C.). Recall that the states, in this data set, are cases. The variable STATE simply labels the states, easing our interpretation of univariate output for CRC347, the rape rates of individual states.

> *Analyze*
> > *Reports*
> > > *Case Summaries*
> > > > *Variables*: STATE
> > > > > CRC347
> > > > *OK*

Note: The variable list on the left should display the variable names in alphabetical order. If your computer shows the variable labels (they will be all in capital letters), or the variable names are not in alphabetical order, you should change the option in SPSS using:

> *Edit*
> > *Options*
> > > *General*
> > > > *Variable Lists*: Display names
> > > > > Alphabetical

Case Summaries[a]

	State name	Rape Rate in 1998
1	Alabama	33.20
2	Alaska	68.60
3	Arizona	31.10
4	Arkansas	35.20
5	California	29.90
6	Colorado	47.40
7	Connecticut	22.20
8	Delaware	67.10
9	District of Columbia	36.30
10	Florida	49.60
11	Georgia	30.40
12	Hawaii	29.50
13	Idaho	31.40
14	Illinois	34.00
15	Indiana	33.10
16	Iowa	25.40
17	Kansas	42.60
18	Kentucky	29.30
19	Louisiana	36.80
20	Maine	18.10
21	Maryland	33.40
22	Massachusetts	27.40
23	Michigan	50.40
24	Minnesota	49.90
25	Mississippi	37.30
26	Missouri	26.90
27	Montana	17.80
28	Nebraska	25.10
29	Nevada	52.10
30	New Hampshire	33.80
31	New Jersey	20.00
32	New Mexico	55.10
33	New York	21.10
34	North Carolina	30.60
35	North Dakota	33.20
36	Ohio	40.50
37	Oklahoma	45.20
38	Oregon	39.80
39	Pennsylvania	26.90
40	Rhode Island	35.50
41	South Carolina	45.70
42	South Dakota	35.00
43	Tennessee	45.80
44	Texas	40.00
45	Utah	41.70
46	Vermont	27.60
47	Virginia	26.70
48	Washington	48.20
49	West Virginia	18.70
50	Wisconsin	19.90
51	Wyoming	27.70
Total N		51 51

a. Limited to first 100 cases.

Table 3.1 Rapes per 100,000 Population

Case Summaries[a]

	State name	Rape Rate in 1998
1	Montana	17.80
2	Maine	18.10
3	West Virginia	18.70
4	Wisconsin	19.90
5	New Jersey	20.00
6	New York	21.10
7	Connecticut	22.20
8	Nebraska	25.10
9	Iowa	25.40
10	Virginia	26.70
11	Missouri	26.90
12	Pennsylvania	26.90
13	Massachusetts	27.40
14	Vermont	27.60
15	Wyoming	27.70
16	Kentucky	29.30
17	Hawaii	29.50
18	California	29.90
19	Georgia	30.40
20	North Carolina	30.60
21	Arizona	31.10
22	Idaho	31.40
23	Indiana	33.10
24	Alabama	33.20
25	North Dakota	33.20
26	Maryland	33.40
27	New Hampshire	33.80
28	Illinois	34.00
29	South Dakota	35.00
30	Arkansas	35.20
31	Rhode Island	35.50
32	District of Columbia	36.30
33	Louisiana	36.80
34	Mississippi	37.30
35	Oregon	39.80
36	Texas	40.00
37	Ohio	40.50
38	Utah	41.70
39	Kansas	42.60
40	Oklahoma	45.20
41	South Carolina	45.70
42	Tennessee	45.80
43	Colorado	47.40
44	Washington	48.20
45	Florida	49.60
46	Minnesota	49.90
47	Michigan	50.40
48	Nevada	52.10
49	New Mexico	55.10
50	Delaware	67.10
51	Alaska	68.60
Total N		51 51

a. Limited to first 100 cases.

Table 3.2 Sorted Distribution

Your output should look very much like Table 3.1, a distribution of the 1998 Rape Rate per 100,000 people in each state. This output is useful in that we can quickly find the rape rates for individual states. However, as the data are currently structured, it takes some effort to find which states have the highest and lowest rates, what is the full range of the data, or which values are most representative of the rape rate in the United States. We need a less cumbersome approach if we are going to understand the general patterns of rape in the United States.

One way of refining the analysis, and gaining further appreciation for the distribution of rate rapes within the United States is to **sort** the data. These data are already sorted by STATE, but let us now impose a new order, by sorting by rape rate CRC347:

Data
　　　Sort Cases
　　　　　Sort By: CRC347
　　　　　　　OK

If you repeat the *Case Summaries* for variable CRC347 and STATE, you should observe that the output has changed, and now displays states in ranked order of the incidence of rape. Output should look like Table 3.2.

Because we can quickly identify which states have the highest and lowest rape rates, our analysis shows some modest improvements. However, creating a description beyond this is still challenging, in that it is difficult to find common or uncommon values. Even when observations are sorted, the analytic potential is limited and meaningful summaries of variables are difficult. These problems escalate for large data sets. A better approach is to summarize the distribution using graphs or summary statistics.

We introduce the *Summarize* and *Sort* features of SPSS here primarily to illustrate the need of using more refined means of describing variables. However, these can be very handy features for performing other operations. Sorting and summarizing, for instance, can be used during **data cleaning**, the phase of a project when researchers examine data for potential errors and make corrections. Sorting is also needed for splitting files into groups for separate analyses, or for preparing data for merging with other data sets.

Histograms
A **histogram** is a graphical summary of the distribution of a numerical variable. In a histogram, classes of values are listed along the horizontal axis. The height of the bar above each class indicates the frequency of occurrence of the values in that class. By indicating how frequently values occur within a class of potential observations, patterns in the data, reflecting distributions, become immediately apparent. Using the STATES data, we can produce a histogram representing the distribution of the rape rates.

Graphs
　　　Histogram
　　　　　Variable: CRC347
　　　　　Titles
　　　　　　　Title: Distribution of Rapes per 100,000 Population
　　　　　　　Continue
　　　　OK

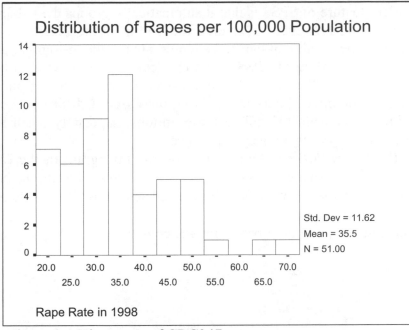

Figure 3.1 Histogram of CRC347

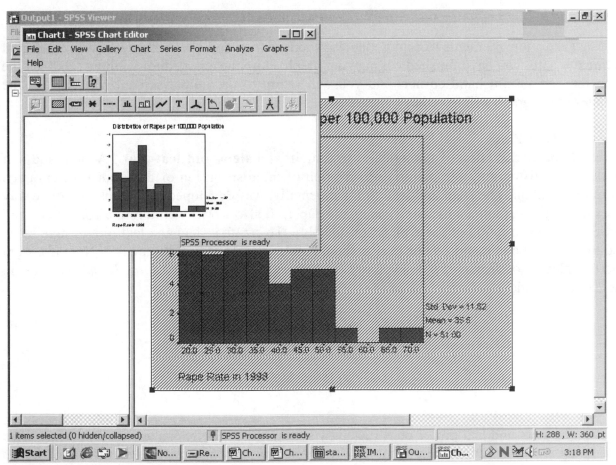

Figure 3.2 The Chart Editor Window

One convenient feature of SPSS is that it automatically groups the values into classes for histograms. It is possible, however, to change the width of the classes into more refined groupings by stipulating the number of bars to be represented in the histogram. In the case of the histogram in Figure 3.1, we allowed SPSS to automatically generate what it believes to be an appropriate number of bars. We could, however, override this function and command it to increase or decrease the number of bars by invoking the **Chart Editor** commands available in SPSS. You will inevitably want to explore these options, especially when it comes time to publish some of the graphic presentations you produce.

To access the *Chart Editor*, double click on the histogram in the *Output Navigator* window (Figure 3.2). This opens the SPSS *Chart Editor* window. To edit the chart, it is usually helpful to expand the *Chart Editor* window to fill the full screen using the icon in the upper right corner of the *Chart Editor* window.

We could change the number of bars using the command:

> *Chart*
> > *Axis*
> > > *Interval: OK*
> > > > *Intervals*: Custom
> > > > > *Define* (Customize your graph)
> > > > > > *Continue*
> > > *OK*

Take a few moments to explore the ways to construct and alter histograms using different options.   After you have finished editing your graph, close the chart editor window (click on the X in the upper right hand corner) and you will return to the output screen, where all of the changes to the graph will have been integrated.

Stem and Leaf Plots

Another depiction of numerical distributions is a **stem and leaf plot**. A stem and leaf plots, like a histogram, is a pictorial description of the distribution of data, but it offers even more information. The stem and leaf plot, incidentally, was developed as a quick and dirty way of examining distributions by using pencil and paper. It also works well through computers, and SPSS eases construction of these plots considerably. To create a stem and leaf plot of rape rates, use the *Explore* command. Your results should look very much like Figure 3.3. Note if a stem and leaf plot is not displayed when you run *Explore*, examine whether *Display Both* is selected in the *Explore* window.

> *Analyze*
> > *Descriptive Statistics*
> > > *Explore*
> > > > *Dependent List:* CRC347
> > > > *OK*

The stem and leaf plot is constructed by sorting the observations and incorporating them in a systematic manner. As the name implies, it has two parts: the stems and the leaves. The initial digits in the value of each observation determine the stems, located on the left of the stem and leaf plot. The leaves are constructed by entering the following digit for each case. For example, on the stem and leaf plot in Figure 3.3, there are four states in the first row: Montana, Maine, West Virginia, and Wisconsin, with rape rates of 17.8, 18.1, 18.7, and 19.9, respectively. The stem indicates that these states have rates in the range of 10-19, and the leaf indicates the exact value of the second digit. The plot indicates that there is one 17, two 18's, and one 19 in the data set.

```
Rape Rate in 1998 Stem and Leaf Plot

      Frequency           Stem  &     Leaf

           4.00              1 .     7889
           3.00              2 .     012
          11.00              2 .     55666777999
          10.00              3 .     0011333334
           7.00              3 .     5556679
           4.00              4 .     0012
           7.00              4 .     5557899
           2.00              5 .     02
           1.00              5 .     5
           2.00          Extremes    (>=67)

Stem width:        10.00
Each leaf:        1 case(s)
```

Figure 3.3 Stem and Leaf Plot of CRC347

The second row represents the states that had a rape rate of 20-24. The stem groups these states using the initial digit 2 (indicating "20 something"). Each leaf represents a state by the second digit. These digits are entered in numeric order. Stems that occur most frequently have the most leaves. In this example, because so many values begin with each digit, the stems have been split in half. Therefore, two stems begin with each of 2, 3, 4, and 5. The first stem for each digit represents the lower values that begin with a single digit (e.g., 20-24) and the second stem represents the higher values (e.g., 25-29). Figure 3.3 reveals that most states have a rape rate somewhere between 25 and 49.

Figure 3.4 illustrates the manual process of building a stem and leaf plot, using the above list of rape rates as the sources for data (this represents the second and third row of the above stem and leaf plot). New Jersey's rape rate is 20, so its stem is represented with a 2; its leaf is 0. New York's rape rate is 21, so its stem is 2; its leaf is 1. Connecticut's rape rate is 22, so its stem is 2; its leaf is 2. Iowa's rape rate is 25, so its stem is 2; its leaf is 5. Nebraska's rape rate is 25, so its stem is 2; its leaf is 5. This continues until the values of the leaves increase to the point where the stem turns to 3 (indicating "30 something").

If a few of the states have extraordinarily low or high stem values, they will be grouped as "extremes" at the top or bottom of the plot. In the case of Figure 3.3, Delaware (67.1) and Alaska (68.6) are classified as extremes.

Stem	Leaf	
2	**0**	New Jersey
2	**01**	New York
2	**012**	Connecticut
2	**5**	Iowa
2	**55**	Nebraska
		Etc.

Figure 3.4 Constructing a Stem and Leaf
Plot Manually

Stem and leaf plots do have some limitations.   They only work with numerical data. They tend to work best in relatively small and compact data sets. If you have 1000 cases, and they all have values in the 20-40 range, the stem and leaf plot will not summarize very well, much less fit on a page! On the other hand, if you have only 10 cases, but the values range from 10 to 1000, there will be so many empty stems that the plot will not be useful. This being said, stem and leaf plots can be a useful way to depict a distribution.

Shapes of Distributions

Histograms and stem and leaf plots offer nice pictorial representations of distributions, and these graphs are often summarized with descriptions of their shapes. There are four common shapes, illustrated in Figure 3.5. A **bell-shaped distribution** is symmetric – both sides look pretty much the same. It has the highest frequency of cases in the middle, and the frequencies taper off at the high and low ends of the distribution, creating "tails" with few cases. A **positively skewed distribution** looks like a bell-shaped distribution that has been shoved to the left side, with a tail that points in the positive direction on the horizontal axis. There are many cases with low values of the variable and there are few cases with high values. A common example of a variable with a positively skewed distribution is the salaries at a company. There are often many workers with relatively low salaries, and fewer and fewer people making higher and higher salaries. A **negatively skewed distribution** is the opposite. These distributions show many cases with high values and few cases with low values. If people rated their health on a 10 point scale, with 10 indicating very good health and 0 indicating poor health, the distribution would be negatively skewed, as most people are in good health. A **bimodal distribution** is also symmetric, but the highest frequencies are at both ends, with few cases in the middle. Although these four patterns above are common, there are many distributions with other patterns or no discernible pattern at all.

When describing the shape of a distribution, it is also important to mention if any outliers are present. An **outlier** is an observation so far removed from the cluster of other observations that it is considered an extreme value. How extreme does an observation have to be to be considered an outlier? There are many different ways of defining a cutoff, but it is sufficient to say that an outlier should be quite different than the rest of the data set. As we will discuss in future chapters, because outliers can have a strong impact on the values of statistics, they can undermine conventional statistical methods. Some researchers will automatically discard any outliers from a data set as "unrepresentative." This is not a sufficiently thoughtful strategy, however, because outliers can be among the most substantively important observations. Knowing that outliers exist is the first step in determining the best way to handle them.

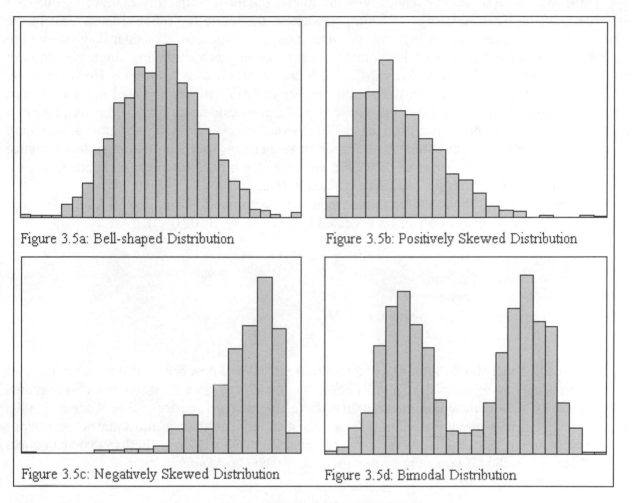

Figure 3.5a: Bell-shaped Distribution

Figure 3.5b: Positively Skewed Distribution

Figure 3.5c: Negatively Skewed Distribution

Figure 3.5d: Bimodal Distribution

Figure 3.5 Histograms of Normal, Skewed, and Bimodal Distributions

Sometimes a researcher can determine that an outlier is a result of an error, either from a measurement or data entry error. For example, one of the authors was once asked to analyze a data set of women's weights, and there was one woman who was listed as weighing 19 pounds. As it is physically impossible for an adult woman to weigh only 19 pounds, we easily concluded that this was a data entry error. It is always a good idea to examine outliers in an attempt to find data entry errors, and if these errors cannot be remedied, they should be removed from the data set.

Measures of Central Tendency

Summarizing data through a frequency distribution graph is very useful for understanding the nature of the distribution. However, sometimes the situation calls for a concise summary. For this reason, univariate analysis often involves summarizing data with a **measure of central tendency**. There are different ways of measuring the central value of a variable, but all attempt to summarize the values with a single number. The central tendency gives an understanding of the "average" or "typical" value. The use of the word "average," however, is not altogether accurate because it implies a mathematical average and ignores other common measures of central tendency.

One measure of central tendency is the **mode**, the most frequently observed value of a variable. Of the three measures of central tendency, the mode is probably used least in the formal reporting of results, but used most in understanding data sets. Consider if we wanted to describe the criminal behavior of the typical teenager. Teenagers vary in how often they commit crimes and there are likely to be many differences in any sample of adolescents. However, if we could describe the most commonly reported number of criminal acts engaged in by each teen (the mode number of crimes), we may have a fairly good understanding of the frequency of criminal behaviors of the "typical" teenager. This would be especially important if a few "hard core" delinquents engage in hundreds of acts of crime per year (outliers) and most teens engage in none or one or two acts per year. If we did not know the mode, we might conclude that most teens engage in more crimes per year than is actually true.

SPSS calculates the mode using the frequencies command. Using the STATES data, run a frequency on the number of prisoners executed from 1977-1998 (PRC72):

Analyze
　　Descriptive Statistics
　　　　Frequencies
　　　　　　Variable: PRC72
　　　　　　OK

Your findings should look like Figure 3.6. If we were to describe the "typical" number of executions occurring in states during this period, the mode is 0, since 22 states (43.1%) executed no prisoners. The next most common number of executions was 1, performed by 4 states (7.8%), as observed in the Frequency column. These statistics indicate that, in most states, executions are uncommon experiences. However, one state executed 164 prisoners. Perhaps you can guess which state this is. See if you were correct using *Sort* then *Case Summaries*.

Prisoners Executed: 1977 to 1998				
		Frequency	Percent	Valid Percent	Cumulative Percent
Valid	.00	22	43.1	43.1	43.1
	1.00	4	7.8	7.8	51.0
	2.00	3	5.9	5.9	56.9
	3.00	3	5.9	5.9	62.7
	4.00	1	2.0	2.0	64.7
	5.00	2	3.9	3.9	68.6
	6.00	1	2.0	2.0	70.6
	7.00	1	2.0	2.0	72.5
	8.00	1	2.0	2.0	74.5
	11.00	2	3.9	3.9	78.4
	12.00	1	2.0	2.0	80.4
	13.00	1	2.0	2.0	82.4
	17.00	2	3.9	3.9	86.3
	20.00	1	2.0	2.0	88.2
	23.00	1	2.0	2.0	90.2
	24.00	1	2.0	2.0	92.2
	32.00	1	2.0	2.0	94.1
	43.00	1	2.0	2.0	96.1
	59.00	1	2.0	2.0	98.0
	164.00	1	2.0	2.0	100.0
	Total	51	100.0	100.0	

Figure 3.6 Frequencies Table of PRC72

The **mean** is generally what people refer to when they say "average." It is the arithmetic average of all the observations of a variable. In all likelihood, your grade point average (GPA) is calculated using a variation of the mean, in which your college averages together all of your course grades (all of which may be weighted differently in the final calculation). This will ultimately produce your mean grade point, which is the indicator of the central tendency of all of your work.

$$\text{MEAN} = \frac{\text{SUM OF THE VALUES OF ALL OBSERVATIONS}}{\text{TOTAL NUMBER OF OBSERVATIONS}}$$

The mean is probably the statistic most commonly used by social scientists. It is especially useful when discussing research findings with the general public, who are less likely to be conversant in interpreting more advanced statistics. For example, newspaper reports of average SAT scores usually refer to the mean SAT scores of all students.

Many of the indicators in your data sets are based upon means, such as the average amount spent per pupil in each state. Another reason why the mean is important is that it is the basis of many of the statistical procedures used to examine relationships between variables.

You have already found one way of locating the mean, by using the *Descriptives* command. Locate the mean of variable PRC72 (Prisoners Executed 1977-98) using the *Descriptives* command. You should find the mean number of executions to be 9.80.

Analyze
> *Descriptive Statistics*
>> *Descriptives*
>>> *Variable*: PRC72
>>> *OK*

The **median** is the value that separates the highest 50% of the cases from the lowest 50% of the cases. It is the center value in the data set. The SPSS *Explore* command finds both the median and the mean of a variable. Take a few minutes to try this. Generate *Explore* output for variable PRC72 (place PRC72 in the *Dependent Variable* box in the *Explore* window). Your output should include a table similar to Figure 3.7.

Analyze
> *Descriptive Statistics*
>> *Explore*
>>> *Dependent List:* PRC72
>>> *OK*

Descriptives

			Statistic	Std. Error
Prisoners Executed: 1977 to 1998	Mean		9.8039	3.5004
	95% Confidence Interval for Mean	Lower Bound	2.7732	
		Upper Bound	16.8346	
	5% Trimmed Mean		5.5196	
	Median		1.0000	
	Variance		624.881	
	Std. Deviation		24.9976	
	Minimum		.00	
	Maximum		164.00	
	Range		164.00	
	Interquartile Range		11.0000	
	Skewness		5.082	.333
	Kurtosis		29.902	.656

Figure 3.7 Descriptives Output of PRC72

In the Descriptives table we find the median value for PRC72 is 1. This indicates that the "typical" state, as indicated by the median, had one execution from 1977-1995. Again, consider whether this seems a more useful assessment than the mode or mean measure of central tendency. In our opinion, the median works quite well for this variable. Because the median operates by locating the point at which 50% of state executions fall above and 50% of state executions fall below, the influence of Texas no longer has such a dramatic influence in determining our estimate of the location of central tendency. At the same time, any summary will need to call attention to the fact that nearly half of the states reported no executions in this time period.

From the above discussion, you might already understand why sometimes researchers choose to concentrate on medians rather than means. The primary reason is that the median often better reflects the central point in the data when the distribution is skewed or when outliers are present.

Measures of Spread

The **standard deviation** is a statistic used to measure the spread of data. It estimates the average distance between each value in the data set and the mean. A large spread of the data away from the mean results in a large standard deviation. Conversely, a tight concentration of data around the mean results in a small standard deviation.

Because the standard deviation is based on the mean, skewed distributions and outliers can greatly affect it. One outlier that is very far from the mean will result in a large distance between it and the mean, and the standard deviation will be inflated. It can make the data set as a whole seem more dispersed than it would otherwise be. Because of this, the standard deviation is most useful for describing symmetric distributions.

If a variable has a bell-shaped distribution, 68% of the cases will have values that fall between the values that are one standard deviation below the mean and one standard deviation above the mean.   Extending the range to two standard deviations above and below the mean captures 95% of the cases and extending it to three standard deviations from the mean captures about 99% of the cases. Therefore, a researcher who knows the mean and the standard deviation has a good indication of whether any case is typical or atypical of the vast majority of cases.

As a point of illustration, look at variable DMS91 (Veterans per 1,000 Population 18 and Older in 1999), which fits a bell-shaped curve quite closely. Using the *Explore* command, you will find that this variable has a standard deviation of 12.46 and a mean of 126.98. If plus or minus one standard deviation from the mean captures 68% of the cases, we know that 68% of the cases of variable DMS91 fall within the range 114.52 – 139.44. How did we arrive at this?

$$\text{Mean} - \text{St Dev} = \text{Low Value} \qquad \text{Mean} + \text{St Dev} = \text{High Value}$$
$$126.98 - 12.46 = 114.52 \qquad 126.98 + 12.46 = 139.44$$

Suppose we do not know anything about this variable except for the standard deviation and the mean and somebody starts talking about the number of veterans in Washington, which has 144 Veterans per 1000 people. We know by looking at the mean and standard deviation that over 68% of the states fall closer to the mean than Washington. If we are to discuss the veteran population, Washington should be considered as having a comparatively high rate. We also know, by looking at the standard deviation in relation to the mean, that there is not much variation in rates of veterans from state to state.

Two other common measures of spread are the **range** and the **interquartile range** (IQR). The range is the distance spanned by the data set. It is calculated by simply subtracting the minimum value from the maximum value. The range for the rate of veterans is 63 (155 – 92). The IQR is the distance spanned by the middle 50% of the cases. Although it is slightly less intuitive than the range, its advantage is that outliers do not affect it, since the ends of the distribution are not used in its calculation.

The IQR is calculated from parts of the **five number summary**, which is a set of five cutoff points in the distribution. These cutoff points include the minimum, the 25th percentile, the median, the 75th percentile, and the maximum. These values split the data set into four equal pieces. The lowest 25% of the cases will have values between the **minimum** and the **25th percentile**. The next 25% of cases will have values between the 25th percentile and the median. The next 25% of cases will have values between the median and the **75th percentile**, and the highest 25% of cases will have values between the 75th percentile and the **maximum**. The IQR is the value of the 25th percentile subtracted from the value of the 75th percentile. Since 25% of cases are below the 25th percentile and 25% of cases are above the 75th percentile, the IQR covers the middle 50% of the data set.

Box Plots

The IQR is easy to see on a **box plot**, a graph that displays the five number summary. Figure 3.8 shows an illustration of a box plot, identifying how these innovative graphs show medians, percentiles, interquartile ranges, extended ranges, and outliers. The main box extends from the 25th to the 75th percentiles. Recall, the distance between them is the interquartile range (IQR). The line inside of the main box represents the median. Remember that 50% of the cases fall above and 50% of the cases fall below this line, and in the case of DMS91, the median is 128. The "whiskers" (the thin lines extending out from the main box) extend 1.5 times the IQR from the top and bottom of the box. Those cases that are outside the whiskers are termed outliers and are signified by small circles.

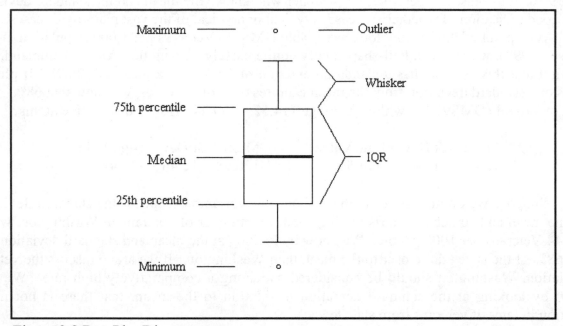

Figure 3.8 Box Plot Diagram

We can also create an actual box plot representing the distribution of proportion of the population that are veterans (DMS91). You can generate this box plot using the *Explore* command. If a box plot is not displayed when you run *Explore*, examine whether "*Display:* Both" is selected in the *Explore* window. A box plot of our veteran rates (DMS91) is shown in Figure 3.9.

> *Analyze*
> > *Descriptive Statistics*
> > > *Explore*
> > > > *Display:* Both
> > > > *Dependent List:* DMS91
> > > > *OK*

Note in Figure 3.9 that the box begins at 119 and ends at 134. From this box plot, we know that 50% of the cases fall between 119 and 134, with an IQR = 15 (134 − 119). Since the median falls in the center of the box and the whiskers are about the same length, the distribution is symmetric. There are two outliers. The number next to the outlier refers to the case number.

Box plots are handy. We can learn whether the data are concentrated at higher or lower values by examining the location of the median in relationship to the box and the whiskers. We can also tell whether outliers are likely to influence our summary descriptions. Chapter 5 describes how outliers can influence our interpretations of how one variable affects another variable. In the case of veteran rates, the box plot reveals that there are two outlying states.

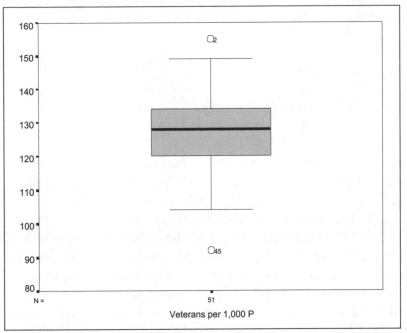

Figure 3.9 Box Plot of DMS91

Exploring Distributions of Categorical Variables

Distributions of categorical variables can be summarized through a **frequency distribution table**. Like a histogram, a frequency distribution table gives the values of a variable and the number of times each value occurs among the cases in the data set. An advantage of this type of output is that it preserves information about all the values, but reduces output to a succinct list. To demonstrate how SPSS produces a frequency distribution for categorical data, open the GSS98 data. These data, recall, represent telephone interviews with people, and measure many of their attitudes.

> *File*
>> *Open*
>>> *Data*
>>>> *File Name*: GSS98.SAV
>>>> *Open*

In this exercise, we examine the degree to which respondents agreed with the statement "a woman has a right to an abortion if she wants one for any reason." If we were to list the responses (you can try this), we would be overwhelmed with information. However, a frequency distribution provides a useful summary of the variable. Try this:

> *Analyze*
> > *Descriptive Statistics*
> > > *Frequencies*
> > > > *Variable:* ABANY
> > > > *OK*

Your output should look like Figure 3.10. This table gives a lot of information about the distribution. The first column of the table lists all the possible values of the variable. In this example, they are "Yes" or "No." Of the 2832 people who were interviewed, only 1778 answered the question. The second column, *Frequency,* indicates how many respondents chose each answer. Notice that the frequencies of people who chose these options add up to 1778 (728 + 1050 = 1778), the total number who answered the question. Adding the frequency of missing values (1054) brings the total number of people who were interviewed to 2832.

Two columns show percentages. The *Percent* column gives the percentage for each response out of all 2832 interviewees. In contrast, the *Valid Percent* column gives the same percentages out of the 1778 people who responded to the question. Both *Percent* columns give important information, because there may be a reason why people chose not to answer the question—perhaps people who feel that their answer is unpopular are less likely to answer. In other circumstances, researchers structure surveys in ways that only subsamples are asked certain questions, which again will create missing values. Realizing that 37.2% of the sample did not answer has implications for any conclusions about the distribution of people's real opinions. Finally, the last column, *Cumulative Percent,* displays the collective number of people who responded to the question, summing row by row in the table. Among those who offered answers to the abortion question, 100% were willing to give a "yes" or "no" answer. Of these three types of percentages, usually researchers report the valid percent when summarizing findings, but also report the percent of cases that proved valid (non-missing), from which these percentages are calculated.

ABORTION IF WOMAN WANTS FOR ANY REASON					
		Frequency	Percent	Valid Percent	Cumulative Percent
Valid	NO	1050	37.1	59.1	59.1
	YES	728	25.7	40.9	100.0
	Total	1778	62.8	100.0	
Missing	DK, NA	98	3.5		
	System	956	33.8		
	Total	1054	37.2		
Total		2832	100.0		

Figure 3.10 Frequency Distribution Table of ABANY

Frequency tables can also be used to analyze numerical data, such as rape rates, but only if the number of values is limited. The execution example in Figure 3.6 illustrates an appropriate frequency distribution of a numerical variable. Because 0 is such a common value, there are only 20 unique values listed. In contrast, the rape rate example in Table 3.2 illustrates an inappropriate frequency distribution. Because of the decimals, almost every value is unique. A frequency distribution that lists almost every value as occurring once does not summarize data efficiently. Instead, it is more useful to group the numerical values into classes and count the frequency of each class. A **class** is a grouping of values that are reasonably comparable, and as such, classes become very similar to ranked categories of numerical data. Although some information is lost when a class is created, the data are simplified so that researchers can interpret them.

Unfortunately, SPSS will not automatically create classes for a frequency distribution table. In order to do this, you have to recode the variable into a new variable. A complete discussion of recoding is in Chapter 4. SPSS will, however, automatically construct classes for histograms.

Pie Charts

The **pie chart** is one of the earliest methods of graphing distributions and is still used heavily in marketing and business presentations of data. One reason for its popularity relates to the underlying conceptualization of the pie chart, that a limited resource (the pie) is being distributed (the wedges). A pie chart quickly reveals if any resource is distributed equitably or inequitably, depending on the size of the wedges. To make a pie chart representing abortion attitudes, perform the following:

> *Graphs*
>> *Pie*
>>> *Data in Chart Are*: Summaries for groups of cases
>>> *Define*
>>>> *Slices Represent*: N of cases (or % of cases)
>>>> *Define Slices By*: ABANY
>>>> *Titles*
>>>>> *Title*: Woman Can Have Abortion for Any Reason
>>>>> *Continue*
>>> *OK*

(If missing values are incorporated into the pie chart, check *Options*.)

You will observe that the pie chart produced on your screen looks slightly different than that in your text. In order to format the pie chart to suit black and white print, we took advantage of some of the Chart Editor commands available in SPSS. You will inevitably want to explore these options, especially when it comes time to publish graphic presentations.

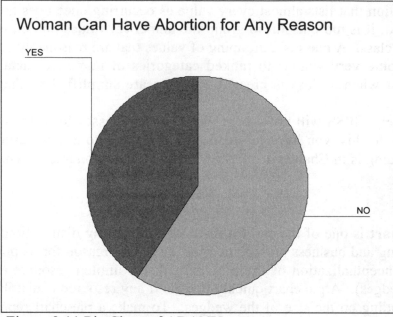

Figure 3.11 Pie Chart of ABANY

In the case of the pie chart in Figure 3.11, we changed the colors of the wedges in the pie chart by using *Chart Editor* command:

> *Format*
>> *Color*
> (You must fist click on the wedge that you want to change the color of.)

We also moved the title to be justified on the left by using the command:

> *Chart*
>> *Title*

Another option for pie charts is altering the fill pattern of the wedges. This can be accomplished by using the command:

> *Format*
>> *Fill Pattern*

It may be useful to take a few moments to explore the capacities of SPSS in creating and modifying pie charts.

Although pie charts remain popular in business and marketing, they have largely fallen out of favor with social scientists. One concern is that pie charts are not always easy to interpret accurately. Discerning small (but sometimes very important) differences based on wedge thickness can be difficult. For this reason, many researchers prefer using bar charts.

Bar Charts

Bar charts are graphs that show how often each category occurs, and in this respect, operate much like histograms. Since bar charts graph the distribution of categorical variables, values do not need to be grouped into classes. The categories of the variable are listed across the horizontal axis. Each category has a bar and the height of each bar represents the frequency of that category in the data set. There are different variations of bar charts, but we will start with a simple bar chart, which places bars side-by-side in a single graph. To produce a bar chart of ABANY, perform the following commands:

> *Graphs*
> > *Bar*
> > > *Simple*
> > > *Data in Chart Are*: Summaries for groups of cases
> > > *Define*
> > > > *Bars Represent*: % of cases
> > > > *Category Axis*: ABANY
> > > > *Titles*
> > > > > *Title*: Woman Can Have Abortion for Any Reason
> > > > > *Continue*
> > > *OK*
> > > (If missing values are incorporated into the graph, check *Options*.)

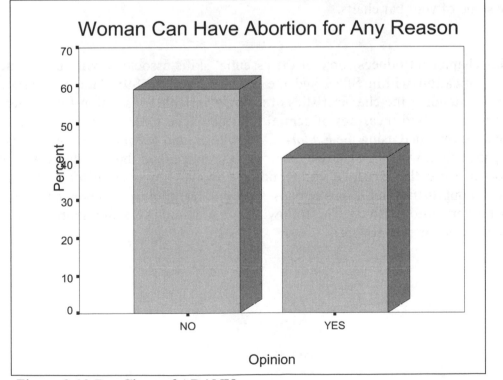

Figure 3.12 Bar Chart of ABANY

Again, you will observe that your bar chart looks slightly different than the one represented in Figure 3.12. You can restructure your chart by using the *Chart Editor* window by double clicking on the graph generated in the *Output Navigator* window. Within the *Chart Editor* window, you can change the bar style to depict a three dimensional bar with the following commands:

> *Format*
>> *Bar Style*: 3-D effect

It is also useful in some circumstances to change the specifications for each axis. In the graph represented above, we made the following modifications:

> *Chart*
>> *Axis*
>>> *Scale: OK*
>>>> *Title Justification*: Center
>>>> *OK*

> *Chart*
>> *Axis*
>>> *Category: OK*
>>>> *Axis Title*: Opinion
>>>> *Title Justification*: Center
>>>> *OK*

You may find it useful to explore some of the other options available in the Chart Editor and customize some of your bar charts.

Summary

This chapter introduces some of the essential skills associated with univariate analyses and their application within SPSS and the STATES and GSS98 data. Univariate analysis involves understanding the characteristics of a single variable in isolation from other variables. One approach is to find measures of central tendency—the mean, median, and mode. These statistics can be obtained using the *Explore, Descriptives,* and *Frequencies* commands. Spread is commonly measured with the standard deviation, the range, and the interquartile range. These can be found using the *Explore* commands. Graphs, however, offer perhaps the most information about distributions. Histograms, stem and leaf plots, pie charts, bar charts, and box plots can be very informative. The following table summarizes the appropriate graphs for numerical and categorical variables:

Variable Format	Graph
Numerical	Box Plot
	Histogram
	Stem and Leaf Plot
Categorical	Pie Chart
	Bar Chart

Table 3.3 Summary of Graph Types

Once researchers have developed a foundation in the skills of understanding individual variables, they are well positioned to perform accurate and informative analyses of the relationships between variables.

Key Terms

25th Percentile	Mean
75th Percentile	Measures of Central Tendency
Bar Chart	Measures of Spread
Bell-shaped distribution	Median
Bimodal distribution	Minimum
Box Plot	Mode
SPSS Chart Editor	Negatively skewed distribution
Class	Outlier
Data cleaning	Pie Chart
Distribution	Positively skewed distribution
Five Number Summary	Range
Frequency distribution table	Sorting data
Histogram	Standard Deviation
Interquartile Range	Stem and Leaf Plot
Maximum	Univariate Analysis

References and Further Reading

Levin, Jack and James Fox. 1997. *Elementary Statistics in Social Research.* New York: Longman.

McGrath, Robert. 1997. *Introductory Statistics: A Research Perspective.* Boston: Allyn & Bacon.

Chapter 3 Exercises

Name_____   Date_____

1. Open your file FAMILY.SAV, run Descriptives, and print the results.
     To print, use:

     File
          Print

     Describe your findings:

2. Using the GSS98 data, construct and print a pie chart displaying opinions concerning sex education in schools (SEXEDUC). Give an appropriate title to the graph and refine the graph so that it is clearly printed and aesthetically appealing. Exclude missing cases. Note if your printer does not support color printing, you will need to change the color of the wedges. Describe this chart below.

3. Using the GSS98 data set, construct and print a bar chart displaying the racial makeup of people's workplaces (RACWORK). Give an appropriate title to the graph and refine the graph so that it is clearly printed and aesthetically appealing. Exclude missing cases. What does this graph inform us of the diversity of workplaces?

4. Using the STATES data set, construct and print a histogram of ENS213 (Hazardous Waste Sites on the National Priority List Per 10K SqMi 98). Give an appropriate title to the graph and refine the graph so that it is clearly printed and aesthetically appealing. What does this graph indicate for the distribution of hazardous waste sites in the United States?

5. Using *Explore,* determine the measures of central tendency and spread for JCC192 (Juvenile Arrest Rate: Violent Crime 1998). Examine the stem and leaf displays and determine which measures of central tendency and spread are most appropriate.

Mean   _____

Median   _____

Standard deviation   _____

Range   _____

Interquartile Range   _____

Circle the measure you would use as the measure of central tendency:

     Mean   Median   Mode

Circle the measure you would use as the measure of spread:

     Standard deviation   Range   IQR

Why did you make these selections?

6. Using *Explore,* determine the measures of central tendency and spread for CRC507 (Rate of Reported Hate Crimes 1998). Examine the stem and leaf displays and determine which measures of central tendency and spread are most appropriate.

Mean   _____

Median   _____

Standard deviation   _____

Range   _____

Interquartile Range   _____

Circle the measure you would use as the measure of central tendency:

  Mean   Median   Mode

Circle the measure you would use as the measure of spread:

  Standard deviation   Range   IQR

Why did you make these selections?

7. Using *Explore,* determine the measures of central tendency and spread for DMS491 (Divorce Rate 1998). Examine the stem and leaf displays and determine which measures of central tendency and spread are most appropriate.

Mean   _____

Median   _____

Standard deviation   _____

Range   _____

Interquartile Range   _____

Circle the measure you would use as the measure of central tendency:

Mean   Median   Mode

Circle the measure you would use as the measure of spread:

Standard deviation   Range   IQR

Why did you make these selections?

8. Using *Explore,* determine the measures of central tendency and spread for DTH107 (Death Rate by AIDS in 1997). Examine the stem and leaf displays and determine which measures of central tendency and spread are most appropriate.

Mean   _____

Median   _____

Standard deviation   _____

Range   _____

Interquartile Range   _____

Circle the measure you would use as the measure of central tendency:

Mean   Median   Mode

Circle the measure you would use as the measure of spread:

Standard deviation   Range   IQR

Why did you make these selections?

Chapter 4
Constructing Variables

Overview

     This chapter shows how to reconfigure existing variables to make them better suited to statistical analysis. We outline the processes involved in recoding and computing new variables, the most common ways of redefining and reorganizing existing data. These functions provide the foundation for categorizing groups of responses, or constructing rates and difference scores. The construction of new variables requires good record keeping, and toward that end, we outline how syntax files can be used to track how data are reorganized. We also show how syntax files can be used to construct new variables, illustrating this process with the construction of an index.

Why Construct New Variables?

     Social science research often involves obtaining data from sources such as police departments, hospitals, and schools. These data can be very informative, but also require refinement before they can be used to answer the types of research questions posed by social scientists. Even when the social scientist is in control of collecting the data, answering research questions often requires manipulating data to form new variables in the process of data analysis. One of the great advantages that SPSS offers researchers is the ease with which data can be reconfigured to suit the analytic needs. In this section, we outline and illustrate some ways to create new variables by combining information held in two or more variables, or by transforming the information held in a single variable using mathematical operations.

Recoding Existing Variables

     There are many circumstances in which a researcher may want to **recode** (or reconfigure) an existing variable. One common case is when the existing variables do not directly measure the concept of interest. For example, alcohol consumption is often measured as a numerical variable (0,1,2,3,4...drinks/day). However, American culture emphasizes the distinction between abstainers, social drinkers, and alcoholics. To bring the data in line with the concept of alcoholism requires recoding the numerical variable into the form of a categorical variable, distinguishing "nonusers" (0 drinks/day) from "moderate users" (1-2 drinks/day) from "heavy users" (3 or more drinks/day). Recoding this way involves making a categorical variable from a numerical variable. The concept of a life stage also requires recoding the numerical variable age, generally measured with birth dates, into categories such as teenager (age 12-17), young adult (age 18-25), establishment stages (age 26-64), and senior years (age 65+).

SPSS offers two choices under the recode command: *Into Same Variable* and *Into Different Variable*. We suggest always selecting *Into Different Variables* to prevent the original information from being overwritten during the recoding procedure. Because recoding *Into Same Variables* replaces the values in that existing variable, it will irrevocably alter a data set, and therefore threaten researchers' abilities to recode the original variable in alternate ways. Also, if the researcher makes a mistake in the logic for the recoding, it is possible to accidentally and permanently alter the data. For these reasons, it is generally best not to recode over an existing variable, unless one is absolutely confident that the lost information will never be needed.

To illustrate how to recode a numerical variable into a categorical variable, we will use the STATES data to create a new variable indicating whether or not a state performed an execution from 1977-1998. Variable PRC72 (Prisoners Executed: 1977-1998) is a numerical variable with the number of executions ranging from 0 to 164. To change this to a categorical variable, use the *Recode* command,

> *Transform*
> > *Recode*
> > > *Into Different Variables*

In the first window select the variable PRC72 and identify the new *Output Variable* as EXECUTE. *Label* the output variable as "Categorical Recode of Executions." You should duplicate Figure 4.1.

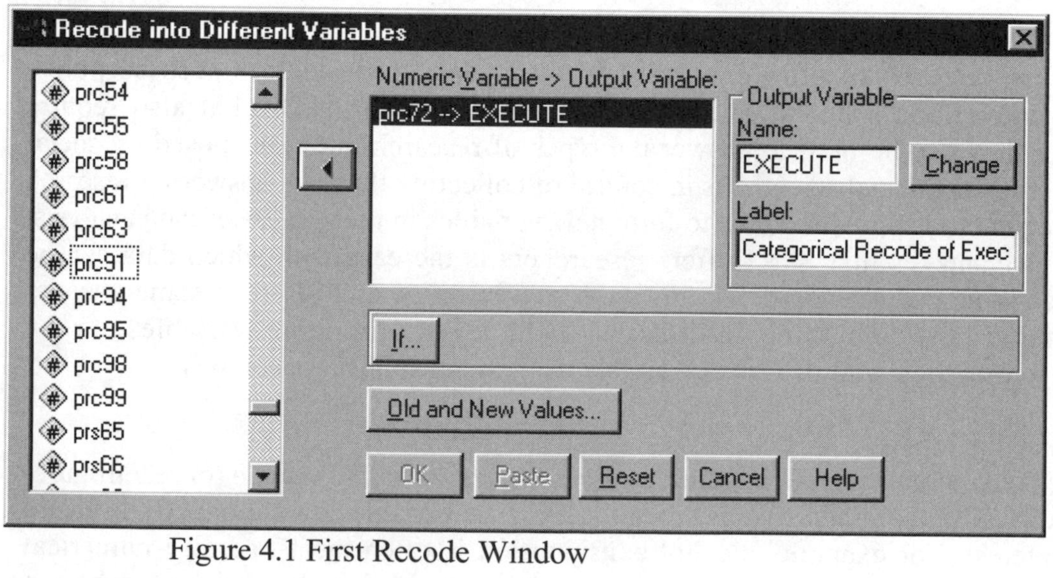

Figure 4.1 First Recode Window

To begin the recode procedure, select *Old and New Values* to reveal another window. On the left side, indicate the values of the old variable, PRC72. On the right side, indicate the corresponding values of the new variable, EXECUTE. States with no executions (PRC72=0) will be coded as 0 and states with executions (PRC72 $\geq$ 1) will be coded as 1 in variable EXECUTE. Note that values can be replaced one at a time, or a range of old values can be recoded as a single value. After entering the old value on the left side and the new value on the right side, click on "Add" to record that pair of corresponding values. After all of the new values have been added, click *Continue*, then *OK*. You should duplicate Figure 4.2.

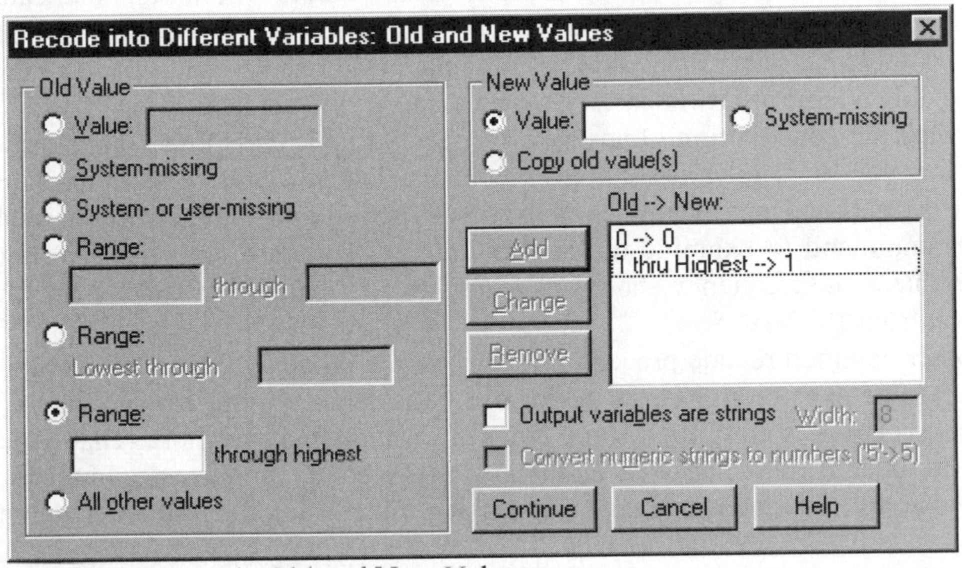

Figure 4.2 Recode Old and New Values

The whole process is as follows:

> *Transform*
>> *Recode*
>>> *Into Different Values*
>>>> *Input variable:* PRC72
>>>> *Output variable Name:* EXECUTE
>>>> *Output variable Label:* Category Recode of Executions
>>>> *Change*
>>>> *Old and New Values*
>>>>> *Old Value: Value:* 0
>>>>> *New Value: Value:* 0
>>>>> *Add*
>>>>>
>>>>> *Old Value: Range:* 1 *through highest*
>>>>> *New Value: Value:* 1
>>>>> *Add*
>>>>> *Continue*
>>> *OK*

After recoding the variable, to make sure that the new variable is recoded accurately, use:

Analyze
> *Reports*
>> *Case Summaries*
>>> *Variables:* PRC72
>>>> EXECUTE
>> *OK*

One very important issue in correctly recoding is the way SPSS deals with missing values. A value that is coded as missing in the original variable will not automatically be coded as missing in the new variable. It will be grouped in with any ranges you specify. Therefore, if the original variable has any values coded as missing, always select that *System or User Missing* values in the old variable are recoded as *System Missing* in the new variable.

To track the construction of any new recoded variable, it is important to label both the variable and its values. The values 0 and 1 can be labeled "no" and "yes" in the *Variable View* spreadsheet, as outlined in Chapter 2. After constructing and labeling the variable, use the *Frequencies* command to examine the distribution and compare it to the distribution of the original variable. The frequency should indicate that 56.9 percent of states performed at least one execution from 1977-1998.

Another common recode procedure is to change a range of values to be missing. Recall that in the case of executions, Texas performed considerably more executions than all other states. Because Texas is an outlier, some types of analyses may be more reliably performed if this case is excluded from the analysis and treated as a separate unique case. In this example, we create a new variable that recodes Texas as a missing value, using the following commands:

Transform
> *Recode*
>> *Into Different Values*
>>> *Input variable:* PRC72
>>> *Output variable Name:* EXECUT2
>>> *Output variable Label:* Category Recode of Executions 1977-1998
>>> *Change*
>>> *Old and New Values*
>>>> *Old Value: Value:* 0
>>>> *New Value: Value:* 0
>>>> *Add*
>>>>
>>>> *Old Value: Range:* 1 *through* 60
>>>> *New Value: Value:* 1
>>>> *Add*
>>>>
>>>> *Old Value: Value:* 164
>>>> *New Value: System Missing*
>>>> *Add*
>>>> *Continue*
>> *OK*

Why would we want both variables EXECUTE and EXECUT2? One reason would be that we could replicate any analysis of executions examining the United States as a whole, and then the United States excluding Texas. If Texas is having an undue influence on the analysis, we will observe different findings, depending on which variable is being used. On the other hand, if both analyses reveal comparable findings, then Texas is not distinguished as a unique case, bolstering our confidence that it can be left in any analysis.

Computing New Variables

Performing a mathematical function on one or more existing variables can also create a needed variable. Consider the types of data needed for research on the most problematic areas of violent crime. One source of these data is police crime reports. They offer indicators of the occurrence of crime and are the basis for a number of variables in the STATES data set.

Use the Sort and Case Summaries functions outlined in Chapter 3 on one of these variables, CRC344 (Rapes 1998). The variable CRC344 indicates that more rapes occurred in California (9,782), for example, than Oklahoma (1,513). These data, while interesting, cannot answer the research question concerning where violent crime is most problematic. An accurate comparison requires taking the populations of both states into account. The question, after all, is not how many rapes occurred, but the probability of an individual falling victim to rape. The answer is to combine each state's incidence of rape with its population to produce a rape rate.

A **rate** is a ratio of two variables that indicates the *measured* number of occurrences in reference to the *potential* number of occurrences. A rape rate allows us to estimate how many rapes occur per every 100,000 people. Because the population base of the statistic is now constant, a comparison between states is possible. In anticipation of many users' needs, we included both rates and incidence variables in our preparation of the STATES data set. The variable CRC347, Rate Rape in 1998, shows that in relationship to its population, California actually has a lower rate of rape (29.9/100,000) than does Oklahoma (45.2/100,000).

Although we tried our best to anticipate user needs, social research usually involves manipulating some variables even in very refined data sets. Suppose, for instance, that a law enforcement agency asks where it should focus financial resources to control violent crime. These agencies have limited funds to fight murders, bombings, rapes, and other violent crimes. One approach is to calculate how much each type of violent crime contributes to the overall number of violent crimes. The STATES data include variables that describe the number of rapes, murders, etc. and the total number of violent crimes. To find the percentage of violent crimes that are made up of rapes, murder, etc. requires computing new variables.

Calculating the percentage of violent crimes that are rapes involves variables CRC315 (Violent Crimes 1998) and CRC344 (Rapes 1998). Use the *Compute* command to calculate a new variable "RAPEPCT." You can also *label* the new variable "Rapes as % of Violent Crimes 1998" from the *Compute* window.

> *Transform*
> > *Compute*
> > > *Target Variable* = RAPEPCT
> > > *Numeric Expression* = (CRC344 /CRC315)*100
> > > *Type&Label*
> > > > *Label:* Rapes as % of Violent Crimes 1998
> > > > *Continue*
> > *OK*

You can enter the information in the *Numeric Expression* box by either typing in the numeric expression (above) or by using the mouse to choose the variables from the list at the left and the mathematical signs from the calculator keyboard. Remember to enter a *Variable Label* right away, to document how you computed RAPEPCT. We suggest "RAPES AS A PERCENT OF VIOLENT CRIMES 1998". Figure 4.3 shows how to generate the new *target* variable name "RAPEPCT" using the *Compute* command.

The speed and ease with which SPSS creates new variables can be seductive, and even when researchers are as careful as possible, mistakes inevitably occur. For this reason, before we make any conclusions about rape as it compares to other violent crimes, it is extremely important to inspect the new variable to confirm that it was accurately calculated. This process is part of **cleaning data**—ridding the data of errors. The types of univariate analyses outlined in the previous chapter offer multiple ways of checking if new variables are accurately computed. For instance, *Frequencies* or *Descriptives* can be used to quickly check that all values fall within possible ranges, a procedure we term **possible code cleaning**. In this case, no percentage should be higher than 100% or lower than 0%.

You can also use intuition to see if variables have likely values and if measures of central tendency (means, medians, or modes) and spread (standard deviations) appear reasonable. Knowing that rapes are often underreported compared to other violent crimes, it would be surprising if rapes constituted the majority of violent crime, or if all states held the exact same rape rate.

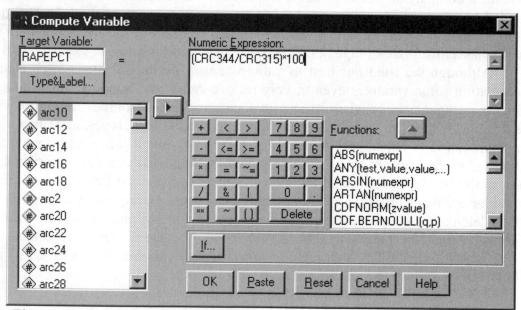

Figure 4.3 Computing a New Variable

	Rapes in 1998	Violent Crimes in 1998	Rapes as % of Violent Crimes 1998	State name
1	1443.00	22286.00	6.47	Alabama
2	421.00	4015.00	10.49	Alaska
3	1451.00	26984.00	5.38	Arizona
4	893.00	12442.00	7.18	Arkansas
5	9782.00	229883.00	4.26	California
6	1883.00	15008.00	12.55	Colorado
7	728.00	11993.00	6.07	Connecticut
8	499.00	5672.00	8.80	Delaware
9	190.00	8988.00	2.11	District of Columbia
10	7404.00	140016.00	5.29	Florida
Total N	10	10	10	10

Case Summaries[a]

a. Limited to first 10 cases.

Figure 4.4 Case Summaries as a Check for Accuracy

Another approach is to engage in **contingency cleaning**—comparing the constructed variables to other existing variables. For instance, because rape is a type of violent crime, we would suspect that rapes are prevalent in states where other types of violent crimes are also prevalent. As a first step in data cleaning, look over the new variable using the command:

> *Analyze*
>> *Reports*
>>> *Case Summaries*
>>>> *Variables:* CRC344
>>>> CRC315
>>>> RAPEPCT
>>>> STATE
>>> *OK*

Using the *Case Summaries* output, you can see if the calculations seem accurate (Figure 4.4). Now that we are sure there are no errors, perform a *Sort* on RAPEPCT to examine which states have the highest proportion of rapes to violent crime. Where does your state rank? In the District of Columbia, rapes constitute only 2.11% of the violent crimes, but in North Dakota, they constitute 37.19% of the violent crimes. These computations place the researcher in a much more informed position to discuss the degree to which law enforcement agencies should funnel limited resources in the fight against violent crime. Recommendations to the District of Columbia and North Dakota may be very different.

Another common reason for computing new variables is to examine the difference between two groups on a similar attribute. For example, a researcher may be interested in how the teenage birth rate has changed from 1980 to 1990 among the states. To look at this we have to create a new variable, TEENCH, using the *Compute* command. This new variable is the difference between the variables BIH38 (Teenage Birth Rate in 1990) and BIH41 (Teenage Birth Rate in 1980). The commands are as follows:

> *Transform*
> > *Compute*
> > > *Target Variable* = TEENCH
> > > *Numeric Expression* = BIH38 – BIH41
> > > *Type&Label*
> > > > *Label:* Change In Teen Birth Rate 1990-1980
> > > > *Continue*
> > *OK*

Descriptive statistics and a histogram of TEENCH give us an assessment of how teen birth rates changed from 1980 to 1990 (Figures 4.5 and 4.6). Positive values indicate that the teen birth rate rose and negative values indicate that it dropped. As these figures show, from 1980 to 1990, the general trend was for teenage birth rates to increase, on average by 2.91. Try to reproduce the figures below using the techniques outlined in Chapter 3.

Descriptive Statistics

	N	Minimum	Maximum	Mean	Std. Deviation
Change in Teen Birth Rate 1990-1980	51	-22.40	30.70	2.9098	8.6448
Valid N (listwise)	51				

Figure 4.5 Descriptives of TEENCH

The most commonly performed computation procedures involve adding, multiplying, dividing, and subtracting variables from one another. There are circumstances, however, when researchers may want to perform other types of computations, such as changing the structure of date variables, calculating time from dates, doing logarithm transformations, or a wide range of other functions. To gain a sense of the range of procedures possible, look through the functions listed in the Compute window. For a description of each function, simply highlight it using the left mouse button, then click on the right mouse button. A text box will explain the type of operation that this function performs, as shown in Figure 4.7.

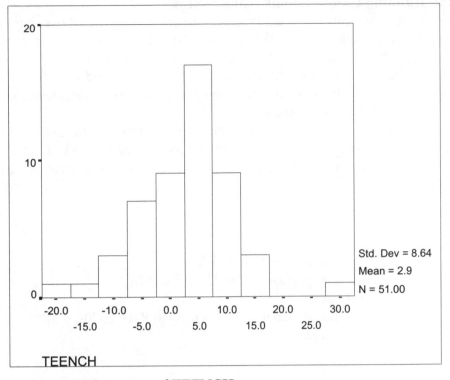

Figure 4.6 Histogram of TEENCH

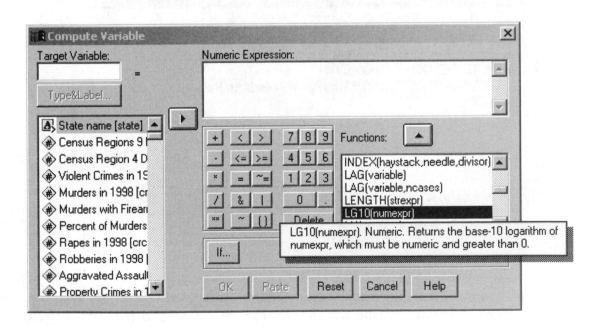

Figure 4.7 Compute Functions

Recording and Running Computations Using Syntax

Computing new variables and using these variables in data analysis require considerable record keeping and data management. We recommend that researchers keep extensive notes on how they computed their variables. One means of doing so is to paste computations into a syntax file using the *Paste* command within the *Compute* window. **Syntax files** contain procedures written in the SPSS command language that, when submitted, cause the SPSS processor to perform statistical operations.

Syntax files are an alternative, as well as a supplement, to the dialogue windows. For most operations within dialogue windows, SPSS offers a command button *Paste*. To illustrate the *Paste* feature and how syntax files work, replicate the above compute procedure creating a new variable TEENCH2

> *Transform*
> > *Compute*
> > > *Target Variable* = TEENCH2
> > > *Numeric Expression* = BIH38 – BIH41
> > > *Type&Label*
> > > > *Label:* Change In Teen Birth Rate 1990-1980
> > > > *Continue*
> > *Paste*

Instead of commanding SPSS to run the procedure immediately using the command OK, order it to *Paste* the command to a syntax file. Your screen should look like Figure 4.8

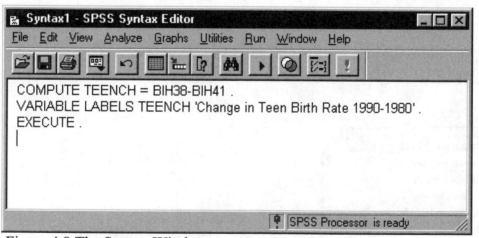

Figure 4.8 The Syntax Window

Observe that the command has now been summarized in syntax, the commands used to make SPSS run procedures. This command has not yet run, however, and the data set remains unchanged. To submit the command to the SPSS processor, highlight the entire command using the mouse, and then select:

Run
> *Selection*

Clicking on the Data Editor Window box at the bottom of the screen will return you to the spreadsheet array of the data, where you can scroll to the end of the data set and see that SPSS created TEENCH2.

Why would anyone want to use syntax files instead of the dialogue windows? There are two general reasons. First, syntax files keep records of how variables were computed and how analyses were performed. Consequently, a researcher can perform extensive analyses and use the syntax files to track data manipulations through the course of the project. Second, syntax files enable researchers to perform repetitious tasks quickly. For example, you can block, move, and copy portions of syntax files just as in word processing programs. Using the syntax to compute many variables using similar procedures can enhance the efficiency of constructing, or even analyzing, variables. Once users become familiar with SPSS, many largely dispense with using the menus and do almost everything through syntax files. The *Help* menu in SPSS shows how to access syntax commands directly, without pasting. For example, syntax commands can label variables (as well as values) directly with:

> Variable labels TEENCH2 "Change In Teen Birth Rate 1980-1990".

Note that the following command can save a syntax file:

File
> *Save As:* Teen Birth.SPS

It can also be reopened and subsequently modified using the command:

File
> *Open*
> > *Syntax*
> > > *File name:* Teen Birth.SPS

Just as managing data is a concern, so is managing syntax files. These files are only useful if researchers can track which commands their analyses rely upon. Different researchers develop their own strategies for managing syntax files, but we suggest creating two general types of syntax files, **preparation files** and **analysis files**. Preparation syntax files contain commands for constructing and modifying variables. Analysis syntax files contain commands for data analysis for a report. This is very helpful when an analysis needs to be replicated later or described accurately in the report.

As you prepare both types of files, it is often helpful to insert notes within the syntax files to track how and why you manipulated data. These notes are text that SPSS ignores when running commands. To insert a note within an SPSS syntax file, use the asterisk (*) character at the beginning and end of the note and separate the note with at least one blank line from the next command within the syntax file. For example:

The following computes and labels a new variable estimating the change in teen birth rates from 1980-1990

```
COMPUTE TEENCH2 = BIH38-BIH41.
EXECUTE.
Variable labels TEENCH2 "CHANGE IN TEEN BIRTH RATE 1980-1990".
```

Using Compute to Construct an Index with Syntax

The creation of indexes is another common use of the compute command. An **index** is a single score that summarizes responses to a number of variables. Indexes are often used when researchers are interested in measuring an underlying concept, such as depression or work commitment, that cannot be reliably measured with a single indicator. In such a situation, the best approach is to combine multiple indicators into an index. One advantage is that analysis becomes less repetitious and statistical summaries become more meaningful. For example, a researcher who is interested in understanding attitudes toward abortion may find it advantageous to ask a number of questions, as most people will fall within a continuum between believing that abortion is wrong in every circumstance and believing that abortion is permissible in any situation.

To illustrate some of the ways to construct indexes, we will use the GSS98 data set. In the following example, we create an index score representing attitudes toward abortion, based on six questions on the GSS98 data set:

ABANY (Abortion If Woman Wants For Any Reason)
ABDEFECT (Strong Chance Of Serious Defect)
ABHLTH (Woman's Health Seriously Endangered)
ABNOMORE (Married—Wants No More Children)
ABPOOR (Low Income—Can't Afford More Children)
ABRAPE (Pregnant As Result Of Rape)

For each question, the respondent indicated if they agreed that abortion should be legal in that situation. We will create an index indicating the degree to which respondents are "pro-life" (against abortion rights) or "pro-choice" (in favor of abortion rights). For each of these variables, a response of 1 indicates "Yes" and a response of 0 indicates "No". The simplest index is a sum of the six variables, so the index could range from 0 to 6. A score closer to 6 indicates the respondent is more in favor of abortion rights; a score closer to 0 indicates the respondent is more opposed to abortion rights. We could use the menus to construct indexes, but we will use syntax to illustrate the process. In the case of a summary score index, the syntax commands would look like this:

```
COMPUTE ABINDX = ABANY+ABDEFECT+ABHLTH+ABNOMORE+ABPOOR+ABRAPE.
VARIABLE LABEL ABINDX "INDEX - RAW SUM OF ABORTION ATTITUDES".
EXECUTE.
```

The above index will be very functional, but we can refine it by making it represent an average of the six items.

NOTE HIGH SCORE INDICATES MORE PRO-CHOICE

COMPUTE ABINDX2 = (ABANY+ABDEFECT+ABHLTH+ABNOMORE+ABPOOR+ABRAPE)/6.
VARIABLE LABEL ABINDX2 "INDEX – AVERAGE RATING OF ABORTION ATTITUDE".
EXECUTE.

Why use an average, rather than a sum? One reason is that SPSS can compute an average that adjusts for missing values for one or more items in the index. In the above examples of index construction, if there were a missing value for any case for any of the six variables, SPSS would drop that case from the index and code it as missing. Missing values can greatly diminish a researcher's ability to perform an analysis. However, if a reasonable number of valid responses are available for the items in an index, they can be included in the analysis. The following syntax computes a mean index score with the command "MEAN.3." This command calculates the mean only if there are three or more valid responses among the six items comprising the scale:

*NOTE HIGH SCORE INDICATES MORE PRO-CHOICE, AVERAGE OF 3 OR MORE
RESPONSES*

COMPUTE ABINDX3 = MEAN.3(ABANY, ABDEFECT, ABHLTH, ABNOMORE, ABPOOR, ABRAPE).
VARIABLE LABEL ABINDX3 "INDEX – AVERAGE RATING OF ABORTION ATTITUDE".
EXECUTE.

In addition to making intuitive sense, it is important that a scale be reliable. As we discussed in Chapter 1, **reliability** indicates how consistently an indicator measures a concept. If an index reliably measures an underlying concept, such as an attitude, respondents should give similar answers to the items on the scale. In general, people who are generally against abortion should tend to answer "no" to most of the abortion attitude questions, those who are in favor of choice should tend to answer "yes." If there is no relationship between the items making up a scale, then researchers need to question the validity of either their underlying concept, or the degree to which these indicators reflect that concept.

One statistic that measures scale reliability is the **Alpha Coefficient**. The Alpha score can range between 0 and 1, with higher numbers indicating higher reliability. As a rule of thumb, an Alpha score of .70 or higher on an index of four or more indicators indicates good reliability. The following SPSS commands will yield the Alpha Coefficient:

Analyze
   Scale
      Reliability Analysis
         Items =   ABANY
                  ABDEFECT
                  ABHLTH
                  ABNOMORE
                  ABPOOR
                  ABRAPE
      OK

The output reveals an Alpha = .8721, which indicates good scale reliability. Pro-life and pro-choice responses to these questions tend to cluster together statistically.

Summary

This chapter demonstrated the two primary ways of reorganizing data within SPSS, computing new variables and recoding existing variables. As new variables are created, they need to be checked for accurate construction. As familiarity with SPSS increases, and as analysis becomes more complex and detailed, there are advantages to working with syntax files. These files can be used to perform repetitious compute or recode procedures. They can also be a valuable means of recording how variables have been constructed and refined. One such circumstance would be in the construction of an index, which often requires many related commands before the final index score is created.

Key Terms

Alpha Coefficient	Possible Code Cleaning
Analysis Files	Preparation Files
Cleaning Data	Rate
Computing Variables	Recode
Contingency Cleaning	Reliability
Index	Syntax Files

References and Further Reading

Du Toit, S. H. C., A. G. W. Steyn, and R. H. Stumpf. 1986. *Graphical Exploratory Data Analysis*. New York: Springer-Verlag.

Levin, Jack and James Fox. 1997. *Elementary Statistics in Social Research*. New York: Longman.

Tufte, Edward. 1986. *The Visual Display of Quantitative Information*. Cheshire, Connecticut: Graphics Press.

Chapter 4 Exercises

Name ——————————————————————————   Date ——————————

1. Generate a new variable MURDPCT and label it "Murders as % of Violent Crimes" using *Compute*. Use the following formula to generate the new variable.

> (CRC325 / CRC315)*100
> (Murders 1998 divided by Violent Crimes 1998) multiplied by 100

What is the mean of this new variable?

————————————————

Which state has the highest percentage of violent crimes that are murders?

————————————————

Which state has the lowest percentage of violent crimes that are murders?

————————————————

What is the percentage of violent crimes that are murders in your state?

————————————————

2. *Compute* a new variable VCPCT that determines the percentage of crimes that are violent crimes. Use variables CRC309 (Crimes 1998) and CRC315 (Violent Crimes 1998) to compute the new variable.

What is the mean of VCPCT?

_____

Which state has the highest percentage of crimes that are violent crimes?

_____

Which state has the lowest percentage of crimes that are violent crimes?

_____

What percentage of crimes are violent crimes in your state?

_____

3. Using the variable REGION4, *Recode* the variable into a new variable SOUTH. SOUTH will be used to indicate whether a state is located in the south or not. Recode states which are coded as "South" in REGION4 to equal 1. Recode all other regions to equal 0.

        REGION4   SOUTH

        1=NorthEast   0=NonSouth
        2=MidWest   0=NonSouth
        3=South   1=South
        4=West   0=NonSouth

To recode these data use the procedure:
> *Transform*
>> *Recode*
>>> *Into Different Variables*

Sort cases by SOUTH, print (and double check) the results using:
> *Analyze*
>> *Reports*
>>> *Case Summaries*
>>>> (Variables: STATE REGION4 SOUTH)

4. Using the STATES data set, *Compute* a new variable, POPCHG, indicating the change in the population from 1970 to 1990. Use variables DMS421 and DMS424.

Which 5 states had the largest population increases?

_____

_____

_____

_____

_____

Which 5 states had the least population change?

_____

_____

_____

_____

_____

5. Using the STATES data set, create an index to measure child abuse using the following variables:

CAC253 (Rate of Physically Abused Children in 1997)
CAC255 (Rate of Sexually Abused Children in 1997)
CAC257 (Rate of Emotionally Abused Children in 1997)
CAC259 (Rate of Neglected Children in 1997)

Use the *Compute* command to create an index using the mean of these four variables. Call this variable ABUSE.

What is the mean value of ABUSE? _____

What is the alpha coefficient of the index? _____

According to the alpha coefficient, is this a good index? _____

Why?

Note that you have some missing values in the new variable ABUSE. Can you write a syntax that would include an additional 5 states and still produce an abuse index for the mean of these variables?

6. Using the GSS data set, create an index to measure suicide acceptance using the following variables:

> SUICIDE1 – Suicide acceptable if incurable disease
> SUICIDE2 – Suicide acceptable if bankrupt
> SUICIDE3 – Suicide acceptable if dishonored family
> SUICIDE4 – Suicide acceptable if tired of living

Use the *Compute* command to create an index using the mean of these four variables. Call this variable SUICAC.

What is the mean value of SUICAC?   _____

What is the alpha coefficient of the index?   _____

According to the alpha coefficient, is this a good index?   _____

Why?

Chapter 5
Assessing Association through Bivariate Analysis

Overview

Many of the most interesting questions addressed by social scientists examine the relationships between two variables. For example:

Is the death penalty associated with lower crime rates?
Does school funding relate to students' educational success?
Do religious people tend to be more politically and socially conservative?

Each of these questions asks if the values of one variable (such as whether a state has the death penalty) are associated with the values of another variable (such as crime rates).

Our introduction to bivariate analysis begins with an explanation of **significance tests**, methods of determining if an observed relationship is the result of chance. We then explain how significance tests apply to bivariate associations. This chapter focuses on two types of associations—cross tabulations and correlations. **Cross tabulations** enable researchers to measure the association between two categorical variables, such as ethnicity and religion. **Correlations** enable researchers to measure the association between two numerical variables, such as income and age. We also illustrate ways of graphing bivariate associations. These graphs are useful for both exploring and disseminating findings in reports and presentations. In Chapter 6, we extend the discussion of bivariate analyses to methods of testing and graphing associations between numerical and categorical variables.

Why Do We Need Significance Tests?

Patterns in data are the result of either relationships between variables or random chance. Intuitively, events that were produced by random chance would look "random" and have no pattern. But random events occasionally form deceptive sequences that imply a relationship between observations. Our friend, Santosh Venkatesh, at the University of Pennsylvania, uses a unique method to illustrate how chance occurrences often look like they have strong patterns. Santosh instructs his students to create what they think a random event looks like, and to document an actual random event. Their challenge is to create such a good fictional depiction of randomness that he will not be able to distinguish it from an actual random event.

Santosh divides his classes into two groups of students. One half of his class creates fake documents illustrating one hundred coin tosses. The other half actually flips a coin 100 times. Thus, in a class of 40 students, he receives 20 documents showing actual coin tosses and 20 documents of fictitious coin tosses. The students record heads with "H" and tails with "T" (HTHTHHTTHTHTHT…etc.). To his students' amazement, our friend can distinguish the faked lists from the actual coin flips with remarkable consistency (he is right about 80% of the time). How does he do this? Not with SPSS or even a hand calculator.

Santosh uses a simple principle to guide his sleuthing—his knowledge that students will tend to be insensitive to the degree of variation normally found in random occurrences. For example, students will tend to fake coin tosses by alternating heads and tails with great regularity (HTHTHTTHTHTHHTHT). In reality (and you can try this), numerous repeats of an event (HTHHHHHTTTH) are commonly observed in a long sequence of coin tosses. In any sequence of 100 coin flips, there is a high probability (approximately .80) that there will be a sequence of at least 5 heads or tails in a row. Very rarely do students produce faked lists containing such a long sequence. His students also tend to make sure there are an equal number of heads (50) and tails (50) in the series. Although a random event will *tend to* produce equal outcomes, unequal outcomes are actually more likely. For example, there is actually a greater likelihood of having an unequal number of heads and tails than achieving exactly 50 heads and 50 tails. Our friend's trick is relevant to the topic of significance tests because it highlights the fact that random events do not necessarily look random. It is common for any set of observations to look like it forms a relationship when, in fact, it is only representing chance occurrence.

In the test of any relationship, one of two hypotheses must be true. Patterns in data are either results of chance (the **null hypothesis**) or a real relationship (the **alternative hypothesis**). Data analysts need to assume that the null hypothesis is true unless chance is a very unlikely explanation for an observed relationship. Only then can an analyst conclude that the alternative hypothesis is true—the relationship is real. Significance tests help data analysts determine the degree to which any differences between groups, or patterns between variables, can be treated as real or as a by product of chance occurrence.

Significance tests rely on **significance levels**, estimates of probabilities that indicate the degree to which chance is a likely explanation for observed patterns. A high significance level indicates a strong possibility that simple random chance could explain a pattern. Such a finding would offer considerable support for the null hypothesis: there is no relationship between the variables. Conversely, a low significance level indicates that simple random chance is unlikely to explain a pattern. This would offer support to the alternative hypothesis: there is a relationship between the variables.

Because significance levels indicate probabilities of chance occurrence, they are handy and intuitively appealing. To understand their logic, consider that a **probability** is a mathematical measurement of the likelihood that an event will occur in the future or has occurred in the past. As examples, one can assess the probability that a family with two children will have a boy and a girl, or the probability that a person in England in the 13th century died of the plague. Probabilities can range from 0 to 1, but can also be expressed in percentages. This simply requires multiplying the probability by 100.

Significance levels give an exact estimate of the probability that chance produced a pattern in the data. Significance tests set thresholds for deciding whether the significance level is low enough to conclude that a relationship is real (not due to chance). If the significance level is low enough, the relationship is considered **statistically significant**. Different disciplines handle the concern of significance levels and statistical significance in different ways, however. Even among the authors of this book, Karen likes to report significance levels because of their exacting detail. On the other hand, Steve prefers judging relationships as being present or absent if they meet the standard of .05, as is common in the discipline of sociology. For beginning data analysts, it is useful to look at significance levels, but then judge them by the standards of significance tests.

At what threshold does a probability value become statistically significant? This is actually a complicated issue, because it depends on the type of question being asked and the types of effects a researcher is looking at. However, norms of social research advocate conservative standards in asserting statistical significance. Usually relationships are only seriously considered if there is only a small chance of the results being due to chance.

Depending on the sample size, typically these thresholds are set at .05 and .01. These two thresholds assert that there is only a 5 in 100 chance (.05) or 1 in 100 chance (.01) that a finding this strong would appear by chance. As you examine relationships, look at the significance level. If it is at or below .10, conclude that the observed relationship suggests the presence of an actual relationship, but more research would be needed before making a firm conclusion. A significance level of .05 or less, or .01 or less, will offer even greater support to concluding the variables are related.

Before judging the statistical significance of any finding, take a few moments to think about significance levels. Seldom can the probability of an event be 0 (impossible) or 1 (inevitable). In the case of a significance test, a significance level close to 1.00 indicates that random chance is a likely cause of the association. In this situation, a researcher will have little confidence that there is an actual relationship between the variables. On the other hand, a significance level close to 0, say .01, indicates that random chance is an unlikely cause, and the researcher can be very confident that the relationship is real. Although chance is still a possible cause, it is so unlikely that most people would rule this explanation out.

In most instances, researchers will find their significance levels falling somewhere in the middle of this potential range. As shorthand, remember that a low significance level indicates that chance is an unlikely explanation for the findings, and that a relationship can be considered real. On the other hand, a high significance level indicates that chance may have played a very big role in creating any observed relationship. In such a circumstance, even if findings look compelling, not much should be made of them, other than to say that no significant relationship was observed.

There are a number of methods for calculating significance levels, and we will not concern ourselves with the formulas involved in these calculations. Our interests are with the interpretation of the statistical significance levels. It is important to understand that significance levels and statistical significance are based on two things: the strength of the association and the **sample size**. Strong associations are needed to produce significant effects in small samples. On the other hand, even weak associations can produce significant effects in very large samples.

Suppose, for example, Springfield has a nuclear power plant and the residents of Springfield are concerned that the power plant might be affecting their community's infant mortality rate. The residents ask a researcher to perform a study to determine if the nuclear power plant is associated with an increase in the infant mortality rate. The researcher understands that infant mortality rates fluctuate on an annual basis in every community. In some years the mortality rates are low, in other years the rates are high. Random chance plays a role in these fluctuations. The researcher needs to rule out the role that random chance plays before concluding that the plant does or does not influence infant mortality rates.

One methodology would be to compare Springfield's mortality rates over time. If the researcher only has two years of observation, one pre-power plant and one post-power plant, it is very likely that the two rates will differ to some extent simply due to chance, since mortality rates naturally fluctuate. However, if the difference in the rates were huge, the researcher could place greater confidence in the findings being real and not just an artifact of random fluctuation. This study can be strengthened considerably by obtaining many years of data. With the increased sample size, magnitudes of effects can actually be smaller and still be statistically significant. With a large enough sample size, even a minute difference in infant mortality rates may register as significant.

Significance levels and significance tests are vital tools because they indicate whether researchers can rule out chance as being the source of findings. However, there are a few things that significant tests cannot do. When a researcher determines that a relationship is statistically *significant*, it does not mean that the relationship is *important*. Rather, it means that random chance is an unlikely explanation for the relationship being discussed. Significance tests can establish associations or relationships between variables, but they do not necessarily indicate that these relationships are causal (one variable affecting the other), only that a discernible pattern is emerging between the variables. Likewise, a significant relationship between the presence of the nuclear power plant and the infant mortality rate does not mean that the plant is causing the babies to die, only that they are associated. It is possible that some third unmeasured factor is creating the appearance of a causal relationship (a spurious effect), where there actually is none.

A low significance level does not necessarily indicate that a relationship is strong. With a large enough sample size, very weak relationships can be statistically significant. Relating this back to the hypothetical nuclear power plant study, suppose we find a statistically significant relationship. It is still possible that the relationship is very weak, say a mortality rate of 2.7/1000 compared to a rate of 2.5/1000. It is also possible that the data could indicate that a power plant is associated with a *lower* infant mortality rate, or that there is some third unmeasured factor causing a spurious relationship. The significance level does not address these other possibilities; it only documents the degree to which random chance is a likely explanation for the findings.

Analyzing Bivariate Relationships Between Two Categorical Variables

Performing bivariate analysis hinges on understanding the structure of variables, as described in Chapter 2. Recall that variables have two general forms, categorical or numerical. This section illustrates how to perform bivariate analysis between two categorical variables. Remember that categorical variables form groupings, such as "employed/unemployed," "White/Black/Hispanic," or "men/women." The applications illustrated here are used to statistically describe and graphically depict the relationship between one categorical variable and another categorical variable.

Cross Tabulations

Cross tabulations (also called **crosstabs**) are simple and highly effective means of showing the association between two categorical variables. A cross tabulation is a grid of all possible combinations of the values of two categorical variables. When the cells of this grid are filled with the frequency of occurrence of the intersecting values, the association between two variables becomes apparent.

To create a cross tabulation, open the GSS98 data and run the following commands (See Figure 5.1):

> *Analyze*
> > *Descriptive Statistics*
> > > *Crosstabs*
> > > > *Rows*: WANTJOB1
> > > > *Columns*: SEX
> > > > *OK*

This creates a table, similar to the one in Figure 5.2, showing the number of men and women (represented in the two columns) and their preferences for full-time work and part-time work (represented in the two rows). This grid shows how respondents are allotted in the "cells," the points of intersection between these two variables.

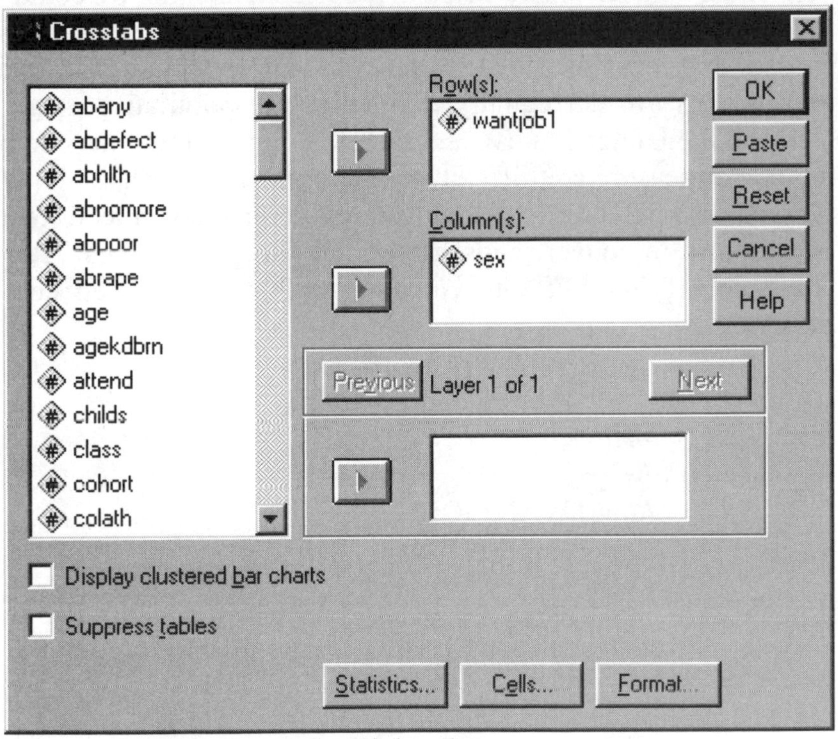

Figure 5.1 The Crosstabs Dialog Box

**WHICH JOB WOULD YOU PREFER * RESPONDENTS SEX
Crosstabulation**

Count

| | | RESPONDENTS SEX | | Total |
		MALE	FEMALE	
WHICH JOB WOULD YOU PREFER	A full-time job	349	323	672
	A part-time job	86	239	325
	Job less 10/wk	21	48	69
	No paid job	35	85	120
Total		491	695	1186

Figure 5.2 The Results Table

The null hypothesis for a cross tabulation says that there is no real association between the variables (all results are due to chance). If no relationship exists, then women and men should be equally represented in each row. For example, a null hypothesis could be structured for the variables work hour preferences and gender:

Null Hypothesis: Women and men do not vary in their preferences for full-time or part-time work.

If there were equal numbers of women and men in our sample, we could just compare the number of men and women who prefer each type of work. However, group sample sizes are rarely equally divided, and most surveys tend to over-sample women and under-sample men. Likewise, religious groups are not equally divided in the population (e.g., there are more Protestants than Jews in the United States), and therefore raw cell numbers comparing religious groups to some outcome measure are difficult to interpret. In this example, 204 more women than men were sampled, making it difficult to do a direct comparison of cell frequencies.

A ready solution is to convert cells from counts to percentages. Rerun the previous command, this time specifying SPSS to calculate both the observed counts and column percentages (See Figure 5.3):

Analyze
      Descriptive Statistics
            Crosstabs
                  Rows: WANTJOB1
                  Columns: SEX
                  Cells
                        Counts: Observed
                        Percentages: Column
                        Continue
            OK

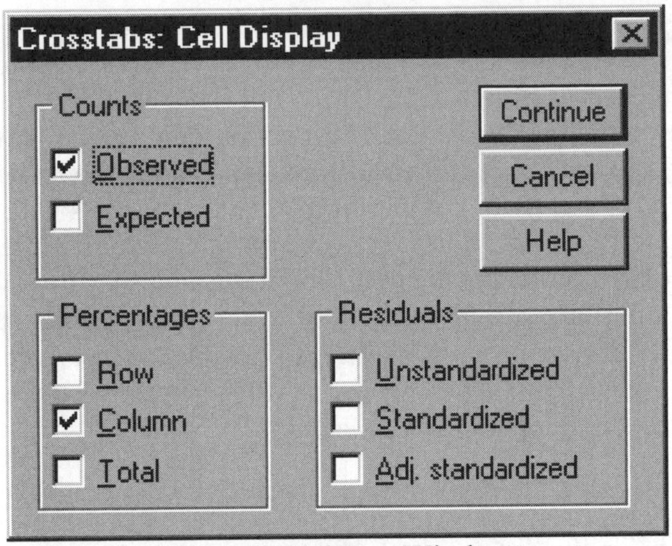

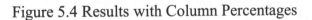

Figure 5.3 The Cell Dialogue Window

WHICH JOB WOULD YOU PREFER * RESPONDENTS SEX Crosstabulation

| | | | RESPONDENTS SEX | | |
			MALE	FEMALE	Total
WHICH JOB WOULD YOU PREFER	A full-time job	Count	349	323	672
		% within RESPONDENTS SEX	71.1%	46.5%	56.7%
	A part-time job	Count	86	239	325
		% within RESPONDENTS SEX	17.5%	34.4%	27.4%
	Job less 10/wk	Count	21	48	69
		% within RESPONDENTS SEX	4.3%	6.9%	5.8%
	No paid job	Count	35	85	120
		% within RESPONDENTS SEX	7.1%	12.2%	10.1%
Total		Count	491	695	1186
		% within RESPONDENTS SEX	100.0%	100.0%	100.0%

Figure 5.4 Results with Column Percentages

You probably noticed that SPSS could compute percentages for rows, columns, or the total number of cases in the entire sample. As a rule, we locate the dependent variable (the hypothesized outcome variable) as the row variable and the independent variable (the hypothesized causal factor) as the column variable. Then we only need the count and the column percent. This provides a standardized and consistent format for output. As this output remains consistent, it makes analyses easier and less mentally taxing. We retain the cell counts because it enables researchers to identify "**thin cells**," intersections between the two variables where there are few cases.

By examining the crosstab table in Figure 5.4, it seems apparent that there is a relationship between sex and work preference. Men (71.1%) are more willing than women (46.5%) to say they prefer to work full-time. The count (located at the top of each cell) provides supplemental information on how many cases fall within each cell. Likewise, women are more willing than men to say they prefer to work part-time, less than 10 hours per week, or not at all.

Our interests are primarily in comparing percentages across cells. Notice, the table in Figure 5.4 shows, proportionately, that over twice as many women prefer part-time work in comparison to men. So, it appears that the null hypothesis is false. However, before making this conclusion, we need to perform a significance test to determine if this apparent relationship is due to chance. SPSS offers a number of different significance tests and we suggest using the most widely accepted one of these, a Chi-square significance test (Figure 5.5). Rerun the cross tabulation commands, specifying this significance test:

Analyze
　　Descriptive Statistics
　　　　Crosstabs
　　　　　　Rows:　　WANTJOB1
　　　　　　Columns: SEX
　　　　　　Statistics: Chi-square
　　　　　　　　　　Continue
　　　　　Cells
　　　　　　　Counts: Observed
　　　　　　　Percentages: Column
　　　　　　　Continue
　　　　OK

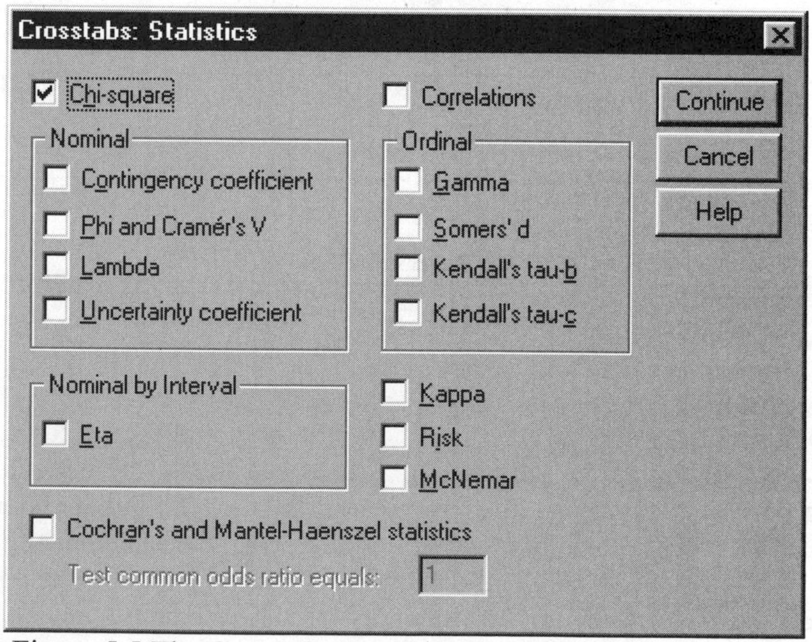

Figure 5.5 The Crosstabs Statistics Window

Chi-Square Tests

	Value	df	Asymp. Sig. (2-sided)
Pearson Chi-Square	71.457[a]	3	.000
Likelihood Ratio	73.034	3	.000
Linear-by-Linear Association	43.057	1	.000
N of Valid Cases	1186		

[a] 0 cells (.0%) have expected count less than 5. The minimum expected count is 28.57.

Figure 5.6 Chi-Square Results

Figure 5.6 shows the results of the significance tests. The test reveals that the relationship is statistically significant because the significance level is .000. This significance level is located in the column labeled "Asymp. Sig." The chance that the observed relationship between sex and work preference is due to random chance is less than 1/1000. Although this value appears to be 0, a significance level of 0 is impossible. The value was actually rounded off to three digits after the decimal point.

Bar Charts

Bar charts offer a highly effective means of displaying bivariate relationships between two categorical variables. As an illustration, construct a bar chart showing the relationship between the variables analyzed in the previous cross tabulation:

> *Graphs*
> > *Bar*
> > > *Clustered*
> > > *Data in Chart Are*: Summaries for groups of cases
> > > *Define*
> > > > *Bars Represent*: % of cases
> > > > *Category Axis*: WANTJOB1
> > > > *Define Clusters By*: SEX
> > > > *Titles*
> > > > > *Line 1*: Job Preference by Respondent's Sex
> > > > > *Continue*
> > > > *Options*
> > > > > Uncheck "Display groups defined by missing values"
> > > > > *Continue*
> > > *OK*

Your bar chart will look slightly different than Figure 5.7. You can restructure your chart using the *Chart Editor* window by double clicking on the graph generated in the *Output Navigator* window, and editing the titles and other format concerns. The bar chart shows, quite dramatically, the degree to which women outnumber men in their preference for part-time jobs.

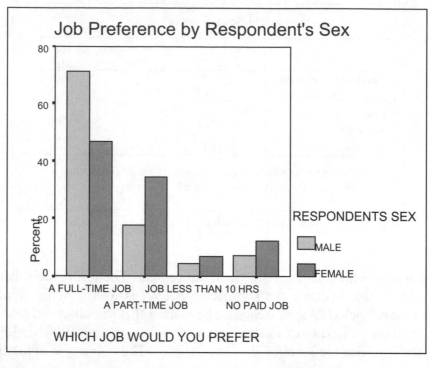

Figure 5.7 Bar Chart of WANTJOB1 By SEX

Analyzing Bivariate Relationships Between Two Numerical Variables

This section illustrates how to perform bivariate analysis between two numerical variables. Numerical variables, unlike categorical variables, display a range of values. Age, income, and miles driven to work are all numerical variables. When analyzing bivariate relationships between two numerical variables, one approach is to recode them into categorical variables and analyze relationships with crosstabs and bar charts. In some circumstances, this is appropriate. Generally, though, it is usually better to retain the numerical information, as it shows the wide range of possible values and offers the most detail for the diversity within the sample.

Correlations

When analyzing bivariate relationships between two numerical variables, most researchers use **correlations**, again a simple and effective means of summarizing the degree to which values in two variables correspond with each another. Generally, when social scientists discuss correlations, they are referring to **Pearson's correlation coefficient**. Pearson's correlation coefficient (from here on the "correlation") measures the strength of the **linear relationship** between two variables. Note that linear relationships are only one potential type of relationship between numerical variables. Other possibilities include **curvilinear**, as well as "**U**" **shaped** and inverted "U" shaped relationships (see Figure 5.8). Correlations identify linear relationships, but researchers should always be sensitive to the possibilities of other kinds of relationships. For example, the most likely relationship between test anxiety and test performance is an inverted U.   People whose anxiety is very low (mentally sleepy) or very high

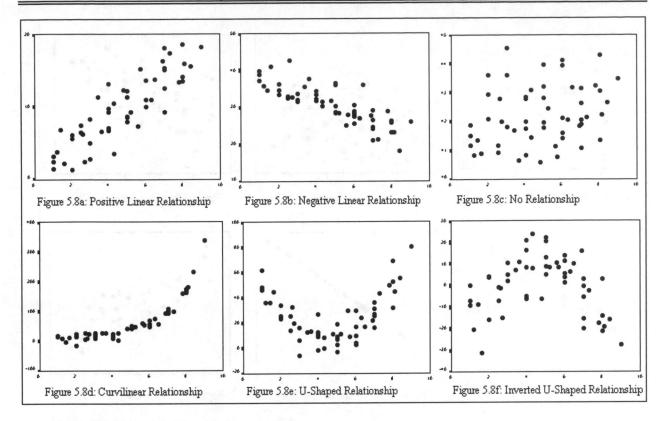

Figure 5.8a: Positive Linear Relationship   Figure 5.8b: Negative Linear Relationship   Figure 5.8c: No Relationship

Figure 5.8d: Curvilinear Relationship   Figure 5.8e: U-Shaped Relationship   Figure 5.8f: Inverted U-Shaped Relationship

Figure 5.8 Various Types of Relationships

(overwrought with anxiety) are likely to perform worse than those whose anxiety is moderate (alert and sharp).

Linear relationships exist when a change in one variable is associated with a consistent change in another variable. For example, if each additional year spent in school is associated with a $1000 increase in starting salary following graduation, this would represent a linear relationship between education and income.

The correlation coefficient can have values ranging between -1 and +1. A correlation of 0 indicates that there is no linear relationship between the two variables. Correlations of -1 and +1 indicate that there is a perfect linear relationship between the two variables. The closer the correlation is to either +1 or -1, the stronger the relationship between the two variables. Conversely, the closer the correlation is to 0, the weaker the correlation. Some examples of linear relationships and their correlations are displayed in Figure 5.9.

The negative and positive signs indicate the direction of the relationship. A positive correlation indicates a relationship in which increases in one variable are associated with increases in the other variable. For example, there is a positive correlation between education and income, in that more educated people tend to have higher incomes. A negative correlation, on the other hand, indicates a relationship in which an increase in one variable is associated with a decrease in the other variable. For example, research has shown a negative correlation between education and obesity in that more educated people are generally less obese.

To illustrate the application of correlation, we will examine the relationship between "social disorganization" and suicide. This relationship was first identified by the sociologist

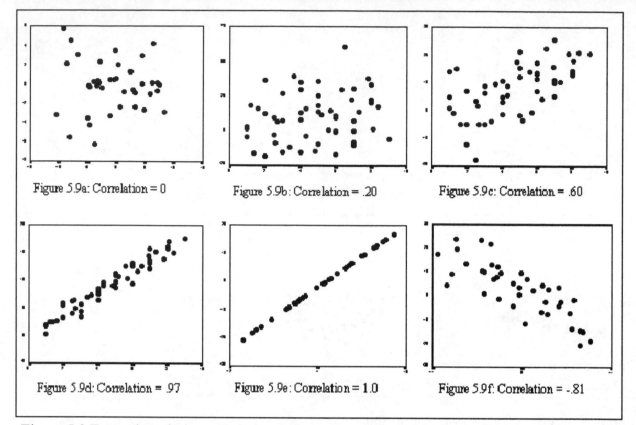

Figure 5.9a: Correlation = 0

Figure 5.9b: Correlation = .20

Figure 5.9c: Correlation = .60

Figure 5.9d: Correlation = .97

Figure 5.9e: Correlation = 1.0

Figure 5.9f: Correlation = -.81

Figure 5.9 Examples of Linear Relationships and Correlations

Emile Durkheim (1897) who found that suicides are influenced by social forces. He suggested that places with high levels of social disorganization (e.g., crime, divorce, substance abuse) also have high levels of suicide. Social disorganization is a concept that can be measured by indicators of the degree to which people are socially tied with one another. One such measure is the divorce rate. People living in areas with high divorce rates live in environments with greater social disorganization than those living in areas with low divorce rates. The null hypothesis for Durkheim's thesis is that there is no real linear relationship between suicide rates and divorce rates. The alternative hypothesis is that there is a positive linear relationship, that areas with high divorce rates will have high suicide rates.

We can test Durkheim's thesis using the STATES data set. Open this data set and run a correlation on the relationship between suicide rates and the divorce rate (Figures 5.10 and 5.11). If Durkheim is correct, we should expect to find a positive correlation between these two variables.

> *Analyze*
>> *Correlate*
>>> *Bivariate*:
>>>> *Variables*: DTH177 (Death Rate by Suicide 1997)
>>>> DMS491 (Divorce Rate 1998)
>>>> *Correlation Coefficients:* Pearson
>>>> *Tests of Significance:* Two Tailed
>>>> *OK*

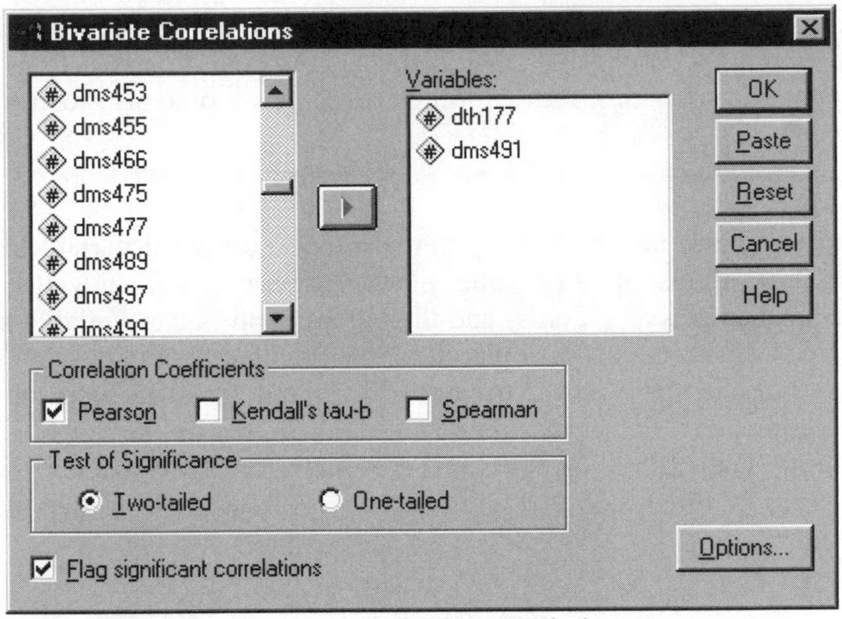

Figure 5.10 The Bivariate Correlations Window

Correlations			
		Death Rate by Suicide in 1997	Divorce Rate in 1998
Death Rate by Suicide in 1997	Pearson Correlation	1.000	.683**
	Sig. (2-tailed)	.	.000
	N	51	46
Divorce Rate in 1998	Pearson Correlation	.683**	1.000
	Sig. (2-tailed)	.000	.
	N	46	46

** · Correlation is significant at the 0.01 level (2-tailed).

Figure 5.11 Correlation Output

The correlation between divorce and suicide offers strong support of Durkheim's thesis. There is a .683 correlation between these two variables, indicating a positive relationship between suicide and divorce rates. This relationship is statistically significant as well. This can be seen in two ways from the Correlations table. The 2-tailed significance test shows a probability of .000, indicating that this is a statistically significant relationship. Also, the correlation tables flag out significance with asterisks (**) next to the coefficients.

Again, it is important to emphasize what correlations can and cannot do. Correlations only show the degree to which two numerical variables "co-relate" in a linear fashion. They cannot measure other types of relationships, such as curvilinear relationships. Also, because two variables are correlated does not necessarily mean that one variable causes the other to occur. One such error would be to fall prey to the **ecological fallacy**—asserting any individual's motivations and experiences from group measures. In the above example, for instance, an ecological fallacy would be to conclude that those experiencing divorces are more likely to kill themselves. We only know that places with high levels of divorce also tend to be places with high levels of suicide.

Scatter Plots

     Scatter plots graph the relationship between two numerical variables. The graphs in Figures 5.8 and 5.9 are all examples of scatter plots. In these graphs, the values of one variable are listed on the horizontal axis (X axis) and the values of the other variable are listed on the vertical axis (Y axis). Each case is then placed on the graph at the intersection of its values for the two variables. For example, Nevada has a suicide rate of 24.5/100,000 people and a divorce rate of 8.5/1000 people, so a dot representing Nevada is plotted on the graph at the intersection of those two values. The scatter plot for DTH177 (Death Rate by Suicide 1997) and DMS491 (Divorce Rate 1998) is illustrated in Figure 5.12. To create this scatter plot, perform the following commands:

Graphs
     Scatter
          Simple
               Define
                    Y Axis: DTH177 (Death Rate by Suicide 1997)
                    X Axis: DMS491 (Divorce Rate 1998)
                    Titles
                         Line 1: Suicide Rate by Divorce Rate.
                         Continue
             OK

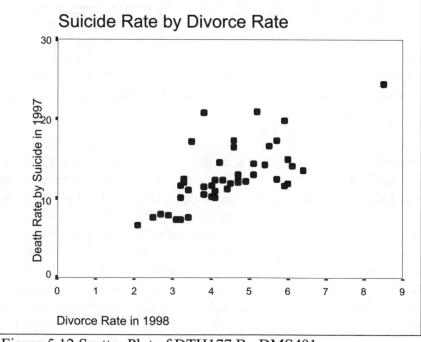

Figure 5.12 Scatter Plot of DTH177 By DMS491

Customarily, the independent variable is placed on the X axis (horizontal axis) and the dependent variable is placed on the Y axis (vertical axis). Because we are testing the effects of divorce rates on suicide rates, we plot divorce rates (the independent variable) on the X axis and suicide rates (the dependent variable) on the Y axis.

Again, there are small differences between the graph you produced and the one in Figure 5.12. We have used the chart editor to change the scale on the X axis. The default minimum value for this axis is 2. Default minimum values can be very misleading because when people look at the graph, there is a natural assumption that the left side of the graph represents 0. To change the minimum value of Divorce Rate in 1998 to 0, enter the Chart Editor by double clicking on the graph, and then double click on the actual X axis (the horizontal line). A window will pop up called "X Scale Axis." Change the minimum displayed value from 2 to 0.

As another example, using the STATES data, we can examine the relationship between infant mortality and poverty using the scatter plot command:

Graphs
> *Scatter*
>> *Simple*
>>> *Define*
>>>> *Y Axis*: DTH86 (Infant Mortality Rate 1999)
>>>> *X Axis*: PVS500 (Poverty Rate 1998)
>>>> *Titles*
>>>>> *Line 1*: Poverty and Infant Mortality.
>>>> *Continue*
>>> *OK*

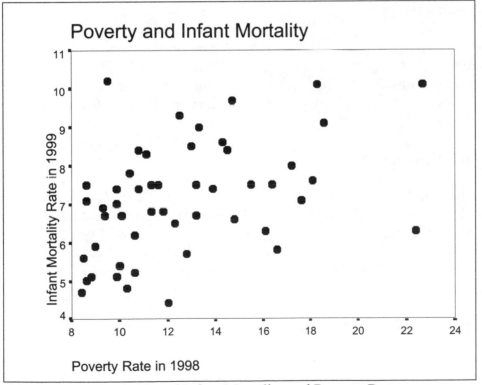

Figure 5.13 Scatter Plot of Infant Mortality and Poverty Rate

In the scatter plot in Figure 5.13, the relationship between poverty and infant mortality becomes quite apparent.   Like the last scatter plot, this one shows a positive linear relationship, although this relationship is weaker. The points still tend to rise as we approach larger poverty rates, but they are more scattered. This is also apparent in the smaller correlation coefficient, .420. This relationship, although weaker, is still significant at .002. We can conclude, therefore, that there is a moderate relationship between poverty and infant mortality, a relationship that is unlikely to be due to chance.

Summary

This chapter has demonstrated methods of establishing the existence of a statistical association using SPSS through crosstabs and correlations. For each method of statistical association, there are accompanying significance tests. The significance tests inform the researcher if the association between the two variables is strong enough so that chance can be ruled out as a likely explanation for the observed relationship. It is up to the researcher to determine the relationship's direction and strength by analyzing the output produced.

Graphing carries considerable persuasive power, especially when used to explain social relationships to people less versed in statistics. Graphing also displays nuances in distributions and relationships between variables that might otherwise go unnoticed. This chapter has introduced bar charts and scatter plots, both offering compelling visual displays of bivariate relationship.

Bivariate analyses are important because they identify the degree to which any two variables are associated with one another. In the following chapter, we extend this discussion, examining ways of analyzing the relationships between a categorical and a numerical variable.

Key Terms

Alternative hypothesis
Bar charts
Correlations
Cross tabulations
Curvilinear relationship
Ecological fallacy
Linear relationship
Null hypothesis
Pearson's correlation coefficient

Probability
Sample size
Scatter plots
Significance level
Significance tests
Statistically Significant
Thin cells
U shaped relationship

References and Further Reading

Du Toit, S. H. C., A. G. W. Steyn, and R. H. Stumpf. 1986. *Graphical Exploratory Data Analysis*. York: Springer-Verlag.

Levin, Jack and James Fox. 1997. *Elementary Statistics in Social Research*. New York: Longman.

Tufte, Edward. 1986. *The Visual Display of Quantitative Information*. Cheshire, Connecticut: Graphics Press.

Chapter 5 Exercises

Name_____   Date_____

1. A police force has increased its employment from five full-time officers in 1998 to eight full-time officers in 1999 in an effort to deter crime. They call you in to analyze whether their program has been effective and give you the following output to analyze. How would you interpret this cross tabulation to the police department?

	Number of Arrests	
	1998	1999
Property Crime Arrests	325	375
Violent Crime Arrests	120	119

Sig. = .03

2. A researcher examines a relationship between "sensitivity" and "cultural acceptance." As a result of her study she finds a correlation of .20 between these variables and a significance level of .25. On the basis of this study, can she conclude that sensitivity is associated with cultural acceptance? Explain.

3. Using the GSS98 data, examine the relationship between attitudes toward abortion (ABANY "Abortion if Woman Wants for Any Reason") and the sex (SEX) of the respondent. Make a bar chart of the relationship. Fill in the following information:

Percentage of men stating this is acceptable   _____

Percentage of women stating this is acceptable   _____

Chi square significance level   _____

Is the relationship statistically significant?   Yes   No

How would you interpret this result?

4. Using the GSS98 data, examine the relationship between race (RACE) and whether a person used a condom during the last experience of intercourse (CONDOM). Make a bar chart of the relationship.

Percentage of whites using condom   _____

Percentage of blacks using condom   _____

Percentage of others using condom   _____

Chi square significance level   _____

Is the relationship statistically significant?   Yes   No

How would you interpret this result?

5. Using the GSS98 data, examine the relationship between race (RACE) and the belief that whites are hurt by affirmative action (DISCAFF). Make a bar chart of the relationship.

Percentage of whites saying
"Somewhat Likely" or "Very Likely"   _____

Percentage of blacks saying
"Somewhat Likely" or "Very Likely"   _____

Percentage of others saying
"Somewhat Likely" or "Very Likely"   _____

Chi square significance level   _____

Is the relationship statistically significant?   Yes   No

How would interpret this result?

6. Using the GSS98 data construct and print a refined graph examining the relationship between HAPMAR and EVSTRAY. Exclude missing cases. Do you observe a relationship between the happiness of people's marriage and whether they have had sex with someone other than their spouse? Test this relationship with the appropriate significance test. Can you conclude that there is a relationship?

7. Is there a relationship between a person's age (AGE) and the number of hours spent per day watching TV (TVHOURS)? Use the GSS98 data to test this relationship.

Correlation   _____

Significance level   _____

Is the relationship statistically significant?   Yes   No

Who tends to watch the most TV?   Young Adults   Middle Age   Seniors

How would you explain these findings?

8. Is there a relationship between the rate of public libraries and branches (SCS153) and the high school dropout rate (JCC239) in an area? Use the STATES data to examine this question. Summarize and interpret your findings below.

Make a scatter plot of the relationship.

_____ Correlation   _____

Significance level   _____

Is the relationship statistically significant?   Yes   No

Make and print a scatter plot of the relationship.

In what ways are libraries associated with high school drop out rates?

How would you explain these findings?

9. Is there a relationship between the average salary of classroom teachers (SCS127) and the percent of population that has graduated from high school (SCS131)? Use the STATES data to examine this question. Summarize and interpret your findings below.

Correlation   _____

Significance level   _____

Is the relationship statistically significant?   Yes   No

Make and print a scatter plot of the relationship.

In what ways are teacher salaries associated with high school graduation rates?

How would you explain these findings?

10. Pose a hypothesis between any two numerical variables in either the STATES or GSS98 data sets.

   A. State the hypothesis:

   B. Construct and print a refined univariate graph of the dependent variable.

   C. Construct and print a refined bivariate graph of the relationship between these two variables.

   D. Determine if the relationship is statistically significant.   Sig.=_____

                                                      Is it significant?   Yes   No

   E. Explain the extent to which your hypothesis is supported by your analysis.

Chapter 6
Comparing Group Means through Bivariate Analysis

Overview

The previous chapter examined ways of studying relationships between two categorical variables and between two numerical variables. This chapter examines ways of studying a relationship between a categorical variable and numerical variable. We first introduce analysis of variance, which compares group means and tests for statistical significance. Bar charts and box plots offer visual comparisons of group characteristics. We also show how to test differences in means with post-hoc tests and t tests. Finally, we explain the assumptions underpinning the analysis of variance.

One-way Analysis of Variance

One-way analysis of variance (ANOVA) tests how much the mean values of a numerical variable differ among the categories of a categorical variable. We could assess the relationship between television viewing and marital status using the GSS98 data set. TVHOURS is a numerical variable indicating the number of hours spent watching television per day. MARITAL is a categorical variable, dividing the sample into groups of married, widowed, divorced, separated, and never married respondents. Neither a correlation nor a cross tabulation would be appropriate because the amount of time that people watch television is a numerical variable and marital status is categorical variable. A cross tabulation would be possible if television viewing is recoded into categorics (e.g., none, 1-3, 4-6, more than 6 hours), but this solution ignores nuances in the data. For example, watching one hour of television is considered the same as watching three hours. If there are differences in the habits of people who watch one and three hours of television, a real relationship may go undetected. A better solution is to compare the mean amount of time that people of each marital status watch television.

The null hypothesis says that there is no relationship—people in all the groups watch, on average, the same amount of television. The alternative hypothesis says that there is a relationship, as different groups may have increased opportunities to watch television or lack opportunities for other recreational activities. One possibility is that married respondents tend to watch the least television. The alternative hypothesis posits that *at least two* of the categories have different means. ANOVA assesses such relationships and can test hypotheses that group means differ.

The GSS98 data include variables on television viewing and marital status, and will work well to illustrate how to perform and interpret an ANOVA. To test the relationship between television viewing and marital status, use the following commands:

> *Analyze*
> > *Compare Means*
> > > *One-way ANOVA*
> > > > *Dependent List*: TVHOURS
> > > > *Factor*: MARITAL
> > > > *Options*
> > > > > *Statistics*: Descriptive
> > > > > *Continue*
> > > > *OK*

The ANOVA will produce output that enables researchers to examine if the means of these groups differ. We concentrate on the Descriptives table (Figure 6.1) and the ANOVA table (Figure 6.2), both of which offer relevant information to the research question.

Descriptives

HOURS PER DAY WATCHING TV

	N	Mean	Std. Deviation	Std. Error	95% Confidence Interval for Mean		Minimum	Maximum
					Lower Bound	Upper Bound		
MARRIED	1121	2.65	2.05	6.14E-02	2.53	2.77	0	20
WIDOWED	229	3.60	2.56	.17	3.27	3.94	0	15
DIVORCED	372	2.85	2.23	.12	2.63	3.08	0	20
SEPARATED	69	3.42	2.80	.34	2.75	4.09	0	21
NEVER MARRIED	546	2.90	2.35	.10	2.71	3.10	0	20
Total	2337	2.86	2.25	4.65E-02	2.77	2.95	0	21

Figure 6.1 Descriptive Statistics

ANOVA

HOURS PER DAY WATCHING TV

	Sum of Squares	df	Mean Square	F	Sig.
Between Groups	198.338	4	49.584	9.972	.000
Within Groups	11595.781	2332	4.972		
Total	11794.119	2336			

Figure 6.2 ANOVA Output

We are interested in testing whether married people spend, on average, less time watching television than the other groups in the study. The Descriptives table gives the number of cases in each group analyzed, the means for these groups, and the spread of the values within each group. The statistics that are most important, when reporting findings, include the means (the average viewing time). The Descriptives table indicates that married people spend less time (2.65 hours) than the other groups, as shown in the column labeled "Mean." The table also documents the number of people represented in each group, as shown in the "N" column. Just as is the case in crosstabs, researchers need to assess if the intersection of two variables creates groups with small representations. In this example, because a total of 2337 people report both marital status and television viewing, and because the smallest group is 69 separated people, we can conclude that the analysis being performed is not threatened by small sample sizes. However, if there were only a few people in a category, we might opt to collapse categories together or exclude small categories from the analysis. Again, we do not need to do this in the present analysis.

The columns for standard deviation, standard error, and confidence intervals all offer information on the spread of values in each group. The standard deviation for married respondents is small, only 2.05, indicating that their television viewing clusters in a restricted range. On the other hand, the standard deviation for separated respondents is larger (2.80). Separated respondents tend to watch more television on average, but as a group tend to have less homogeneous (similar) television viewing habits.

Even when means appear very different, if observations are not closely clustered around those means or if samples are small, there may be little basis for concluding that there is an actual difference between groups. To test if a difference in groups could be attributed to chance, we need to perform a significance test. In the case of ANOVA, this test is reported in the ANOVA table (Figure 6.2). For television viewing and marital status, the significance level (Sig.) is .000. This indicates that the differences in the mean values between these groups, given this sample size, is so large that similarly strong findings would be unlikely to recur by chance, even if we were to replicate this study a thousand times. We therefore conclude that there is a relationship between marital status and television viewing.

Graphing the Results of an ANOVA

Two common ways of graphing group comparisons are bar charts and box plots. Bar charts are familiar to many people and are appropriate for presenting findings to the general public or people not well versed in statistical analysis. Box plots, however, offer more detailed information, showing both the central tendencies and distributions of each category.

Bar Charts

Bar charts allow a researcher to quickly compare the means of different categories. The categories are placed along the horizontal axis and the height of each bar indicates the mean value of the numerical variable within that category. To construct a bar chart showing how television viewing varies by marital status, use the following commands:

Graphs
> *Bar*
>> *Simple*
>> *Data in Chart Are*: Summaries for groups of cases
>> *Define*
>>> *Bars Represent*: Other summary function
>>> *Variable*: TVHOURS
>>> *Category Axis*: MARITAL
>>> *OK*

The resulting bar chart, in Figure 6.3, clearly shows that separated and widowed people watch more television, on average, than married, never married, and divorced people. Notice that the bars replicate the findings reported in the ANOVA table. For example, married people watch, on average, 2.65 hours of television per day. SPSS automatically scales bar charts, and in some circumstances, researchers will desire rescaling the graph. In this example, the graph that SPSS automatically generates (if only viewed quickly) appears to suggest that separated people watch an average of 3 times as much television as married people do. Rescaling the graph so that the Y axis (the vertical axis) ranges from 0 to its high value results in a more appropriate representation. To fix this, double click on the graph to open the *Chart Editor*, then do the following operations:

Chart
> *Axis*
>> *Scale*
>> *OK*
>>> *Range: Minimum Displayed:* 0
>>> *OK*

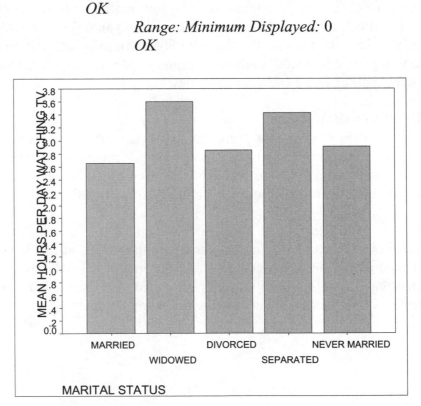

Figure 6.3 Bar Chart Output

Box Plots

Recall from Chapter 3 that a box plot displays a variable's distribution, showing the distribution of cases, including the median. Box plots are useful for showing relationships between categorical and numerical variables as they can depict differences in both the spread and center among groups. By placing box plots side-by-side, comparing the distributions is easy. Use the following commands to construct box plots of television viewing and marital status:

> *Graphs*
>> *Boxplot*
>>> *Simple*
>>> *Data in Chart Are*: Summaries for groups of cases
>>> *Define*
>>>> *Variable*: TVHOURS
>>>> *Category Axis*: MARITAL
>>>> *OK*

As you can see in Figure 6.4, a separate box plot is produced for each marital category. An advantage of generating box plots, as opposed to bar charts, is that they show the spread of values for each category. These box plots show that most people in each category watch between 0 and 8 hours per week (even less for married and divorced people), but that a few people in each category watch much more television.

One thing to remember is that a box plot displays the median, not the mean, so its results will only match those of the ANOVA if the distributions are symmetric. Although this limits the degree to which box plots and ANOVAs are compatible when variables are not normally distributed, box plots are particularly advantageous when examining variables that have slightly skewed distributions, such as television viewing.

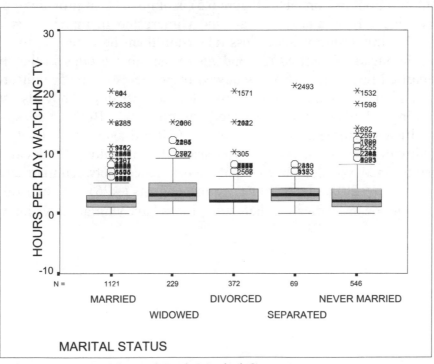

Figure 6.4 Box Plots of Each Marital Category

Post-hoc Tests

The ANOVA informed us that there is a difference among the groups in their television viewing habits. However, the ANOVA does not indicate which group means are significantly different, only that a difference exists somewhere among the groups. A significant ANOVA could mean that only two means are significantly different, that all of them are significantly different, or anything in between. For example, married people appear to spend much less time than separated people do watching television. However, is there a statistically significant difference between married people (2.65 hours) and divorced people (2.85 hours) in their television viewing? The answer requires a post-hoc test. **Post-hoc tests** indicate which group means differ from one another. To add a post-hoc test to the ANOVA, perform the following command:

> *Analyze*
> > *Compare Means*
> > > *One-way ANOVA*
> > > > *Dependent List*: TVHOURS
> > > > *Factor*: MARITAL
> > > > *Options*: *Statistics*: Descriptive
> > > > > *Continue*
> > > > *Post-hoc*: *Equal Variances Assumed*: Tukey
> > > > > *Continue*
> > > *OK*

As is apparent from the Post-hoc window in SPSS, there are many post-hoc tests to choose from. Although their methods are different, they generally test the same thing. A **Tukey test** is one of the most commonly used post-hoc tests, and is the one we will use here.

The Multiple Comparison table (Figure 6.5) is of interest. It provides a comparison of all the category means.   In our case, we are most interested in married respondents, as our hypothesis was that this group watches less television than the other groups. The first set of rows compares the mean of married respondents to the other groups in the study. The mean difference of married respondents from widowed respondents is −0.95, indicating that married respondents watch, on average, 0.95 hours less television per day. They also spend 0.77 hours less time watching television than separated respondents. Both of these differences are statistically significant, with significance levels of .000 and .043, respectively. Significance is also highlighted with a "*" in the mean difference column, making the location of significant differences easy to find. We also observe that the differences between married respondents and divorced respondents (−.20) and never married respondents (−.25) in television viewing are not flagged as being significant, indicating that these groups have similar television viewing habits.

Multiple Comparisons

Dependent Variable: HOURS PER DAY WATCHING TV

Tukey HSD

(I) MARITAL STATUS	(J) MARITAL STATUS	Mean Difference (I-J)	Std. Error	Sig.	95% Confidence Interval	
					Lower Bound	Upper Bound
MARRIED	WIDOWED	-.95*	.16	.000	-1.39	-.51
	DIVORCED	-.20	.13	.541	-.57	.16
	SEPARATED	-.77*	.28	.043	-1.52	-1.55E-02
	NEVER MARRIED	-.25	.12	.185	-.57	6.30E-02
WIDOWED	MARRIED	.95*	.16	.000	.51	1.39
	DIVORCED	.75*	.19	.001	.24	1.26
	SEPARATED	.18	.31	.976	-.65	1.02
	NEVER MARRIED	.70*	.18	.001	.22	1.18
DIVORCED	MARRIED	.20	.13	.541	-.16	.57
	WIDOWED	-.75*	.19	.001	-1.26	-.24
	SEPARATED	-.57	.29	.299	-1.36	.23
	NEVER MARRIED	-4.99E-02	.15	.997	-.46	.36
SEPARATED	MARRIED	.77*	.28	.043	1.55E-02	1.52
	WIDOWED	-.18	.31	.976	-1.02	.65
	DIVORCED	.57	.29	.299	-.23	1.36
	NEVER MARRIED	.52	.28	.368	-.26	1.29
NEVER MARRIED	MARRIED	.25	.12	.185	-6.30E-02	.57
	WIDOWED	-.70*	.18	.001	-1.18	-.22
	DIVORCED	4.99E-02	.15	.997	-.36	.46
	SEPARATED	-.52	.28	.368	-1.29	.26

*. The mean difference is significant at the .05 level.

Figure 6.5 Multiple Comparisons Output

Assumptions of ANOVA

ANOVAs and post-hoc tests are helpful in comparing groups. However, because they are based on means, care must be taken to use these tests only on data that conform to some underlying assumptions. ANOVA assumes the samples are independent and the distributions are normal, concerns we address below.

Independence Assumption

One assumption of one-way ANOVA is that the individual observations in different categories are **independent** of each other. This means that the observations in one category are not paired up in some way with the observations in any other category. For example, if we analyzed television viewing by gender, and if both husbands and wives were interviewed in the study, measures of television viewing for married couples would be interdependent. Because husbands and wives form television-viewing habits together, they cannot comprise independent observations. However, ANOVA will treat them as such. In the case of the GSS98, it is unlikely that any observations are interdependent, as the study relies on a random sample of individuals who are unlikely to be connected with each other in meaningful ways.

Normality Assumption

The other important assumption is that the observations of the numerical variable within each category have a normal, or bell-shaped distribution. In practice, distributions that are slightly skewed generally do not pose a problem for ANOVA. However, distributions that are highly skewed or U-shaped do pose a problem, and ANOVA is not the appropriate analysis in such cases. Because the application of advanced data analytic techniques relies on understanding the structure of variables, this highlights the skills learned earlier in univariate analysis. For instance, forming a histogram of television viewing is one way of checking that this variable reasonably conforms to the normality assumption. Recall that this can be tested by performing:

> *Graphs*
> > *Histogram*
> > > *Variable:* TVHOURS
> > > *OK*

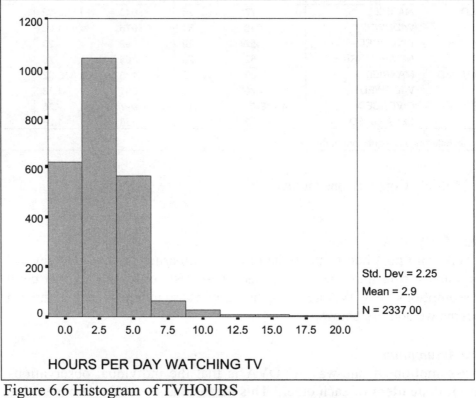

Figure 6.6 Histogram of TVHOURS

As Figure 6.6 shows, television viewing has a moderate skew. Although not a fully normal distribution, it conforms reasonably well enough to meet the normality assumption.

T tests

A **t test** is a special case of analysis of variance that compares the means of only two groups. There are two types—an independent samples t test and a paired samples t test. An independent samples t test is equivalent to a one-way analysis of variance with only two groups. We introduce it here because the t test is a very popular test that you will see often when reading research articles and in future statistics classes.

Independent Samples t Test

An **independent samples t test** would be appropriate if we wanted to compare the mean time spent watching TV for men and women. To do so, use the following commands:

> *Analyze*
>> *Compare Means*
>>> *Independent-Samples T Test*
>>>> *Test Variables:* TVHOURS
>>>> *Grouping Variable:* SEX
>>>> *Define Groups: Group 1:* 0 (Male)
>>>>> *Group 2*: 1 (Female)
>>>>> *Continue*
>>> *OK*

The Define Groups window tells SPSS the two categories to be compared. It is important that you type in the values for the categories exactly as they were entered into the data set. If you typed in "M" and "F" in Define Groups, but they were entered into the data set as 1 and 2, SPSS would give you an error.

		Levene's Test for Equality of Variances		t-test for Equality of Means					95% Confidence Interval of the Difference	
		F	Sig.	t	df	Sig. (2-tailed)	Mean Difference	Std. Error Difference	Lower	Upper
HOURS PER DAY WATCHING TV	Equal variances assumed	.807	.369	-.959	2335	.338	-8.99E-02	9.37E-02	-.27	.09
	Equal variances not assumed			-.958	2178.44	.338	-8.99E-02	9.39E-02	-.27	.09

Independent Samples Test

Figure 6.7 Independent Samples T Test Output

The independent samples t test output in Figure 6.7 can be tricky to read. Essentially, only the top row of the columns labeled "t" and "Sig. (2 tailed)" is of interest. "t" is the test statistic and Sig., once again, is the significance level. A t value that is close to 0 indicates that the two means are very similar and will result in a large significance value. A t value that is far from 0, in either a positive or negative direction, will result in a small significance level, indicating a difference in the means. This output has a t = -.959 and a significance level = .338. Since the significance level is above .05, there is no significant association between sex and amount of time spent watching television—men and women watch about the same amount of television (2.81 and 2.90 hours per week). The Group Statistics table (Figure 6.8) shows these means.

Group Statistics					
	RESPONDENTS SEX	N	Mean	Std. Deviation	Std. Error Mean
HOURS PER DAY WATCHING TV	MALE	1019	2.81	2.26	7.08E-02
	FEMALE	1318	2.90	2.24	6.16E-02

Figure 6.8 Mean TVHOURS By SEX

Paired-samples t test

In situations in which the data in the two categories are related, a **paired samples t test** is appropriate. For example, a researcher could test if the rate of incarceration was the same for Whites and Blacks using the STATES data set. Since each state (case) contributed data on both the incarceration rate for Blacks (PRC61) and the incarceration rate for Whites (PRC58), it is likely that these values will be correlated. States with high overall incarceration rates will tend to have high rates for both Blacks and Whites. Therefore, the samples for each category are not independent and the paired t test is appropriate. To perform this paired t test:

> *Analyze*
> > *Compare Means*
> > > *Paired-Samples T Test*
> > > > *Paired Variables*: PRC58 (White State Prisoner Incarceration Rate in 1997)
> > > > PRC61 (Black State Prisoner Incarceration Rate in 1997)
> > > > (Note: Click on both variables before clicking the arrow)
> > > *OK*

The two tables of interest are the Paired Samples Statistics table and the Paired Samples Test table, shown in Figures 6.9 and 6.10. The Paired Samples Statistics table indicates that the mean incarceration rate for Whites is 212 per 100,000 people, whereas the mean incarceration rate for Blacks is 1676 per 100,000 people. The Paired Samples Test table indicates that this difference is highly significant, Sig. = .000. In conclusion, there is a large association between the incarceration rate and race—the rate is much higher for Blacks than for Whites.

Paired Samples Statistics

		Mean	N	Std. Deviation	Std. Error Mean
Pair 1	White State Prisoner Incarceration Rate in 1997	211.7059	51	82.6850	11.5782
	Black State Prisoner Incarceration Rate in 1997	1676.0196	51	607.6076	85.0821

Figure 6.9 Sample Statistics for PRC58 and PRC61

Paired Samples Test

		Paired Differences							
					95% Confidence Interval of the Difference				
		Mean	Std. Deviation	Std. Error Mean	Lower	Upper	t	df	Sig. (2-tailed)
Pair 1	White State Prisoner Incarceration Rate in 1997 - Black State Prisoner Incarceration Rate in 1997	-1464.3	588.6248	82.4240	-1629.87	-1298.76	-17.766	50	.000

Figure 6.10 Paired T Test Output

Summary

Researchers can test for an association between a numerical and a categorical variable by performing an ANOVA and creating bar graphs and box plots. Performing post-hoc tests can further refine these results. Additional comparisons can be made with independent samples t tests and paired samples t tests, which compare the mean values of two independent or related groups. As researchers perform these analyses, they should keep a watchful eye for characteristics of variables that may influence the decision to use these applications. Some concerns include adequate sample sizes for all groups, distributions of numerical variables that conform to normality assumptions, and independent observations.

Key Terms
Bar Charts
Box Plots
Independence Assumption
Independent Samples T Test
Normality Assumption
One-way Analysis of Variance
Paired Samples T Test
Post-hoc tests
Tukey Test

References and Further Reading

Keppel, Geoffrey. 1991. *Design and Analysis: A Researcher's Handbook*. Upper Saddle River, NJ: Prentice Hall.

Levin, Jack and James Fox. 1997. *Elementary Statistics in Social Research*. New York: Longman.

McGrath, Robert. 1997. *Introductory Statistics: A Research Perspective*. Boston: Allyn & Bacon.

Montgomery, Douglas. 1997. *Design and Analysis of Experiments*. New York: John Wiley & Sons.

Chapter 6 Exercises

Name_____   Date_____

1. Astrologers assert that our birth dates influence our success (or lack thereof) in life. Test this assumption with the GSS98 data by analyzing the relationship between ZODIAC (Respondent's Astrological Sign) with SEI (Respondent's Socioeconomic Index). The SEI is an indicator of economic and social-economic attainment. The higher the SEI score, the more successful the respondent.

Mean SEI of Pisces   _____

Mean SEI of Taurus   _____

Mean SEI of your astrological sign   _____

ANOVA significance level   _____

Is the relationship statistically significant?   Yes   No

On the basis of these data, would you say that astrologers are correct in their assertion of the power of the stars? Why?

2. Test whether there is an association between a person's educational attainment and the age at which they have children. Use the GSS98 data set to perform an ANOVA on respondents' highest educational degree (DEGREE) and their age when they had their first child (AGEKDBRN).

Independent variable   _____

Dependent variable   _____

Mean age for people with less than a high school degree   _____

Mean age for people with a high school degree   _____

Mean age for people with a junior college degree   _____

Mean age for people with a Bachelor's degree   _____

Mean age for people with a graduate degree   _____

ANOVA significance level   _____

Is the relationship statistically significant?   Yes   No

According to the Tukey test, which groups have means that are significantly different from the means of those with a high school degree?

On the basis of these data, would you say that education is associated with the age at which people have children? Why?

3. Construct and print a refined boxplot graph of the relationship between AGEKDBRN and DEGREE.

4. Using the STATES data set construct, refine, and print a bar graph showing the distribution of hazardous waste sites (ENS213) according to the 9 Census Regions (REGION9). Describe your findings below and explain how this analysis could influence decision making on where to allocate funding for hazardous waste site clean up.

5. Perform a one-way ANOVA to test the relationship you graphed between ENS213 and REGION9. Include a Tukey test in your analysis.

Mean hazardous waste level in New England   _____

Mean hazardous waste level in Mid Atlantic   _____

Mean hazardous waste level in East North Central   _____

Mean hazardous waste level in South Atlantic   _____

Mean hazardous waste level in East South Central   _____

Mean hazardous waste level in West South Central   _____

Mean hazardous waste level in West North Central   _____

Mean hazardous waste level in Mountain   _____

Mean hazardous waste level in Pacific   _____

ANOVA significance level   _____

Is the relationship statistically significant?   Yes   No

According to the Tukey test, are any Regions significantly different than the Middle Atlantic States? If so, which ones?

What do you think are some of the reasons for the different number of waste sites in different geographic regions?

6. Pose a hypothesis between a categorical independent variable and a numerical dependent variable in either the STATES or GSS98 data sets.

    A. State the hypothesis:

    B. Construct and print a refined univariate graph of the dependent variable.

    C. Construct and print a refined bivariate graph of the relationship between these two variables.

    D. Determine if the relationship is statistically significant.   Sig.=_____

                                                 Is it significant?   Yes   No

    E. Explain the extent to which your hypothesis is supported by your analysis.

7. Pose another hypothesis between a categorical independent variable and a numerical dependent variable in either the STATES or GSS98 data sets.

   A. State the hypothesis:

   B. Construct and print a refined univariate graph of the dependent variable.

   C. Construct and print a refined bivariate graph of the relationship between these two variables.

   D. Determine if the relationship is statistically significant.   Sig.=_____

                                                      Is it significant?   Yes   No

   E. Explain the extent to which your hypothesis is supported by your analysis.

Chapter 7:
Multivariate Analysis with Linear Regression

Overview

Chapters 5 and 6 examined common methods for testing relationships between two variables. Many research projects, however, require testing the association of multiple independent variables with a dependent variable. This is the task of multivariate analysis. In this chapter, we outline the reasons why researchers may want to use multivariate models in their analysis of data. We then examine one of the most powerful approaches to performing multivariate analyses: linear regression. We illustrate how to interpret regression statistics and show how to graph linear regressions using the STATES data. We conclude with a brief discussion of the considerations researchers need to address in their application of linear regression, including concerns of data structure and approaches to model building.

What Are the Advantages of Multivariate Analysis?

Multivariate analysis often constitutes the final stage of data analysis. It is best performed after researchers understand the characteristics of individual variables (univariate analysis) and the relationships between any two variables (bivariate analysis). Multivariate analyses are more complex because they examine the simultaneous relationship of many variables. Why do we need multivariate approaches to studying data? There are two general reasons: documenting collective effects and accounting for potentially spurious factors.

First, by including more than one variable in statistical models, researchers can create more sophisticated (and often more accurate) models to predict or explain social behavior. In reality, social behavior is usually associated with many factors and cannot be explained by the association of a single variable. For example, a researcher might be interested in testing how family background is related to a person's educational attainment. One bivariate analysis might examine the association with father's education, then another bivariate analysis might examine the association with mother's education, then another analysis for the number of brothers and sisters in the family, etc. Including all of these variables in one model is a more powerful examination of the same issue. It enables the researcher to understand the individual contribution of each independent variable to the association with the dependent variable as well as the collective contribution of all the independent variables.

Second, multivariate analyses can account for the influence of **spurious factors** by introducing **control variables**. Recall from Chapter 1 that a relationship is spurious when it can be explained by a third unmeasured variable. We used the example of the correlation of ice cream consumption and drowning deaths. Unless we use temperature as a control variable, it can appear that eating ice cream causes people to drown. If we made a regression model that included a variable for temperature, the relationship between ice cream consumption and drowning would likely disappear. We could then rightly attribute the increase in drowning to the temperature.

To test the impact of parents' education on a child's education, we would want to select the most important independent variables reflecting family background. We would also want to control for any factors that might cause spurious relationships. For instance, we would want to include age in the model because it may be strongly associated with educational attainment. The same would be true for ethnicity. Therefore, an improved model would include age and ethnicity as control variables. Our models could then examine the combined effects of father's education and mother's education, above and beyond the association of age and ethnicity. The results would then show how parents' education is associated with a child's educational attainment, while accounting for the association of factors that might "explain away" these findings.

When Can I Do a Linear Regression?

Because linear regressions require complex mathematical procedures, this chapter will be less concerned with how the regression statistics are created than with their interpretation. However, toward the conclusion of this chapter we outline a number of assumptions that are required for reliable significance values. One immediate concern, though, is identifying the circumstances under which a researcher can perform a linear regression.

First, linear regressions are used when the increase in an independent variable is associated with a consistent and constant increase or decrease in the dependent variable. Recall from Chapter 5 that there are many types of relationships between variables. Linear regressions measure only one of these, the **linear** form. The relationship between years of education that a father has and years of education that his son or daughter achieves is likely to be linear. Perhaps each additional year of schooling that a parent received is associated with an additional two years of schooling that his or her children receive. If so, linear regression is a good means of testing the relationship. On the other hand, linear regression cannot test non-linear relationships, such as the inverted U shaped relationship between anxiety and test performance. In the case of a non-linear relationship, regression often will not find a relationship because it assumes the relationship will take on an entirely different form.[1]

The consideration in using linear regression concerns the structure of the dependent variable. To accurately make inferences from a linear regression, the dependent variable should be numeric and should reasonably conform to a normal distribution. The distribution can be checked with histograms to see if the dependent variable has a "bell shape." Linear regressions

---

[1] In some circumstances, linear regressions can be used to test nonlinear relationships, but this first requires changing variable values to accommodate nonlinear forms. For a description of these methods, see Kutner, Nachtschiem, Wasserman, & Neter.

are quite accommodating of variables that do not exactly conform to normal distributions, but the better the dependent variable conforms to a "bell shaped" distribution, the more accurately the significance levels will reflect the probability that the relationship is a result of chance.

This information is probably sufficient for most researchers to gauge whether their study should, or should not, use linear regression. Later, we examine in more detail some other assumptions that underpin linear regressions.

Linear Regression: A Bivariate Example

Chapter 5 introduced correlation as a means of measuring the strength of the linear relationship between two numeric variables. A linear regression is a model of the line that best describes that relationship. The model allows precise understanding of the relationship between the two variables. It also allows us to predict values of the dependent variable from values of the independent variable.

To illustrate how to perform and interpret a linear regression, we first examine a bivariate relationship, studying the relationship between poverty and teen births using the STATES data. Our model predicts the association of poverty (the independent variable) with the teenage birth rate (the dependent variable). Figure 7.1 shows a scatter plot of these two variables. Looking at the scatter plot, one can observe that the relationship tends to flow from the lower left-hand corner of the graph to the upper right. The purpose of a linear regression is to create an equation that can be used to illustrate this tendency for the values of the variables to coincide.

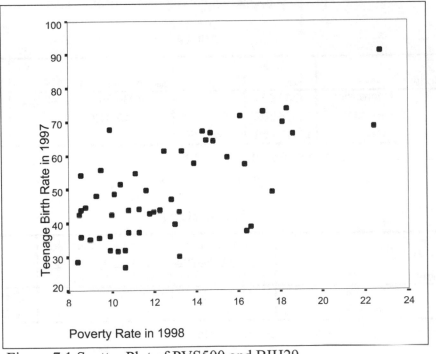

Figure 7.1 Scatter Plot of PVS500 and BIH29

Using the STATES data, we will create a linear regression of the poverty rate on teenage birth rates. The output from this regression can be used to describe this relationship, as well as create a regression line that can be plotted over the scatter plot shown in Figure 7.1. This line will show the relationship between the two variables.

Analyze
> *Regression*
>> *Linear*
>>> *Dependent*: BIH29 (teenage birth rate in 1997)
>>> *Independent(s)*: PVS500 (Poverty Rate 1998)
>>> *OK*

Figure 7.2 shows the output generated from the linear regression. We will concentrate on three groups of statistics from this output: the coefficients, the significance tests, and the R Square statistic.

Model Summary

Model	R	R Square	Adjusted R Square	Std. Error of the Estimate
1	.675[a]	.455	.444	10.7633

a. Predictors: (Constant), Poverty Rate in 1998

ANOVA[b]

Model		Sum of Squares	df	Mean Square	F	Sig.
1	Regression	4739.251	1	4739.251	40.909	.000[a]
	Residual	5676.602	49	115.849		
	Total	10415.853	50			

a. Predictors: (Constant), Poverty Rate in 1998

b. Dependent Variable: Teenage Birth Rate in 1997

Coefficients[a]

Model		Unstandardized Coefficients		Standardized Coefficients	t	Sig.
		B	Std. Error	Beta		
1	(Constant)	15.160	5.650		2.683	.010
	Poverty Rate in 1998	2.735	.428	.675	6.396	.000

a. Dependent Variable: Teenage Birth Rate in 1997

Figure 7.2 Regression Output

Interpreting Linear Regression Coefficients

The **Unstandardized Coefficient** of an independent variable (also called **B** or **slope**) measures the strength of its relationship with the dependent variable. It is interpreted as the size of the difference in the dependent variable that corresponds with a one-unit difference in the independent variable. If a **coefficient** were 0, it would indicate that the values of the dependent variable do not differ as the values of the independent variable increase or decrease. In such a circumstance, we would conclude that there is no linear relationship between the two variables. However, in our model, the coefficient for poverty rate is 2.735. This indicates that for every one-percentage increase in the poverty rate, there is a predicted increase in the teen birth rate by nearly 3 births (2.735) per 1000 teenage women. A regression coefficient with a negative sign indicates that a one-unit increase in the independent variable is associated with a predicted decline in the dependent variable. In this way, regression coefficients operate like correlations, but they offer more information about the relationship between the variables.

The next question concerns whether this relationship is statistically significant. Moving across the row for "Poverty Rate in 1998" in the Coefficients Table, we find a significance (Sig.) score of .000. This is a statistically significant relationship, since the probability of random chance producing these findings is less than 1/1000. As the relationship is significant, we can be confident of an actual statistical association between poverty and teen births.

The coefficients column also shows the **constant**, a statistic indicating the **intercept**—the predicted value of the dependent variable if the independent variable had a value of 0. In this example, the constant indicates the predicted number of births per 1000 teenage women if a state had no one living below the poverty rate (a poverty rate of 0). Even if there were no poor people living in a state, we could still expect about 15 births (15.160) each year for every 1000 teenage women.

Interpreting the R-Square Statistic

The R-Square is a general measure of the usefulness of the regression model. It indicates how well the statistical model explains variation in the dependent variable. In other words, the R-Square indicates how much of the fluctuation in the dependent variable is produced by its relationship with the independent variable(s).

An R-Square of 1.00 indicates that 100% of the variation in the dependent variable is explained by the independent variables. Conversely, an R-Square of 0.0 indicates that none of the variation in the dependent variable is explained by the independent variables. In the case of the regression of the poverty rate on the teenage birth rate, the R-Square is .455, as found in the Model Summary Table. This indicates that 45.5% of the variation in the teenage birth rate from state to state can be explained by variations in the poverty rates. The remaining 54.5% can be explained by other factors that we did not include in the model. Some possibilities might be differences in sex education in schools or the presence of religious groups that forbid the use of birth control or abortion. Human behavior is complex and is influenced by a number of factors. However, it is remarkable that poverty can account for nearly half of the variation in the teen birth rates between the states.

Using Linear Regression Coefficients To Make Predictions

Regression lines can be used to predict values for a dependent variable. Regression lines are calculated using the following formula:

$$\hat{Y} \quad = \quad A \quad + \quad B \quad (X)$$

Predicted Value of Y (Dependent Variable)	=	Y axis intercept (The constant)	+	predicted increase of Y for 1 unit increase in X (The slope)	Multiply value of X (Independent Variable)

This equation posits that the predicted value of the dependent variable ($\hat{Y}$) is a function of a constant (A) plus the value of the regression coefficient (B) multiplied by the values of the independent variable (X). This formula enables researchers to calculate predicted values for a dependent variable. A predicted value is the best estimate of the value of the dependent variable, given a value for the independent variable. Suppose, for example, that we wanted to predict the teenage birth rate if the poverty rate is 20%. To do this, simply substitute the selected value of 20 for X in the regression equation.

$$\hat{Y} \quad = \quad A \quad + \quad B \quad (X)$$
$$\text{Predicted} \quad = \quad 15.160 \quad + \quad 2.735 \quad (20)$$

$$\hat{Y} \quad = \quad A \quad + \quad B \quad (X)$$
$$69.86 \quad = \quad 15.160 \quad + \quad 2.735 \quad (20)$$

By using the coefficient, the constant, and the selected value of X (the poverty rate), we are able to quickly calculate that a state with a poverty rate of 20% will have a predicted teenage birth rate of 69.86, approximately 70 births per 1000 teenage women.

Making predictions from regression coefficients can also be helpful in gauging the effects of implementing a social policy. For example, if poverty is related to teenage pregnancy, we could predict how much the teenage birth rate could decline if government leaders were able to reduce the poverty rates in their states. Let us assume a state had an existing poverty rate of 15% and we wanted to know what the teenage birth rate would be if the state were able to reduce its poverty rate to 10%.

$$\hat{Y} \quad = \quad A \quad + \quad B \quad (X)$$
$$56.185 \quad = \quad 15.160 \quad + \quad 2.735 \quad (15)$$

$$\hat{Y} \quad = \quad A \quad + \quad B \quad (X)$$
$$42.51 \quad = \quad 15.160 \quad + \quad 2.735 \quad (10)$$

Teen births at 15% poverty rate = 56.185/1000
Teen births at 10% poverty rate = 42.510/1000
Reduction in teen births   = 13.675/1000 teenage women

Generally, it is a good practice to limit predictions to the available range of values of the independent variable. Because we used data that had poverty rate values between 1% and 22% to construct the regression line, we predict values of teen pregnancy only for poverty rates within this range. The relationship between these variables could differ for poverty rates beyond 22%. Perhaps the relationship starts to level off, or even decrease. Alternatively, the rates could skyrocket, as some sociological studies indicate. Because we do not know what the relationship is like for these places of highly concentrated poverty, we should be very cautious using the regression line to make predictions in these situations.

Using Coefficients to Graph Bivariate Regression Lines

Because regression coefficients offer so much information, they are commonly reported in journal articles. However, lay audiences, who are less conversant in statistical methods, are usually unable to interpret these statistics. Therefore, it is helpful to graph regression lines to create a visual representation of the coefficients.

We will calculate a regression line using the independent variable, PVS500, the coefficients, and the predicted values of the dependent variable.

> *Transform*
> > *Compute*
> > > *Target Variable*: BIRTHPRE
> > > *Numeric Expression*: 15.160+2.735*PVS500
> > > *Type and Label*
> > > > *Label*: Predicted Teen Birth Rate From Poverty Rates
> > > > *Continue*
> > > *OK*

> Note: BIRTHPRE = predicted teen birth rate
> > 15.160 = constant
> > 2.735 = coefficient for poverty rates
> > PVS500 = poverty rates for states

This line can then be plotted, using the SPSS graphing commands. The resulting graph should look like Figure 7.3.

> *Graphs*
> > *Scatter*
> > > *Overlay*
> > > *Define*
> > > > *YX Pairs*: BIH29 – PVS500
> > > > BIRTHPRE – PVS500
> > > *OK*

> Note: PVS500 should be listed second in both YX pairs. If it is not, click *Swap Pair*.
> Note: Highlight both variables before moving them into the YX pair box.

We use this approach as an introduction to the fundamental method for generating the regression line. However, for bivariate regressions SPSS also offers an automated means of producing this line. First, recreate the scatter plot between Poverty Rate and Teenage birth rate using the following commands:

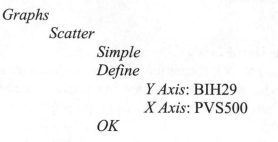

> *Graphs*
>> *Scatter*
>>> *Simple*
>>> *Define*
>>>> *Y Axis*: BIH29
>>>> *X Axis*: PVS500
>>> *OK*

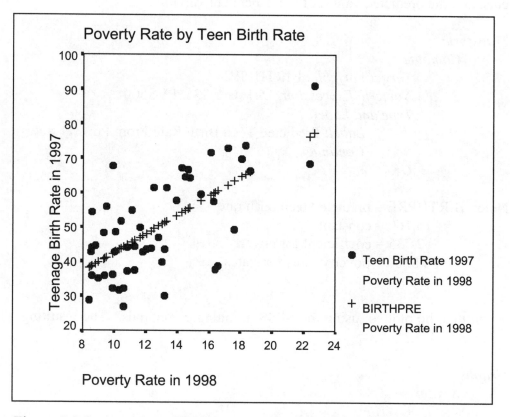

Figure 7.3 Scatter Plot of BIH29 and PVS500 with Regression Line

Then add the regression line to the scatter plot using the Chart Editor. Double-click on the graph to invoke the Chart Editor, then

> *Chart*
>> *Options*
>>> *Fit Line:* Total
>>> *OK*

Multiple Linear Regression

In a multiple linear regression, more than one independent variable is included in the regression model. As discussed above, multiple regression examines how two or more variables act together to affect the dependent variable. It also enables researchers to introduce control variables that may account for observed relationships.

To illustrate how to perform a multiple linear regression, we will expand the study of the teenage birth rate (BIH29) into a multivariate analysis. Our interest is in examining some of the factors that may relate with the teenage birth rate, particularly those frequently forwarded in the popular press and academic literature. We will test the following hypotheses:

Hypothesis 1: Teenage birth rate is positively associated with poverty.
　　Independent Variable: PVS500

Hypothesis 2: Teenage birth rate is negatively associated with expenditures per pupil.
　　Independent Variable: SCS141

Hypothesis 3: Teenage birth rate is positively associated with the unemployment rate.
　　Independent Variable: EMS171

Hypothesis 4: Teenage birth rate is positively associated with the amount of welfare (TANF)[2] a family receives.
　　Independent Variable: PVS526

To run this regression, use the following commands:

Analyze
　　Regression
　　　　Linear
　　　　　　　　Dependent:　BIH29 (Births to teenagers/1000 1997)
　　　　　　　　Independents: PVS500 (Poverty Rate 1998)
　　　　　　　　　　　　　　 SCS141　 (Expenditures per Pupil in 1999)
　　　　　　　　　　　　　　 EMS171　 (Unemployment Rate in 1999)
　　　　　　　　　　　　　　 PVS526 (Maximum Monthly TANF Benefit for
　　　　　　　　　　　　　　 Family of Three in 1999)
　　　　　　　OK

The result of this regression is interesting (Figure 7.4). We will interpret this regression equation by first looking at the regression coefficients, then the significance tests, and finally the R-Square value.

---

[2] TANF stands for "temporary assistance to needy families," the most commonly understood program equated with "welfare."

Interpreting Multiple Linear Regression Coefficients

In scanning through the significance tests in the Coefficients Table, we find that only two of these variables are significant. But do they support the hypotheses? To find out, we need to interpret the coefficients.

Hypothesis 1 predicts that states with higher poverty rates will have higher teenage birth rates. The hypothesis is supported, since the coefficient is positive. Although it is still significant, you may notice that the coefficient is smaller than it was in the bivariate regression model (1.506 vs. 2.735).

Hypothesis 2 predicts that the more a state spends on a pupil, the lower the teenage birth rate will be. The Coefficients Table does not support this hypothesis because the relationship is not statistically significant (Sig.=.411). Although the coefficient shows a tendency for the teen birth rate to decline (indicated by the negative coefficient) with increased expenditures on students, we cannot assert any relationship between student funding and teen birth rates because the relationship is not statistically significant. This suggests that expenditures per pupil are not associated with the teen birth rates above and beyond the effects of the other variables in the model.

Model Summary

Model	R	R Square	Adjusted R Square	Std. Error of the Estimate
1	.791[a]	.626	.594	9.2020

a. Predictors: (Constant), Maximum Monthly TANF Benefit for Family of Three in 1999, Unemployment Rate in 1999, Expenditures per Pupil in Elementary and Secondary Schools in 1999, Poverty Rate in 1998

Coefficients[a]

Model		Unstandardized Coefficients		Standardized Coefficients	t	Sig.
		B	Std. Error	Beta		
1	(Constant)	41.874	9.279		4.513	.000
	Poverty Rate in 1998	1.506	.536	.371	2.812	.007
	Expenditures per Pupil in Elementary and Secondary Schools in 1999	-9.59E-04	.001	-.090	-.831	.411
	Unemployment Rate in 1999	2.515	1.672	.183	1.504	.139
	Maximum Monthly TANF Benefit for Family of Three in 1999	-3.79E-02	.010	-.426	-3.725	.001

a. Dependent Variable: Teenage Birth Rate in 1997

Figure 7.4 Multiple Regression Output

Hypothesis 3 asserts that the high unemployment rates are related to high teenage birth rates. The coefficient shows a positive relationship between these two variables. The Coefficients Table shows the regression coefficient is 2.515. This, too, is not statistically significant (Sig.=.139). Lacking a significant finding, our hypothesis is not supported and we find no relationship between unemployment and teen births.

Hypothesis 4 predicts that the more a state spends on welfare per recipient family, the higher the teenage birth rate will be. We find this is a statistically significant relationship (Sig.= .001). However, the negative regression coefficient indicates a relationship *opposite* the one predicted in the hypothesis. The more a state spends on welfare per recipient family *the lower the teenage birth rate will be*. We need to convert the coefficient B (-3.785E-02) to the natural number -.03785 to fully appreciate the relationship. This indicates that for every $1 a family receives in TANF payments each month, the teenage birth rate is lower by .037%. If we multiply this times 250, we can predict how much an increase in $250 expenditures per welfare family per month will "buy" in lower teenage birth rates. Controlling for all other factors, an increase in TANF payments of $250 is related to 9.25 fewer births per 1000 teenage women.

While the liberal-conservative debate concerning social policy and social behavior cannot be settled with one regression and one set of data, these data seem to offer much stronger support for liberal theories concerning the causes of teenage births. Based on this analysis, teenage births are associated with poverty. Contrary to our hypothesis, higher welfare payments (as indicated by TANF) are associated with lower teenage birth rates. Teen birth rates are not associated with expenditures on students or unemployment.

Interpreting the Adjusted R-Square Statistic

The Adjusted R-Square statistic is used in multiple regression instead of the R-Square because adding even unfounded independent variables to a model will raise the R-Square statistic. The **Adjusted R-Square** statistic adjusts for the number of variables in the model and it will only increase if added variables contribute significantly to the model. Therefore, the adjusted R-Square is often used to compare which of several models is best.

How good is the model? The Adjusted R Square statistic in the Model Summary Table indicates that 59.4% (Adj R-Square=.594) of the variation in the teenage birth rate can be attributed to these four variables! This is an excellent model. In fact, it is rare to find a model for social behavior that has such a high explanatory power.

Graphing a Multiple Regression

Graphing relationships from multiple regressions is more complex than graphing relationships from bivariate regressions, although the approach is the same. In bivariate regressions, there is only one independent and one dependent variable, which are the only variables on the graph. However, because there are many variables in the multivariate models, the two-dimensional graphs need to control for the other variables when plotting only two variables. To graph a regression line from a multivariate model requires selecting one independent variable (X axis variable). The rest of the variables in the model will be held constant. To hold these values as constants, any value could be chosen, but the most common choice is the mean value (which we generate using *Descriptives*). Again, we will use the regression formula, now expanding it to include the other variables in the model.

$$\hat{Y} = A + B_1(X_1) + B_2(X_2) + B_3(X_3) + B_4(X_4)$$

$\hat{Y}$ = Predicted Value of the dependent variable

A = Constant
B$_1$ = Slope of Variable 1   X$_1$ = Chosen value of Variable 1
B$_2$ = Slope of Variable 2   X$_2$ = Chosen value of Variable 2
B$_3$ = Slope of Variable 3   X$_3$ = Chosen value of Variable 3
B$_4$ = Slope of Variable 4   X$_4$ = Values of Variable 4

This example will show how to graph the association of welfare benefits and teenage birth rates, holding poverty rates, school expenditures, and unemployment rates at their means. This requires computing a new variable (TEENPRE), the predicted value of teen birth rate. Input the following equation into the *Compute* command to generate the new variable TEENPRE and label the variable "Predicted Teenage Birth Rate."

> *Transform*
> > *Compute*
> > > *Target Variable*: TEENPRE
> > > *Numeric Expression*: 41.874 + (1.506*12.73) + (−.0009*6341.98) + (2.515*4.16) + (−.037*PVS526)
> > >
> > > *Type and Label*
> > > > *Label*: Predicted Teenage Birth Rate
> > > > *Continue*
> > *OK*

Sources of numbers in the above equation.

Constant (A) = 41.874

Variable	B	Mean Value
PVS500	1.506	12.73
SCS141	−.0009	6341.98
EMS171	2.515	4.16
PVS526	−.037	------

To graph this relationship, use the scatter plot command (Figure 7.5):

> *Graphs*
> > *Scatter*
> > > *Overlay*
> > > *Define*
> > > > *YX Pairs*: BIH29 – PVS526
> > > > > TEENPRE – PVS526
> > *OK*

Note: PVS526 should be listed second in both YX pairs. If it is not, click *Swap Pair*.

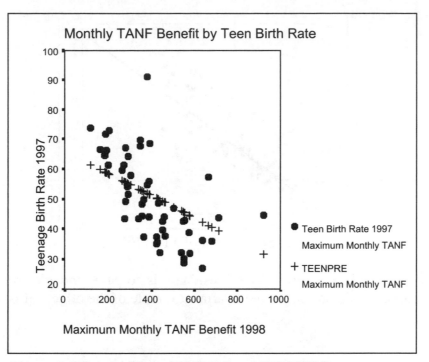

Figure 7.5 Scatter Plot of PVS526 and TEENPRE

Other Concerns of Linear Regression

Earlier we introduced a few concerns that researchers should consider as they decide whether linear regression is the appropriate statistical technique for multivariate analysis, including the need for linear relationships and a numerical dependent variable. Here we outline some other considerations researchers should keep in mind when using regressions.

Constant Variance and Normality of Residuals

Residuals represent the distance between the actual observations contained in the data and their distances from the predicted regression line. Regressions are best suited to analyzing relationships in which the residuals are randomly distanced from this line. In some circumstances the regression line is not well suited to analysis, such as in the case of Figure 7.6, which shows a "fan effect." As this figure shows, the regression line is much better at predicting low values of the dependent variable than it is at predicting high values.

Ideally, the residuals will follow a normal distribution, with a mean of 0. Recall that a normal distribution is shaped like a bell—it is symmetric, and most points are in the middle, with fewer and fewer farther from the mean. Since the residuals measure where the points fall in relation to the line, a symmetric distribution of the residuals means that the same number of points fall above and below the line. Since a residual of 0 means a point is right on the line, a mean of 0 means the line is in the middle of the points—once again, some are above and some are below. And the bell shape indicates that most are close to the line, and there are fewer points farther from the line.

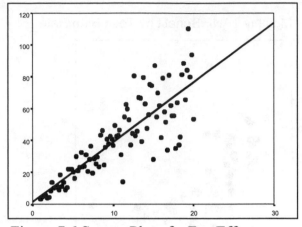

Figure 7.6 Scatter Plot of a Fan Effect

One way to check the normality of residuals is to save and plot residuals from the regression command. To do so for our multivariate example of the effects of poverty on teenage births:

Analyze
> *Regression*
>> *Linear*
>>> *Dependent*: BIH29 (teenage birth rate in 1998)
>>> *Independents*: PVS500 (Poverty Rate 1998)
>>>> SCS141   (Expenditures per Pupil in 1999)
>>>> EMS171   (Unemployment Rate in 1999)
>>>> PVS526 (Maximum Monthly TANF
>>>> Benefit for Family of Three in 1999)
>>> *Save*
>>>> *Residuals:* Unstandardized
>>>> *Continue*
>> OK

This will create a new variable RES_1, which can be graphed using the Graph command (Figure 7.7).

Graphs
> *Histogram*
>> *Variable:* RES_1
>> Check *Display Normal Curve*
>> OK

As Figure 7.7 shows, the residuals form a normal distribution. A normal distribution of the residuals is a good indication that the regression is working well.

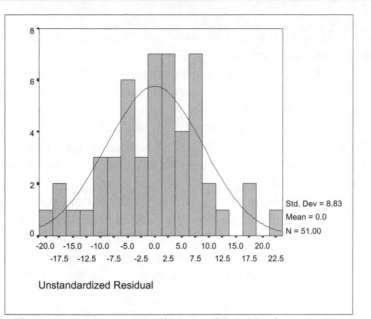

Figure 7.7 Histogram of Normal Residuals

Building Multivariate Models

One might suspect that the most efficient manner of analyzing data would be to load all of the variables in the data set into a regression to observe which have significant associations with the dependent variable. Although this may seem an appealing (albeit lazy) approach, it suffers from a number of problems.

Degrees of Freedom

The first problem concerns **degrees of freedom.** Degrees of freedom refers to the number of observations in a sample that are "free to vary." It is a means of compensating for the possibility of drawing inaccurate conclusions from a sample to the population. Every variable in a regression equation reduces the degrees of freedom by one and consequently reduces the researcher's ability to test the effects of individual variables. When choosing variables for multivariate analysis, it is in the researcher's interest to be highly selective in determining which variables to include in the statistical model. Therefore, the selection of variables in a regression should be hypothesis driven.

We also suggest, in large models, introducing new variables in a sequential manner. For example, rather than loading all of the variables at once, examine a smaller group of variables before introducing another large group of variables. Also, researchers should only proceed with multivariate analysis only after sufficiently exploring the data with univariate and bivariate analysis.

Collinearity

Collinearity occurs when variables have strongly redundant information. If variables are collinear, there is not enough distinct information in these variables for the multiple regression procedure to operate correctly. A multivariate analysis that includes two independent variables that measure essentially the same thing will produce errant results. An example is the percent of the population living below the poverty line (PVS500) and the percent of school age children living in poverty (PVS502). These are two different variables, but they are so strongly collinear (correlation of .85) that they do not really vary sufficiently from one another to be distinguishable in the regression equation.

Collinear variables often result in peculiar outcomes in regression outputs. In the case of the above variables and their relationship to teenage birth rate, we would assume that because both poverty variables are strongly associated with one another, both would be significantly related to teenage birth rates. However, if we run a multiple regression of PVS500 and PVS502 on teenage birth rates (BIH29), one variable fails to become significant (even though both are significant in separate regressions). In even more extreme cases, none of the variables in the multivariate analysis will be significant.

The implication is that researchers should be careful about putting collinear variables in regression equations. To check for collinearity, examine the correlation between the independent variables. A correlation coefficient above .50 is an indicator that collinearity might be present. In such a situation, it is a good idea to follow up with specific diagnostic procedures to confirm if collinearity is a problem. If so, variables may need to be analyzed in separate regression equations.

Dummy Variables

Recall that the coefficients for independent variables reflect incremental differences in the dependent variables. For this reason, all independent variables must reflect some type of continuum. For example, linear regression cannot analyze the impact of ethnicity when it is coded as 1 "Black" 2 "Hispanic" 3 "Asian" 4 "White" 5 "other," because the values do not comprise a continuum (they could be put in any order). Categorical independent variables, such as ethnicity, can be made to reflect a one-unit increase through **dummy variables**. Dummy variables split the observations into two categories. One category is coded as "1" and the other as "0." When a categorical variable is coded like this, the coefficient can be interpreted as the average difference in the dependent variable between the two categories. The conventional practice in constructing dummy variables is to code the comparison group as "1" and the reference group as "0." Although values of "1" and "2" are also one unit apart, there are mathematical conveniences that make "1" and "0" preferable.

Take as an example a model to predict the impact of employment status on saving for retirement. Since we would like to compare employed people to unemployed, employed would be coded as 1 and unemployed would be coded as 0. If the coefficient for employment status were 4600, it would mean that in general, employed people have saved an average of $4600 more than unemployed people.

Sometimes a categorical variable has more than two categories, as is the situation with ethnicity. We would need to construct dummy variables for each ethnic group. The variable "Black" would be coded 0/1, with all African American respondents coded as 1 and all other respondents with known ethnicity coded 0. The variable "Hispanic," likewise, would be coded 0/1 with all Hispanic respondents coded 1 and all others coded 0. We would do this for all but one ethnic group, and then include all the dummy variables in the model. In this example, we would exclude Whites, which would serve as the reference group. Our regression output would then be interpreted as being relative to White respondents. For example, if we were predicting how much money people saved for retirement and the variable "Black" had a coefficient –3200, it would indicate that Blacks save, on average, $3200 less than Whites. If the variable "Asian" had a coefficient of 6700, it would indicate that Asians save $6700 more for retirement than

Whites. In each case, the dummy variable is interpreted relative to the excluded group in the regression.

Outliers

Linear regressions can be greatly influenced by outliers, which are atypical cases. Outliers can "pull" the equation away from the general pattern of the relationship and can greatly influence the regression output. If there is an exceptional case in the data, having atypical high or low values, one solution is to rerun the regression analysis without the outlier and report both results in the text of the report.

In some situations it is reasonable to simply delete an outlier from the analysis. These situations occur when the outlier is not measuring the same thing as the rest of the observations. For example, perhaps the outlier was a mistake – a data entry error or data recording error. Another example is when there are special circumstances surrounding a specific case. For example, Nevada has a very high divorce rate. Because of its laws, it attracts people from outside the state for "drive by divorces." Consequently, Nevada has an inflated divorce rate and would be an outlier for analyses examining the social causes of divorce. Because Nevada's divorce rate does not accurately measure the rate of divorce for Nevada residents, as do the divorce rates in other states, it is reasonable to completely remove Nevada from any analysis of divorce rates.

In other situations, outliers should remain in the analyses, as an outlier may be the most important observation. In these circumstances, it is a good idea to run the analysis twice, first with the outlier in the regression and second with it excluded. If the outlier is not exerting an undue influence on the outcomes, both models should reasonably coincide.

Causality

Finally, researchers should take care when concluding that the results of a linear regression reflect a causal relationship. As discussed in Chapter 1, regressions show associations. They usually do not document time order. For example, we have been careful to say that poverty is associated with teen births, not that it causes them (although this is a likely conclusion). Careful readers will have also noticed that some of our variables indicate information that was generated after the teen birth rates were established. For example, our measure of poverty rates are for 1998 and the teen birth rate is for 1997. These inconsistencies in years resulted from our efforts to create a data set that includes the most current information for all of the measures. Because poverty rates and birth rates are slow to change, this inconsistency is probably not a major threat to the findings, but ideally a more refined analysis would use indicators of the social context in the same year as the teen birth rate is measured. Another causal concern is that it is possible that teen births are a contributing cause to poverty, a reversal of the independent and dependent variables (also a likely conclusion).

One of the strengths of multiple linear regressions is that researchers can include factors (if they are available) that can control for spurious effects. However, there always remains the possibility that a spurious factor remains untested. Even though multiple variables may be included in the statistical model, it is still possible to have spurious relationships if important variables are left out. Therefore, no matter how tempting, it is very important to use caution when concluding that the relationships between an independent and dependent variable are causal.

Summary
Multiple linear regression offers researchers many advantages, as they can examine the multiple factors that contribute to social experiences and control for the influence of potential spurious effects. They also enable us to create refined graphs of relationships through regression lines. These can be a powerful means of presenting analyses to audiences needing complex analyses presented in a straightforward and accessible manner.

Knowing how to interpret linear regression coefficients allows researchers to understand both the direction of a relationship (whether one variable is associated with an increase or a decrease in another variable) and strength (how much of a difference in the dependent variable is associated with a measured difference in the independent variable). Knowing about the R-Square helps researchers understand how powerful their model is, the degree to which it can explain variation in the dependent variable. As with other statistical measures, the significance tests in regressions address the concern of random variation and the degree to which it is a possible explanation for the observed relationships.

As regressions are complex, care is needed in performing them. Researchers need to examine the variables and construct them in forms that are amenable to this approach, such as creating dummy variables. They also need to examine findings carefully and test for concerns such as collinearity or patterns among residuals. This being said, linear regressions are quite forgiving of minor breaches of these assumptions and can produce some of the most useful information on the relationships between variables.

Key Term

Adjusted R-Square	Intercept
B	Linear Relationship
Coefficient	Outliers
Collinearity	Normality of Residuals
Constant	Residuals
Constant Variance	R-Square
Control Variables	Slope
Degrees of Freedom	Spurious Factors
Dummy Variables	Unstandardized coefficient

References and Further Reading
Grimm, Laurence and Paul Yarnold. 1995. *Reading and Understanding Multivariate Statistics*. Washington, DC: American Psychological Society.

Kutner, Michael, Christopher J. Nachtschiem, William Wasserman, and John Neter. 1996. *Applied Linear Statistical Models*. Columbus, OH: McGraw-Hill.

Levin, Jack and James Fox. 1997. *Elementary Statistics in Social Research*. New York: Longman.

Sen, Ashish and Muni Srivastava. 1990. *Regression Analysis: Theory, Methods and Applications*. New York: Springer-Verlag.

Tarbach, Barbara and Linda Fidell. 1983. *Using Multivariate Statistics*. New York: Harper and Row.

Chapter 7 Exercises

Name_____   Date_____

1. Using the STATES data, test the hypothesis that states with large African American populations receive lower educational funding than predominantly White states. Test this hypothesis by performing a bivariate linear regression on SCS143 (Per Capita State and Local Gvt Expenditures for Higher Education 1999) and DMS449 (Percent of Population Black 1998). Fill in the following statistics:

Regression Coefficient B for DMS449   _____

Significance level   _____

Is the relationship significant?   Yes   No

Adjusted R Square   _____

In your own words, describe the relationship between SCS143 and DMS449. How would you explain these findings?

2. Using the STATES data set, examine the relationship between the AIDS death rate (DTH107) and the percent of the population of a state that is urban (DMS437).

Regression Coefficient B for DMS437   _____

Significance   _____

Is the relationship significant?   Yes   No

Adjusted R Square   _____

In your own words, describe the relationship between DTH107 and DMS437. How would you explain these findings?

3. Perform a regression on the relationship between the property crime rate (CRC383) as predicted by the percent of the population of a state that is living below the poverty level (PVS500).

Regression Coefficient B for PVS500   _____

Significance   _____

Is the relationship significant?   Yes   No

Adjusted R Square   _____

In your own words, describe the relationship between CRC383 and PVS500. How would you explain these findings?

4. Perform a multiple regression to determine if social stress predicts the rape rate (CRC347). Include as indicators of potential social stress the percentage of the population that is urban (DMS437), the divorce rate (DMS491), and the business failure rate (ECS104).

Constant   _____

Adjusted R Square   _____

Regression Coefficient B for DMS437   _____

Significance   _____

Is the relationship significant?   Yes   No

Regression Coefficient B for DMS491   _____

Significance   _____

Is the relationship significant?   Yes   No

Regression Coefficient B for ECS104   _____

Significance   _____

Is the relationship significant?   Yes   No

In your own words, describe these relationships and whether the theory that social stress predicts the rape rate is supported by these statistics.

5. Using the output from the regression of social stress and the rape rate in Exercise 4, write the formula which would be used to generate a line showing the association of the divorce rate with the rape rate. Hold constant DMS437 and ECS104 at their mean values. You will need to generate the mean values using the *Descriptive Statistics - Descriptives* command.

$$\hat{Y} \quad = \quad A \quad + \quad B_1(X_1) \quad + \quad B_2(X_2) \quad + \quad B_3(X_3)$$

6. Compute a new variable "RAPE2" using the above equation. Label RAPE2 "Predicted Rape Rate 2." Graph and print the relationship between RAPE2 and DMS491 using the command:

Graphs
    Scatter
        Simple
            Y Axis: RAPE2
            X Axis: DMS491

7. Using the output from the regression of social stress and the rape rate in Exercise 4, write the formula which would be used to generate a line showing the association of the urban population with the rape rate. Hold constant DMS491 and ECS104 at their mean values. You will need to generate the mean values using the *Descriptive Statistics - Descriptives* command.

$$\hat{Y} \quad = \quad A \quad + \quad B_1(X_1) \quad + \quad B_2(X_2) \quad + \quad B_3(X_3)$$

8. Compute a new variable "RAPE3" using the above equation. Label RAPE3 "Predicted Rape Rate 3." Graph and print the relationship between RAPE3 and DMS437 using the command:

> *Graphs*
>> *Scatter*
>>> *Simple*
>>>> *Y Axis*: RAPE3
>>>> *X Axis*: DMS437

Chapter 8
Multivariate Analysis with Logistic Regression

Overview

The previous chapter explained how to analyze multivariate relationships using linear regression. This chapter introduces multivariate analysis using logistic regression. Like linear regression, logistic regression can analyze the relationships of multiple independent variables to a dependent variable. Logistic regression is useful in some situations when the assumptions of linear regression fail. It requires a different type of data and its coefficients have different interpretations. Like linear regression, logistic regression allows results to be graphed with regression lines and predictions to be made given a set of conditions. We outline these methods within SPSS.

What Is Logistic Regression?

Both linear and logistic regression analyze the relationship between multiple independent variables and a single dependent variable. As previously discussed, linear regressions analyze linear relationships, which requires a numerical dependent variable (such as age) that follows a normal distribution. In contrast, logistic regressions require **binary dependent variables,** categorical variables with two categories. Like dummy variables, these are coded 0/1 and indicate if a condition is or is not present, or if an event did or did not occur. For example, logistic regression might use mortality as a dependent variable, which would be coded 0 (alive) and 1 (dead). Recidivism (repeat crimes) would be measured with 0 (no new crimes) and 1 (committed a new crime). As each of these codes constitutes an "either/or" condition, predictions will necessarily fall into one group or the other.[3]

Because there are only two values of the dependent variable (which we will call occurrence or non-occurrence), predicting the probability of occurrence is theoretically interesting. Logistic regressions find the relationship between the independent variables and a function of the probability of occurrence. This function is the logit function (hence, the name logistic regression), also called the log-odds function. It is the natural logarithm of the odds of occurrence. We discuss the relationship between odds and probability below.

As it turns out, using the log-odds creates an equation very similar to the linear regression equation. As you can see, by using the log-odds instead of Y on the left hand side of the equation, the right hand side is identical:

<table>
<tr><td>Linear Regression</td><td>Logistic Regression</td></tr>
<tr><td>$Y = A + B(X)$</td><td>$\text{log-odds} = A + B(X)$</td></tr>
</table>

SPSS will be able to calculate the coefficients, which are interpreted similarly to linear regression coefficients.

What Are the Advantages of Logistic Regression?

Logistic regression is highly effective at estimating the probability that an event will occur. For this reason, it has been applied to medical research, where it is used to estimate the likelihood of individuals recovering from surgery. In education research, it has been used to gauge the probability that an individual will graduate from high school. Criminologists have used it to understand the factors that may lead a criminal to become a repeat offender.

Logistic regression differs from other analytic techniques in a number of ways. These differences offer some great advantages to researchers. As the above examples indicate, logistic regression creates estimates for the likelihood that an event occurs, given a set of conditions. For example, a researcher can use information about criminals, such as the type of crime they committed, the amount of time they spent in jail, and their age, to create a model that estimates the likelihood of a repeat offense. Although a logistic regression model is unable to predict the behavior of any individual criminal, it gives the likelihood that a type of person, given a set of conditions, will become a repeat offender. For instance, what is the likelihood of a young female nonviolent criminal becoming a recidivist compared to an older male violent criminal? This is something that a logistic regression can test.

In summation, logistic regressions offer the same advantages as linear regression, including the ability to construct multivariate models and include control variables. It can perform analysis on two types of independent variables—numeric and dummy variables—just like linear regression. Logistic regression opens the possibility for multivariate analysis for data that are incompatible with linear regression. In addition, logistic regressions offer a new way of interpreting relationships by examining the relationships between a set of conditions and the probability of an event occurring.

---

[3] There are also multinomial logistic regressions, which can predict the likelihood of more than two conditions. In this circumstance, for instance, we might predict the likelihood that a man would see an action movie, a comedy, or a love story if he is going on a date to the cinema on a Friday evening. This chapter will only focus on binomial logistic regressions, where only two possible outcomes exist.

When Can I do a Logistic Regression?

Logistic regression is used when the dependent variable is binary, but can be useful for other dependent variables if they are recoded to binary form. For example, a variable might indicate the highest degree earned, and have values 1 "High School" 2 "Bachelors" 3 "Masters" 4 "Ph.D." A researcher who is interested in predicting the likelihood that a person would attain at least a college degree could recode this variable to a binary form: 0 "High School" or 1 "Bachelors or higher."

Likewise, a highly skewed numeric variable is not well suited to linear regression analysis, because linear regression requires a normal distribution. For example, a study by Straus and Sweet (1992) studied the incidence of verbal aggression, such as yelling and name calling, in American families. They found that most couples report never yelling at their partner. However, there are some couples where yelling and threatening is an everyday occurrence. This resulted in a very skewed distribution of the dependent variable—number of verbal assaults in a year. Consequently, linear regression could not be used reliably, even though the dependent variable was numeric. Their solution was to recode the numeric variable into a binary categorical variable of verbally aggressive and verbally non-aggressive couples. Verbally aggressive couples yelled or threatened more than once per month (13+ per year) and were coded as "1." The other couples were coded as "0," indicating that they were comparatively non-aggressive. Straus and Sweet analyzed the data with multivariate logistic regression models. These models examined the influence of gender, socioeconomic status, children, drinking, and drugs on verbal aggression.

When constructing the binary dependent variable, it is important that the categories be **mutually exclusive**, so that a case cannot be in both categories at the same time. For instance, a researcher might want to test whether a person owns a truck or a car. If this variable was coded as 0 "truck" and 1 "car," logistic regression would not be appropriate because a person could own both (thereby falling into both categories). A better approach would be to create two binary variables. One variable would indicate if the person owned a car, coded 0 "does not own" and 1 "owns." Then a second variable would indicate if the person owned a truck, coded 0 "does not own" and 1 "owns." Then two logistic regressions could predict car ownership and truck ownership.

Understanding the Relationships through Probabilities

Logistic regressions predict likelihoods, measured by probabilities, odds, or log-odds. Often, people speak of "probabilities" and "odds" as being the same thing, but there is an important distinction. A **probability** is the ratio of the number of occurrences to the total number of possibilities. For example, what is the probability of drawing a spade from a deck of cards? Considering that there are 52 cards in a deck (52 possibilities), and that there are 13 spades in that deck, the probability of randomly choosing a spade from a deck of cards is 13/52, or 1/4. In contrast, the **odds** describe the ratio of the number of occurrences to the number of non-occurrences. If we drew all of the cards in the deck to determine the odds of choosing a spade, we would find the odds as 13/39 or 1/3. For every spade in the deck, there are 3 non-spades.

As another example, the probability of catching a flu during any given winter is about 0.10, or 1/10. This means that out of every 10 people, approximately one will catch the flu. In contrast, the odds of catching a flu during any given winter is 1/9—for every one person who catches the flu, nine do not. It is easy to convert back and forth between probability and odds, as they give the same information. Table 8.1 shows the correspondence between some probabilities and odds.

Number of occurrences in 100 trials	Probability	Odds
0	0	0
10	1/10	1/9
25	1/4	1/3
33	1/3	1/2
50	1/2	1
75	3/4	3
90	9/10	9
100	1	∞ (infinity)

Table 8.1 Common Values of Probability and Odds

As you can see, probabilities range from 0 to 1, whereas odds range from 0 to infinity. An odds of one indicates equal probability of occurrence and non-occurrence (.50). An odds less than 1 indicates that occurrence is less likely than non-occurrence. An odds greater than 1 indicates that occurrence is more likely than non-occurrence. Distinguishing probabilities from odds is important, not only for accuracy in reporting findings, but also for the interpretation of the logistic regression coefficients and graphs that we will be creating. Note here that even when findings are reported as odds, they can be converted to probabilities using the following formula:

$$Probability = \frac{Odds}{1 + Odds}$$

We will use this formula to convert the logistic regression results from log-odds into probabilities.

Logistic Regression: A Bivariate Example

To illustrate the construction and interpretation of a logistic regression, we will use an example generated from the GSS98 data. Our question concerns the relationship between political orientation and gun ownership and our interests are in predicting the types of people most likely to report owning a gun. For this bivariate example, we will examine the influence of political views. The guiding hypothesis is that conservative people are more likely to own guns because political conservatives tend to support gun ownership rights. We will use the GSS98 data to analyze this hypothesis.

The first step in the analysis involves examining the structure of the dependent and independent variables, making sure that they conform to the structures needed in logistic regression. For the dependent variable OWNGUN, the variable should take on the form of a 0/1 binary variable, with 1 indicating gun ownership. To check this, perform:

Utilities
         Variables: OWNGUN

It indicates that OWNGUN is a nominal categorical variable with two values: No and Yes. The remaining values are coded as missing. The independent variable in a bivariate logistic regression should be numeric. The Utilities command can check this as well. The variable POLVIEWS is an ordinal variable, but can also be considered numerical, locating respondents on a scale ranging from 1 (extremely liberal) to 7 (extremely conservative). The higher the value, the more conservative the respondent. We would expect to see a positive relationship between POLVIEWS and OWNGUN. Having confirmed that both variables have the right structures for bivariate logistic regression, we can now test the relationship:

Analyze
         Regression
                  Binary Logistic
                           Dependent: OWNGUN
                           Covariates: POLVIEWS
                           OK

Your output should look similar to Figure 8.1. Our examination of this output will focus on the odds ratios, coefficients, significance tests, and the model chi-square.

Interpreting Odds Ratios and Logistic Regression Coefficients

The first step is to interpret the hypothesized relationship by examining the **logistic regression coefficients** or **log-odds**. Logistic regression coefficients, in the column "B" in the *Variables in the Equation* box, perform the same function as regression coefficients in linear regressions, in that they indicate the direction and strength of the relationship between the independent and dependent variables. However, these logistic regression coefficients are a little bit more complicated to intuitively gauge, as they represent the influence of a one-unit change in the independent variable on the log-odds of the dependent variable. It is difficult to visualize a log-odds relationship, and as we show below, the interpretation is greatly assisted by graphing these relationships. Given the complexity of understanding the coefficients, on face value, most researchers initially concentrate on the directionality of the relationships. In this example, we observe a positive relationship (.190), indicating that the more conservative a person is, the greater the likelihood of he or she owning a gun.

The next step is to gauge the strength of the relationship with the odds ratio, shown in the column Exp(B) in the *Variables in the Equation* box. The **odds ratio** is a ratio of the odds at two values of the independent variable that are one unit apart. It indicates how many times higher the odds of occurrence are for each one-unit increase in the independent variable. The odds ratio for POLVIEWS is 1.210. Again, this shows that a higher score (being more conservative) increases the odds of owning a gun. How much more? Each one-unit increase on the political views scale increases the odds of owning a gun by a factor of 1.21. People who consider themselves liberal (with a score of 2) are 1.21 times as likely to own a gun than people who consider themselves very liberal (with a score of 1). Likewise, people who consider themselves slightly liberal (with a score of 3) are 1.21 times as likely to own a gun than people who consider themselves liberal (with a score of 2), and so on.

Omnibus Tests of Model Coefficients

		Chi-square	df	Sig.
Step 1	Step	28.625	1	.000
	Block	28.625	1	.000
	Model	28.625	1	.000

Model Summary

Step	-2 Log likelihood	Cox & Snell R Square	Nagelkerke R Square
1	2266.345	.016	.022

Classification Table[a]

			Predicted		
			HAVE GUN IN HOME		Percentage Correct
	Observed		NO	YES	
Step 1	HAVE GUN IN HOME	NO	1136	0	100.0
		YES	627	0	.0
	Overall Percentage				64.4

a. The cut value is .500

Variables in the Equation

		B	S.E.	Wald	df	Sig.	Exp(B)
Step 1[a]	POLVIEWS	.190	.036	28.032	1	.000	1.210
	Constant	-1.379	.158	75.902	1	.000	.252

a. Variable(s) entered on step 1: POLVIEWS.

Figure 8.1 Logistic Regression Output

The next step is to see if the relationship is statistically significant. The output from the logistic regression shows a significance level for POLVIEWS of .000. The probability that the observed relationship can be attributed to chance is extremely low, and we conclude there is a relationship between political views and gun ownership.

Using Logistic Regression Coefficients to Make Predictions

Like linear regressions, logistic regression coefficients can be used to make predictions for the dependent variable. Suppose, for example, that we wanted to know the exact probability of gun ownership for someone who is extremely conservative (POLVIEWS=7). To do this requires plugging in a seven for POLVIEWS and mean values for the other independent variables into the logistic regression equation and converting the log-odds to probabilities.

The logistic regression equation is:

$$Log\text{-}odds = A + B(X) \tag{1}$$

Because the logistic regression represents the log-odds, we have to take the antilog (Exp) as we convert the formula to represent probability, as shown in this equation:

$$Odds = Exp(A + B(X)) \tag{2}$$

Recall that the formula for converting odds to probabilities is:

$$Probability = \frac{Odds}{1 + Odds} \tag{3}$$

Putting it all together by replacing *Odds* with equation 2, gives:

$$Probability = \frac{Exp(A + B(X))}{1 + Exp(A + B(X))} \tag{4}$$

In this example:

$$Probability = \frac{Exp(-1.379 + .190(7))}{1 + Exp(-1.379 + .190(7))}$$

$$Probability = \frac{Exp(-.049)}{1 + Exp(-.049)}$$

$$Probability = \frac{.95}{1.95}$$

Probability of a very conservative person owning a gun = .49

Likewise, we could predict gun ownership for someone who is extremely liberal (POLVIEWS–1):

$$Probability = \frac{Exp(A + B(X))}{1 + Exp(A + B(X))}$$

$$Probability = \frac{Exp(-1.379 + .190(1))}{1 + Exp(-1.379 + .190(1))}$$

$$Probability = \frac{Exp(-1.189)}{1 + Exp(-1.189)}$$

$$Probability = \frac{.306}{1.306}$$

Probability of a very liberal person owning a gun = .23

Predicting probability based on logistic regressions is helpful for presenting findings to lay audiences. In the current case, we can succinctly state our findings in the following way.

Political attitudes are significantly associated with gun ownership. The probability of a very conservative person owning a gun is .49. In comparison, people identifying themselves as being very liberal have a much lower probability (.23) of owning a gun.

Using Coefficients to Graph a Logistic Regression Line

We find graphing logistic regressions very helpful. Our approach draws upon the way we constructed a regression line for a linear regression, modifying it to accommodate the log-odds represented in the coefficients column (B). To graph the logistic regression, we will find the predicted probabilities for different values of the independent variable. Unlike the linear relationship in linear regressions, the logistic regression graphs will show a **sigmoidal** or **S-shaped** relationship, as represented in Figure 8.2.

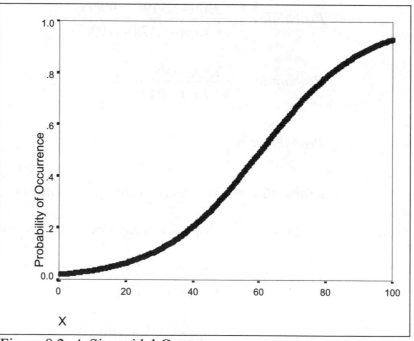

Figure 8.2: A Sigmoidal Curve

The reason relationships for probabilities are sigmoidal, not linear, can be illustrated by the relationship between the probability of injury in a car accident and driving speed. Think of the X axis in Figure 8.2 as speed in miles per hour (mph), and the Y axis as the probability of being seriously injured. People traveling at *any* low speed are unlikely to be seriously injured. The probability of serious injury changes little between one mph or six mph. This relationship is shown in the lower left hand quadrant of the graph. Likewise, people traveling at *any* high speed are very likely to be seriously injured. A 5 mph change from 90 to 95 mph has little effect on the probability of being injured in an accident, because almost everyone traveling this fast would be injured. Now consider what happens in the middle portion of the graph. The influence of an incremental change becomes greater. Traveling 40 versus 45 mph will have a marked influence on the probability of injury in a crash. There are bounds to the probability of serious injury at both ends, and the sigmoidal curve does not exceed these boundaries the way a linear one can.

Our approach to generating graphs relies on the values in the data set, and as such, each graph might contain only a portion of the sigmoid curve, such as the upper end, lower end, or middle portions. To make the graphs, we will use the same formula we used earlier to find predicted probabilities. Rather than compute the predicted probabilities by hand, we will allow SPSS to calculate the predicted probabilities from the constant and coefficient using the *Compute* command. Particular attention should be paid to bracketing "()" the information in the formula, as failing to do so will produce errors.

> *Transform*
> > *Compute*
> > > *Target Variable*: GUNPRE
> > > *Numeric Expression*: (*Exp* (-1.379 + (.190*POLVIEWS)))/ (1+*Exp* (-1.379 + (.190*POLVIEWS))).
> > > *Type&Label*
> > > > *Label:* Predicted Gun Ownership
> > > > *Continue*
> > > *OK*

Then we use GUNPRE to graph the logistic regression line, using the *Scatterplot* commands (Figure 8.3).

> *Graphs*
> > *Scatter*
> > > *Simple*
> > > *Define*
> > > > *Y Axis*: GUNPRE
> > > > *X Axis*: POLVIEWS
> > > > *OK*

Figure 8.3 enables us to visually observe the degree to which political attitudes are associated with gun ownership. Note how the regression represents both the direction of the relationship and the relative impact of being very liberal, to liberal, to conservative, to very conservative. In this example, the graph represents the central portion of the sigmoid curve, as all political groups have between a .20 and a .50 probability of owning a gun. Although it appears almost linear, this is in fact a sigmoidal curve, representing the steepest portion of the curves.

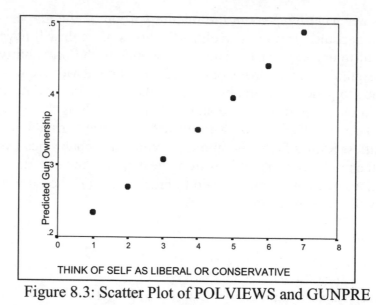

Figure 8.3: Scatter Plot of POLVIEWS and GUNPRE

Model Chi-Squares and Goodness of Fit

There is no single well accepted measure in logistic regression that performs the function of the R-Square statistic of linear regression. Recall that the R-Square statistic offers information on goodness of fit and the degree to which the model can account for the variance in the dependent variable. There have been some attempts by statisticians to create an equivalent statistic, but there is no agreement on which statistic is best. We recommend examining the **Model Chi-Square**, which tests whether the model as a whole predicts occurrence better than chance. It is located in the table called "Omnibus Tests of Model Coefficients." Since it has a low significance value (.000), we conclude that this is a useful model.

Multivariate Logistic Regression: An Example

In the bivariate logistic regression, we found a relationship between political views and whether someone owns a gun, but other variables may also predict gun ownership. We predict that racial minorities, younger people, less educated people, and those without children are more likely to own guns. We will use the following variables:

RACE (Race of respondent)
AGE (Age of respondent)
EDUC (Highest year of school completed)
CHILDS (Number of children)

The first step is to make sure that the variables are structured correctly. Recall, you can check the structures using the *Utilities* command. One concern is that the variable CHILDS represents the number of children in the family. Our interest, however, is whether having any children influences the likelihood of owning a gun. Therefore, we need to recode CHILDS into a dummy variable indicating whether the respondent has, or does not have, any children:

Transform
 Recode
  Into Different Variable: CHILDS → CHILDREN
  Label: Does Respondent have Children?
  Old and New Values:
   Value: 0 → 0
   ADD

   Range: 1 *through highest* → 1
   ADD

   System or user missing → System Missing
   ADD
   Continue
 OK

Remember to add value labels in the Variable View window. Note also that RACE is a categorical variable. One approach to analyzing RACE would be to recode it into dummy variables, as discussed in the previous chapter. If we specify variables as categorical in the logistic regression procedure, SPSS will automatically dummy code them. We will use this approach. The following commands run the multivariate logistic regression:

Analyze
 Regression
  Binary Logistic
   Dependent: OWNGUN
   Covariates: POLVIEWS
         AGE
         CHILDREN
         RACE
         EDUC
  Categorical:
   Categorical Covariates: RACE
                 CHILDREN
   Reference Category: First, Change (while RACE is
                 highlighted)
   Reference Category: First, Change (while CHILDREN is
                 highlighted)
   Continue
  OK

Our analysis of the multivariate logistic regression (Figure 8.4) shows that many of these variables are statistically significant, showing relationships to gun ownership. As we found in the bivariate logistic regression, the more conservative someone is (higher values of POLVIEWS), the more likely that person is to own a gun. In fact, the odds that someone owns a gun is 1.15 times higher for each one-unit increase on the POLVIEWS scale, as shown in the

Exp(B) column of the Variables in the Equation box. Notice that although political view is still significant, the odds ratio has changed slightly from the earlier bivariate logistic regression. Once the other variables have been taken into account, the predictive power of political orientation on gun ownership is slightly less. This is because political orientation is associated with the other independent variables. As we have controlled for their influence, a more accurate analysis of the influence of political orientation emerges.

CHILDREN is also significant. You may notice a (1) after Children in the Coefficients Table. It means that the odds ratio compares those who have CHILDREN (coded 1) to those who do not have children (coded 0), the reference group. How do we know which is the reference group? This information is in the "Categorical Variables Codings" Table. The value of CHILDREN, which is 0.000 in the "Variable Coding" column, is the reference category. We also specified this in our model, choosing the reference category to be the "first" value when we set up the categorical variable. In this example, the first value is "0," our code for those who do not have children. The odds ratio for CHILDREN is 1.738. This means that people with children are nearly twice as likely to own a gun as people without children. (Remember this

Categorical Variables Codings

		Frequency	Parameter coding (1)	Parameter coding (2)
RACE OF RESPONDENT	WHITE	1400	.000	.000
	BLACK	245	1.000	.000
	OTHER	107	.000	1.000
Does Respondent have Children?	No	493	.000	
	Yes	1259	1.000	

Omnibus Tests of Model Coefficients

		Chi-square	df	Sig.
Step 1	Step	138.344	6	.000
	Block	138.344	6	.000
	Model	138.344	6	.000

Variables in the Equation

		B	S.E.	Wald	df	Sig.	Exp(B)
Step 1[a]	POLVIEWS	.140	.037	13.973	1	.000	1.150
	AGE	-.001	.003	.068	1	.795	.999
	CHILDREN(1)	.553	.128	18.612	1	.000	1.738
	RACE			67.761	2	.000	
	RACE(1)	-1.233	.180	47.114	1	.000	.291
	RACE(2)	-1.538	.305	25.330	1	.000	.215
	EDUC	-.058	.018	10.439	1	.001	.943
	Constant	-.535	.343	2.428	1	.119	.586

a. Variable(s) entered on step 1: POLVIEWS, AGE, CHILDREN, RACE, EDUC.

Figure 8.4 Multivariate Logistic Regression Output

comparison is for people with the same political views, race, education, and age, so these are not factors in the comparison.) We hypothesized that people with children would be *less* likely to own guns. Our hypothesis was not supported, and the opposite conclusion appears to be true.

RACE is also significant. Since there are three categories of race, there are two sets of coefficients, odds-ratios, and significance values for race. Each set represents the comparison between one racial category and the reference category. Again, the "Categorical Variables Coding" table indicates that Whites are the reference category, Blacks are Category (1), and Others are Category (2). We also structured our model to use White as the reference group, as White is the lowest value in the variable RACE. The odds-ratio for RACE(1), therefore, is the comparison between Blacks and Whites. It indicates that Blacks are .291, about 1/3 as likely to own a gun as Whites. Likewise, other minorities are about 1/5 as likely to own a gun as Whites, as indicated by the odds ratio for RACE(2), .215. Again, our hypothesis that racial minorities are more likely to own guns was not only unsupported, the opposite hypothesis was supported. African Americans and other racial minorities are considerably less likely to own guns in comparison to whites.

EDUC is also significant, at .001. The negative relationship (-.058) revealed in the coefficient column (B) shows that the more educated people are, the less likely they are to own guns. The odds ratio-column (Exp(B)) indicates that for each additional year of education a person has, his or her odds of owning a gun are only .943 as large. This hypothesis was supported.

Because AGE shows a significance value of .795, it is not significant and we find no evidence that age is related to gun ownership.

Using Multivariate Logistic Regression Coefficients to Make Predictions

Like linear regressions, logistic regression coefficients can be used to make predictions. Suppose, for instance, that we wanted to predict the likelihood that a person who holds a Bachelor's degree owns a gun. We will write out the regression equation, inserting the mean value for POLVIEW and AGE, the most common value for CHILDREN, RACE1, and RACE2, and 16 for EDUC (the number of years of education it takes a person to achieve a BA). We draw the coefficients for this equation from the logistic regression output. We then use the relationship between odds and probabilities as we did in the bivariate case to find predicted probabilities.

$$Log\text{-}odds\ = A + B_1(X_1) + B_2(X_2) + B_3(X_3) + B_4(X_4)...$$

$$Odds = Exp(A + B_1(X_1) + B_2(X_2) + B_3(X_3) + B_4(X_4)...)$$

$$\begin{array}{ccccc} \text{POLVIEW} & \text{AGE} & \text{CHILDREN} & \text{RACE1} & \text{RACE2} & \text{EDUC} \end{array}$$

$$Probability = \frac{(Exp\,(-.535+(.140*4.28\,)+(-.001*45.56)+(.553*1)+(-1.233*0)+(-1.538*0)+(-.058*16)))}{(1+Exp\,(-.535+(.140*4.28\,)+(-.001*45.56)+(.553*1)+(-1.233*0)+(-1.538*0)+(-.058*16)))}$$

$$Probability = \frac{Exp(-.36)}{1+Exp(-.36)}$$

$$Probability = \frac{.70}{1.70} = .41$$

We conclude that a 45-year-old white person with children, average political views, and a Bachelor's degree has a .41 probability of owning a gun.

Sources of the numbers in the above equations:

Constant = -.535

	B	Value
POLVIEW	.140	4.28 (mean value)
AGE	-.001	45.56 (mean value)
CHILDREN	.553	1 (value of yes, has a child)
RACE1	-1.233	0 (value of White)
RACE2	-1.538	0 (value of White)
EDUC	-.058	16 (years of education for Bachelor's degree)

Using Multivariate Coefficients to Graph a Logistic Regression Line

Graphs of multiple logistic regression lines are produced in much the same way as bivariate logistic regression lines. In the previous section, we showed how to predict probabilities from a multiple logistic regression. Graphing requires the same formula, without entering a specified value for the variable to be graphed on the X axis.

The logistic regression for the model predicting gun ownership includes political views, age, children, race, and education. We will create a regression line for the relationship between education and gun ownership, holding all of the other variables constant at selected values. We use the same regression formula outlined above, only instead of inserting 16 for education, we will allow it to vary.

Multivariate Model Predicting Log-odds Of Gun Ownership by Education

POLVIEW   AGE   CHILDREN RACE1 RACE2   EDUC

Log-odds = -.535+(.140*4.28)+(-.001*45.56)+(.553*1)+(-1.233*0)+(-1.538*0)+(-.058*EDUC)

To create the regression line, we use the *Compute* procedure, and include in the formula our method of converting the log-odds back to probabilities:

Transform
    Compute
        Target Variable: GUNPRE2
        Numeric Expression: (*Exp* (-.535+(.140*4.28)+(-.001*45.56)+(.553*1)+
                (-1.233*0)+(-1.538*0)+(-.058*EDUC)))/
                (1+*Exp* (-.535+(.140*4.28)+(-.001*45.56)+(.553*1)+
                (-1.233*0)+(-1.538*0)+(-.058*EDUC))).
        Type and Label:
                Label: Predicted Gun Ownership by Education
                Continue
        OK

The results can be graphed using the *Scatterplot* command. The resulting graph will look like Figure 8.5.

> *Graphs*
>> *Scatter*
>>> *Simple*
>>> *Define*
>>>> *Y Axis*: GUNPRE2
>>>> *X Axis*: EDUC
>>>> *OK*

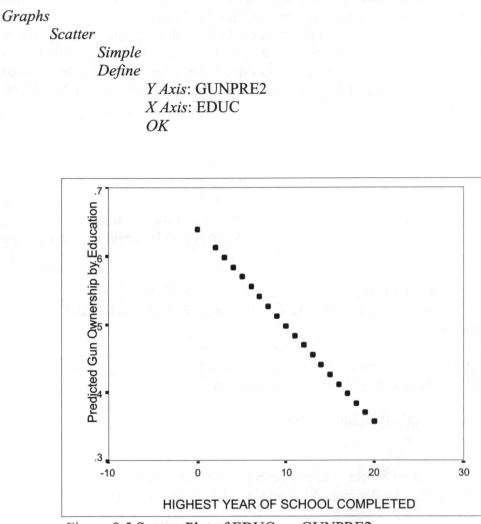

Figure 8.5 Scatter Plot of EDUC vs. GUNPRE2

Graphing these multivariate lines is intense. It requires keen attention to transferring information from the regression equation, converting the log-odds into probabilities, and controlling for the influence of variables by setting values at their mean. There are numerous sources for error. There are a few tricks to checking that the graphs accurately represent the information in the logistic regression. First, the Y axis must always have values between 0 and 1, as these are the minimum and maximum possible probabilities. If the Y axis extends above or below these values, the regression line was incorrectly computed. Second, the direction of the relationship should be consistent with the directionality indicated in the regression coefficients. In this example, the negative coefficient for EDUC signals that the regression line should flow from the upper left corner of the graph to the lower right.

Summary

Logistic regression operates like linear regression. However, unlike linear regression, logistic regression requires a binary dependent variable. Since coefficients are in terms of the log of the odds, it is necessary to interpret the odds ratios. Logistic regression is often a viable alternative when the dependent variable does not conform to the expectations required for linear regression, particularly when the variable can take on the form of a binary variable, indicating either the presence or absence of an event, condition, or behavior. Logistic regressions can be graphed by converting the log-odds, and predictions of probabilities can be calculated for specific sets of conditions.

Key Terms

Binary Variable

Log-odds

Logistic Regression

Logistic Regression Coefficients

Model Chi-square

Mutually Exclusive

Odds

Odds Ratio

Probability

Sigmoidal Relationship

S-shaped Relationship

References and Further Reading

Aldrich, John and Forrest Nelson. 1984. *Linear Probability, Logit and Probit Models*. Beverly Hills: Sage Publications.

Grimm, Laurence and Paul Yarnold. 1995. *Reading and Understanding Multivariate Statistics*. Washington DC: American Psychological Association:

Hosmer, David and Stanley Lemeshow. 1989. *Applied Logistic Regression*. New York: John Wiley and Sons.

Straus, Murray and Stephen Sweet. 1992. "Verbal/Symbolic Aggression in Couples: Incidence Rates and Relationships to Personal Characteristics." *Journal of Marriage and the Family* 54:346-357.

Chapter 8 Exercises

Name_____   Date_____

1. Using the GSS98 data and the variable GRASS, examine whether the respondent's socioeconomic index score (SEI) has an effect on the likelihood of supporting the legalization of marijuana. Use logistic regression to generate the following information:

Constant   _____

Logistic Regression Coefficient for SEI   _____

Odds ratio for SEI   _____

Significance   _____

Is this relationship statistically significant?   Yes   No

Do people scoring high on SEI have a greater
or lesser probability of supporting legalization
in comparison to people scoring low on SEI?

                Greater   Lesser   No Effect

2. Using the GSS98 data and the variable GRASS, examine whether the respondent's education (EDUC) has an effect on the likelihood of supporting the legalization of marijuana. Use logistic regression to generate the following information:

Constant   _____

Logistic Regression Coefficient for EDUC   _____

Odds ratio for EDUC   _____

Significance   _____

Is this relationship statistically significant?   Yes   No

Do people with high levels of education
have a greater or lesser probability of
supporting the legalization of marijuana in
comparison to people with low education?

            Greater   Lesser   No Effect

3. Using the GSS98 data and the computed variable COLHOM2, examine whether the respondent's education (EDUC) has an effect on the likelihood of his/her accepting homosexuals as teachers. Use logistic regression to generate the following information:

Constant   _____

Logistic Regression Coefficient for EDUC   _____

Odds ratio for EDUC   _____

Significance   _____

Is this relationship statistically significant?   Yes   No

Do people with higher educational attainment
have a greater or lesser probability of
supporting homosexuals as teachers
in comparison to people with less education?

                                Greater   Lesser   No Effect

4. Using the output from the previous logistic regression, predict the probability of a person being in support of a homosexual's right to teach if the respondent has a high school education (12 years).

Step 1. Generate the log-odds using the formula: *Log-odds = A+B(X)*

Log-odds _____

Step 2. Generate the odds using the formula: *Odds = Exp(A+B(X))*

Odds _____

Step 3. Generate the probability using the formula: $Probability = \dfrac{Odds}{1+Odds}$

Probability _____

5. Using the output from the previous logistic regression, predict the probability of a person being in support of a homosexual's right to teach if the respondent has a college education (16 years).

Step 1. Generate the log-odds using the formula: *Log-odds = A+B(X)*

Log-odds_____

Step 2. Generate the odds using the formula: *Odds = Exp(A+B(X))*

Odds_____

Step 3. Generate the probability using the formula: $Probability = \dfrac{Odds}{1+Odds}$

Probability_____

6. Generate and print a scatter plot showing the predicted relationship between COLHOM2 and EDUC. Do your answers in questions 5 & 6 correspond with this graph?

Yes   No

7. Using the GSS98 data and the computed variable COLHOM2, examine whether the respondent's education (EDUC), controlling for the variable age (AGE), has an effect on the likelihood of his/her accepting homosexuals as teachers. Use logistic regression to generate the following information:

Constant   _____

Logistic Regression Coefficient for EDUC   _____

Odds ratio for EDUC   _____

Significance   _____

Is this relationship statistically significant?   Yes   No

Logistic Regression Coefficient for AGE   _____

Odds ratio for AGE   _____

Significance   _____

Is this relationship statistically significant?   Yes   No

Are older people more or less likely
to accept homosexuals as teachers in
comparison to younger people?   More   Less   No Effect

8. Using the output from the logistic regression in question 7, predict the probability that a 65-year-old person with 10 years of education will be in favor of homosexuals teaching.

Step 1. Generate the log-odds using the formula: $Log\text{-}odds = A + B_1(X_1) + B_2(X_2)$

Log-odds _____

Step 2. Generate the odds using the formula: $Odds = Exp(A + B_1(X_1) + B_2(X_2))$

Odds _____

Step 3. Generate the probability using the formula: $Probability = \dfrac{Odds}{1 + Odds}$

Probability _____

9. Generate and print a scatter plot showing the predicted relationship between age and supporting a homosexual teaching college. Control for education by setting this value at 10 years in your equation.

Does your graph correspond with the calculations you made for these probabilities?

Chapter 9
Writing a Research Report

Overview

After completing data analysis, researchers are professionally obligated to conclude their projects by writing a **research report**. This report is an organized presentation of all phases of the research project, from beginning to end. It should present research questions, relevant literature, key findings, and the limitations of the study. Writing a good report is one of the most important phases of the research project because it is the avenue to making study findings known and accessible to the wider scientific community. Without the report, knowledge remains trapped within the researcher.

Writing the research report can be very challenging because it requires demonstrating a mastery of the research question, the analytic methods, and the findings. Readers should be able to understand the complexities of the data analyses without becoming lost in the minutia of the data analysis process. They need to understand the limitations, but also to appreciate the insights the study offers. Furthermore, many readers will not be conversant in all of the statistical methods used, and therefore analyses need to be accompanied with a written explanation of the findings. At the report phase of the project, the data analyst shifts from being an explorer to being a writer.

In this chapter, we offer an overview of the composition of a good report. This includes a scholarly but accessible writing style and a structure offering systematic and organized information.

Writing Style and Audience

The main purpose of a research report is to condense the questions and findings so that the reader can understand the study's implications and limitations. It should introduce the reader to the research question and offer a concise overview of the project. The first question a researcher should consider before writing the report is "who is the audience?" Not all readers have the same skills or abilities to comprehend statistics, and therefore the style needs to be appropriate for the audience. Scientists writing to other scientists can take for granted that their readers will understand fundamental statistical methods, such as those discussed in this book. However, even this audience will need to have findings and methods summarized so that they can critically evaluate the research project. On the other hand, writing to a general audience requires an entirely different style. Statistical results will be meaningless to those who have little understanding of "coefficients," "standard errors," or "significance tests." Writing a graded research report for a college professor requires yet a different style. Professors are usually concerned with not only the most important findings, but also an in-depth discussion of the process used to produce those findings.   In comparison, scientists and general audiences are more interested in the findings than in the process.

In all cases, constructing a report does not consist of churning out lots of statistical output and leaving it for readers to decipher (frequently they will lack these skills). Rather, it requires analyzing lots of statistical output, weeding out analyses that are peripheral to the research question, and keeping only analyses that are central. Further, it involves reconfiguring statistics into a format that is reader friendly, in the form of tables, graphs, and written text. Statistical output, such as that produced by SPSS, is designed to give researchers information for a variety of purposes other than hypothesis testing. For instance, some statistics are used for diagnostic purposes, and as such, have little interest to readers. Therefore, researchers often need to distill hundreds of pages of output into a modest number of graphs and tables.

The Structure of a Report

Reports vary in their structures, but usually include the sections that constitute journal articles. Researchers can modify this structure depending on the needs of the audience, but even then, the following information is important:

> *Title*
> *Abstract*
> *Introduction*
> *Literature review*
> *Methods*
> *Findings*
> *Conclusion*
> *References*

Journal articles require researchers to present this information succinctly, in about twenty pages. **Evaluation reports**, which are written for practitioners or administrators, are somewhat longer, with slightly altered section headings, but hold the same overall format. Theses and dissertations also have the same format, but the literature review, methods, and conclusion each comprise full chapters. Findings can be many chapters, each examining part of the research question. Below, we examine each of the eight sections of a research report and highlight the concerns researchers should consider as they write their report.

The Title

The **title** is a concise description of the research project and can make or break a report. Because computer searches use titles as one means of locating research articles, a title is one of the primary means of attracting readers in the first place. If a title lacks necessary information, or presents the subject in an unsatisfactory manner, it may discourage potential readers. The minimal standard for a title is that it be short (5-10 words) and that it offer some information about the research topic.

It is not in a researcher's interest to pick the types of titles that appear in *Cosmopolitan* or *People* magazines. Consider the merits of these titles:

"Who Will Save the Children?"

"A Struggle Against All Odds"

"Desperate, But Not Defeated!"

While these titles are catchy, they share two problems. The first problem is that they do not offer enough information to describe the issue being addressed in the report. The reader does not know what is threatening children, what is the struggle against the odds, or who is desperate but not defeated. It is better to sacrifice "pizzazz" in favor of information. The second problem is that these titles imply that the researcher is an advocate of a political cause, rather than an objective analyst of data. Because our reports are generally written to the scientific community, or to people who trust our attempts at objectivity, it is to the writers' advantage to write in a non-inflammatory style.

Here are a few more titles, drawn from the American Sociological Review:

"The Democratic Class Struggle in the United States, 1948-1992"

"The Impact of Reagan's New Federalism on Business Failures"

"Organizational Mortality in Peace Movement Organizations."

These titles are less "catchy," but they are much better than the previous titles. Each title offers substantial information about the article's research topic. Furthermore, the tone implies that the study will offer a balanced evaluation of the data. For example, while it is possible that Reagan's new federalism increased business failures, the title also makes clear that it is possible that it may have decreased it.

The Abstract

Although the abstract is the first major section of a research report, it is usually written last. This is because the **abstract** is a concise summary of the report. The length of the abstract can vary, but it should be under 150 words (approximately half a page of double spaced text). It serves very much like an **executive summary** in business reports. The abstract should contain information about the research question, data, findings, and conclusions of the study. The trick to creating a good abstract is using words as effectively as possible.

Everyday Forms of Employee Resistance

Drawing on empirical material collected from over 250 individuals employed in a variety of short-term positions, this article examines how temporary employees pursue grievances against their employing organizations. The findings indicate that temporary employees generally respond to offensive behavior on the part of their employers in nonaggressive ways. Gossip, toleration, and resignation are popular, while occasionally grievances are expressed by theft, sabotage, or noncooperation. Collective responses, formal complaints, and legal action are rare. These restrained responses are traced not to the severity of injustices but to the social environment associated with temporary employment, where workers are loosely tied to their organizations and one another. This research may help explain the decline of organized resistance in the contemporary workplace.

Source: Tucker, James. 1993. "Everyday Forms of Employee Resistance." *Sociological Forum* 8:25-45.

The above example is a good illustration of a well-written abstract and a few things deserve note. The author starts the abstract by immediately discussing the research question and the data. The author then discusses the findings and briefly explains the relationships (in order of magnitude) without using any statistics. The author then concludes with a brief statement about the relevance of this research to our understandings of social relationships.

A similar approach should be used when creating an "executive summary." One could recast the above abstract into an executive summary using a "bulleted" format:

Everyday Forms of Employee Resistance
Executive Summary

Drawing on empirical material collected from over 250 individuals employed in a variety of short-term positions, this article examines how temporary employees pursue grievances against their employing organizations. The findings indicate that:

- Temporary employees generally respond to offensive behavior on the part of their employers in nonaggressive ways
- Gossip, toleration, and resignation are popular, while occasionally grievances are expressed by theft, sabotage, or noncooperation
- Collective responses, formal complaints, and legal action are rare
- These restrained responses are traced not to the severity of injustices but to the social environment associated with temporary employment, where workers are loosely tied to their organizations and one another

This research may help explain the decline of organized resistance in the contemporary workplace.

Again, we suggest not writing the abstract or executive summary until all of the other sections of the research report have been written. Once the rest of the report is constructed, this section will fall into place quite readily.

The Introduction

The **introduction** invites the reader to examine the rest of the report. It "sells" the report to readers, informing them of the research question and why this question is important. It can be quite short (1-3 double spaced typed pages) and the length will depend on the type of research question addressed.

After reading through the introduction, the reader should have a very clear idea of the question the writer is addressing. Good introductions will often include the phrase "In this paper I...." This brief phrase forces the writer to come to terms with the specific purpose of the paper and to focus the rest of the report accordingly.

When writing an introduction, global and unsupported statements should be avoided. Consider this introductory sentence: "The growth in teenage births is a huge social problem." While this may seem intuitively appealing, the statement is factually incorrect because teenage births have declined rather than increased over the past 24 years. This introduction could be improved significantly by providing facts, such as "According to National Vital Statistics Reports (2001), the teenage birth rate has declined from 69.5/1000 teenage women in 1970 to 49.6/1000 in 1999." The introduction then can build a compelling argument why it is still important to study teenage births in the context of current demographic trends.

Generally, the introduction should not serve as the conclusion of the study. Consider this introductory sentence: "In this paper I will prove that teenagers get pregnant because they lack solid moral values." It is important to remember that scientific methodology cannot prove anything; it can only find support for some hypotheses and refute other hypotheses. It would be a considerable improvement to rephrase this sentence as: "In this paper I will examine the degree to which personal values influence teenagers' risks for pregnancy." The introduction is designed only to open the research question.

The Literature Review

Because this book has emphasized the data analysis stage of research, we have not given much attention to the **literature review**. This is, however, a critical stage of the research process because it places the current study within a body of research. The sociologist Max Weber (Gerth and Mills 1946) argued that science is a cumulative endeavor and that all of scientists' work rests on the shoulders of preceding scientists. The literature review is aimed at simultaneously acknowledging other researchers' contributions to the collective knowledge while also informing the reader of how these contributions relate to the current research project. The literature review is an appraisal of what is known and what is not known about the research question. Depending on the scope of the research project, typical literature reviews in journal articles range from 5-15 pages of double spaced type. For reports to professionals, the literature review will be briefer; for theses and dissertations, it is generally a chapter in length.

At a bare minimum, a literature review is an overview of the essential findings from articles related to the research question. However, creating a structure that links these articles will significantly improve a literature review. For example, in a study of factors associated with family violence, one of the authors organized the literature review by first writing about studies that looked at gender and family violence, then age and family violence, then race/ethnicity and family violence, then socioeconomic status and family violence. Providing a structure enables the reader to get a solid understanding of specific relationships (see Straus and Sweet 1992).

This is not the only way to structure a literature review. In some circumstances, it may make sense to link studies based on methodologies. For example, a study on behaviors of the poor could first discuss participant-observation studies, then cross sectional survey studies, and then panel design studies. Each methodology will reveal different aspects of the behaviors of concern. In rare circumstances, it is appropriate to structure a literature review by the dates of the studies: for example, comparing studies on television viewing behavior performed in the 1950s with studies examining television viewing behavior in the 1990s.

By far, though, the weakest literature review discusses studies in random order or in the order in which the researcher read the articles (a common error for novice researchers). A writer should not forget the audience. The audience does not care about the sequence that the researcher read articles, or whether the researcher found the articles interesting or boring. They do care, however, about the research question, the knowledge that the scientific community has already developed, and how the current project fits into this body of literature.

The Methods

As with every other section, the **methods section** should be concise. It explains data collection, sampling strategies, sample sizes, indicators, and any reworking of the data. It is helpful to take the perspective of an intelligent and skeptical reader while writing the methods section. This reader looks for weaknesses and flaws in the study and will only trust conclusions if given reasons to. With this in mind, the intelligent and skeptical reader will ask questions such as:

Are the data suited to the research question?
Is the sample size large enough?
Is the sample representative of the population?
Is the sample appropriate to the study?
Are the indicators reliable and valid?
Does the researcher measure factors that could eliminate spurious findings?
Does the researcher use analytic techniques suited to the data?

With each of these questions, the reader is asking, "To what degree will this research project effectively answer the research question?" The methods section builds that trust by carefully laying out the empirical basis of the study. It should, at a minimum, address the following information:

- The methods of data collection or sources of data
- The sample size and sample characteristics
- Modifications made to the data
- The types of statistical procedures used

The length will vary, depending on the complexity of the data collection and analysis procedures, but generally, this section can be written in 2-5 double spaced typed pages. A report to a professional or administrative audience will often have a very brief methods section, but include relevant information in an appendix. Theses and dissertations tend to have an entire chapter dedicated to methodology.

The Findings

The **findings section** details the results of the study. Although the researchers may have found many interesting results, the findings should include only those results that directly relate to the research question posed in the introduction. This section includes graphs, tables, and text that describe relevant relationships.

There is an old maxim that social scientists read tables and ignore the text and "regular people" read the text and ignore the tables. There is truth to this statement and the findings section should be written accordingly. Tables and graphs should be rich with statistical information relating to the research question and should have enough information for the reader to interpret the table without having to simultaneously read the accompanying text. The text serves the purpose of translating these statistics into a form that "regular people" can understand. This involves describing the relationships without statistics. Tables may show percentages or regression coefficients, but the text accompanying the tables should be phrased in terms of "positive" and "negative" relationships.

One of the best ways to organize the findings section is to address results in relation to hypotheses. Your study should come to some conclusion in relation to each testable hypothesis posed in the introduction. With some thought, you may be able to construct a modest number of tables that can effectively display all of the information needed to make conclusions, including significance tests, sample sizes, etc.

Table 1. Logistic Regression of Verbal/Symbolic Aggression

| | Verbal/Symbolic Aggression | | | |
| | Man-to-Woman | | Woman-to-Man | |
Variable	Coefficient	SE	Coefficient	SE
Gender	0.20**	.077	0.39**	.077
Age	-0.02**	.003	-0.02**	.003
Number of children	-0.09**	.033	-0.05	.030
Drunk	0.01**	.003	0.04**	.009
High on drugs	0.00	.001	0.01**	.002
Physical aggression	1.35**	.082	1.30**	.074
Couple conflict	0.93**	.052	0.83**	.050
Logit Constant	-1.82**	.162	-1.66**	.163

$*p<.05$ $**p<.01$

Source: Straus, Murray and Stephen Sweet. 1992. "Verbal/Symbolic Aggression in Couples." Journal of Marriage and the Family 54:346-357.

Figure 9.1 A Sample Table

Figure 9.1 illustrates how a well-constructed table improves raw SPSS output. One of the chief advantages is that the table effectively conveys a lot of information concisely. The table includes the logistic regression coefficients, standard errors, the constant, and significance tests for two different regressions. Academic journals commonly present the results of many regressions in a single table.

Depending on the complexities of the study, the findings section typically ranges from 6-12 pages in a journal article. Findings will comprise the greatest amount of space in a report to a professional or administrative audience, and this audience will be better able to interpret graphs than tables. In theses and dissertations, findings can comprise many separate chapters.

The Conclusion

The **conclusion** relates the findings back to the research question posed in the introduction. The conclusion section should also discuss the limitations of the study and acknowledge any ways the data or analyses fall short of establishing causal relationships.

The conclusion reinforces the theoretical or practical implications of the study findings. A good conclusion **generalizes** findings, relating the findings to social behavior outside of the study. Generalizing the findings requires consideration of **external validity**, the degree to which study findings accurately describe social behavior outside the confines of the study. In order to assess external validity, the researcher should consider the study's limitations. For example, laboratory experiments on human subjects often have little external validity because they place people in very contrived situations (Campbell and Stanley 1963). A biased sample also threatens external validity. If a sample consists of college freshman, for example, the researcher should be cautious in generalizing the findings to the general population.

One positive way to conclude a research report is to open the topic to additional related questions. The researcher can state "In this study I showed..." and then go on to say, "Further research needs to be done to find out if...." Science is a never-ending process and a strong conclusion acknowledges this.

The References

The **reference section** provides a list of sources cited in the report. Each discipline specifies different formats for referencing sources. It is important that the reference provide sufficient information so that a reader can locate the original source, no matter what the format.

The following are some examples of how the American Sociological Association suggests referencing books, articles, and government documents.

Books
Berlin, Gorden and Andrew Sum. 1988. *Toward a More Perfect Union: Basic Skills, Poor Families, and Our Economic Future.* New York: Ford Foundation.

Articles from Collected Works
Clausen, John A. 1972. "The Life Course of Individuals." Pp. 457-514 in *Aging and Society*, vol. 3, *A Sociology of Age Stratification*, edited by M. W. Riley, M. Johnson, and A. Foner. New York: Russell Sage.

Articles in Journals
Goodman, Leo A. 1947. "The Analysis of Systems of Qualitative Variables When Some of the Variables Are Unobservable. Part 1 - A Modified Latent Structure Approach." *American Journal of Sociology* 79:1179-259.

<u>Articles from Newspapers and Magazines</u>
Guiles, Melinda and Krystal Miller. 1990. "Mazda and Mitsubishi-Chrysler Venture Cut Output, Following Big Three's Lead." *Wall Street Journal*, January 12, pp. A2, A12.

<u>Government Documents</u>
U.S. Bureau of the Census. 1960. *Characteristics of Population*. Vol 1. Washington, DC: U.S. Government Printing Office.

Source: American Sociological Association. 1996. *American Sociological Association Style Guide*. Washington, DC: American Sociological Association.

Summary

SPSS can generate a great variety of statistical output. Researchers face considerable challenges as they organize and describe their statistical analysis so that a variety of audiences can understand it. The research report is essential in conveying this information. A well-written report is concise, conveys statistical information in numeric form, and describes relationships with prose. All good reports explain the relevance of the study, as well as acknowledge limitations of the study.

Key Terms

Abstract	Introduction
Conclusion	Literature Review
Evaluation Report	Methods Section
Executive Summary	Reference Section
External Validity	Research Report
Findings Section	Title
Generalization	

References and Further Reading

American Psychological Association. 1995. *Publication Manual of the American Psychological Association*. 4th ed. Washington, DC: American Psychological Association.

American Sociological Association. 1996. *American Sociological Association Style Guide*. Washington DC: American Sociological Association.

Becker, Howard. 1984. *Writing for the Social Sciences*. Chicago, IL: University of Chicago Press.

Bem, Darryl J. (in press). "Writing the Empirical Journal Article." In Darley, John M., Mark P. Zanna, and Roediger III, H. L. (Eds.), *The Complete Academic: A Practical Guide for the Beginning Social Scientist* (2nd Ed.). Washington, DC: American Psychological Association.

Campbell, Donald and Julian Stanley. 1963. *Experimental and Quasi-Experimental Designs for Research*. Chicago: Rand McNally.

Gerth, Hans and C. Wright Mills. 1946. From *Max Weber: Essays in Sociology.* New York: Oxford University Press.

Straus, Murray and Stephen Sweet. 1992. "Verbal/Symbolic Aggression in Couples: Incidence Rates and Relationships to Personal Characteristics." *Journal of Marriage and the Family* 54:346-357.

Tucker, James. 1993. "Everyday Forms of Employee Resistance." *Sociological Forum* 8:25-45.

Weber, Max. 1946. From *Max Weber: Essays in Sociology.* London: Routledge & Kegan Paul.

Ventura, S., J. Maritin, S. Curtin, F. Menacker, and B. Hamilton. 2001. *National Vital Statistics Report: Births: Final Data for 1999.* Vol 49 #1. Washington, DC: Center For Disease Control.

Chapter 10
Research Projects

Potential Research Projects

In the following pages we describe some potential research projects that can be tackled with the data included with this book. Before embarking on these projects, it may be helpful to review some of the central lessons forwarded in this book in order to guide your approach.

Research projects are guided by developing research questions and using data that fits a research question. Each of these projects we outline are introduced by topical area. We suggest restructuring these projects into a set of research questions. After formulating these questions, it will be necessary to evaluate the degree to which the STATES data and the GSS98 data will be suited to providing answers. One of the first tasks you will need to perform is locating variables that relate to that research question. This includes finding relevant independent and dependent variables and assessing the degree to which these variables are accurate indicators of the concepts you want to examine.

It is to the researcher's advantage to understand what is already known about a research question. Therefore many will find it useful to engage in a literature review on the subject. The depth of this literature review can be of your (or possibly your instructor's) discretion. However, you should have a reasonable understanding of what to anticipate in the data analysis based on previous research in this area. Although this may seem like extra work, it will actually help push the analysis in fruitful directions more efficiently and effectively.

Empirical studies are hypothesis driven. Once you have developed an understanding of the relationships previously revealed by other researchers, you should be able to develop clearly framed hypotheses concerning the relationships between each independent and dependent variable. These hypotheses should be embedded in a larger theoretical understanding of the basis of social behavior and social experience.

Analysis of the data occurs in three stages. The first stage is univariate analysis, where you will examine the structure, central tendency, and spread of individual variables. The second stage is bivariate analysis, where you will examine the relationships between pairs of variables in isolation from other variables. The third stage is multivariate analysis, where multiple variables are examined together to control for extraneous factors and examine cumulative effects.

Once you analyze your data and understand the implications, write the research report. The report distills the analysis to the most essential information so that readers can understand the relationships revealed in the data analysis. The report will contain carefully constructed tables and yield maximum content in minimal space. It also includes written descriptions of the relationships revealed.

The report will conclude with a summary of supported and unsupported hypotheses. In some circumstances you will likely find that the data do not support your hypothesis. You may sometimes conclude that the relationship is nonexistent. However, it is also important at this stage of the study to critically evaluate the limitations of the data. State level data, for instance, cover very large geographic regions. Therefore in some circumstances the data may gloss over important variations within each state. For example, we are writing this book in Tompkins County, a very rural part of New York State. Our experiences are likely very different than those of residents of Brooklyn County in New York City. However, because New York State, not the individual counties, is our unit of analysis in the STATES data, the variation between counties is lost. In some circumstances, lumping of social experience into such a large geographic area may limit the validity of the measures. This may be one consideration (among others) in evaluating the degree to which a theory is ultimately maintained or rejected. The research report should conclude with a discussion of these limitations, as well as with some suggestions for future research.

Finally, it is important to understand that analysis almost always involves some backtracking, reevaluation, restructuring of models, and recoding variables. The best approach is an inquisitive one. Always think, is there a better or more eloquent way to test this relationship? Is there some possible alternate explanation for my findings? If there is, how can I test this? Data analysis, after all, is driven by a desire to understand the world that surrounds us. Enjoy!

Research Project 1: Racism

Social theory posits that people sometimes have prejudicial thoughts, which in turn lead them to discriminate against members of particular racial groups in society. This constitutes overt discrimination. Social theory also posits that there are structural factors that limit the opportunities of group members. Social structure includes the ways in which schools are funded, jobs distributed, infrastructure maintained, etc... If a racial group resides in an area that is deprived, they become deprived as a result. Can you determine, based on the GSS98 data and the STATES data, the degree to which prejudice, overt discrimination, and structural discrimination against African Americans persists in the United States?

Suggestions for Data Analysis:

A.   Make a list of variables from the STATES data and the GSS98 data that relate to this research question.

B.   Determine which variables are independent variables and which variables are dependent variables.

C.   Examine the structure of each of these variables to determine if they are numerical or categorical variables.

D.   Develop a clear hypothesis as to how each independent variable will be related to the dependent variable.

E.   Perform Univariate Analysis
            Means, Medians, Modes, Standard Deviations, Stem and Leaf Plots, Box Plots, Histograms, Pie Charts, Bar Charts.

F.   Perform Bivariate Analysis
            Crosstabulations, Comparison of Means, Correlations, Significance Tests, Box Plots, Bar Charts, Scatter Plots.

G.   Perform Multivariate Analysis
            Linear Regression, Logistic Regression, Significance Tests, Scatter Plots.

Research Project 2: Suicide

What explains why a person chooses to terminate his or her own life? On the one hand, this can possibly be attributed to psychological factors, such as depression. On the other hand, it can be caused by social forces such as living in a society that is characterized as socially disorganized (e.g., lots of crime, unemployment, etc.). Can you determine the degree to which social psychological factors influence a person's willingness to accept suicide as a viable alternative to life's problems using the GSS98 data? Can you then determine the degree to which social structural factors influence variation in suicide rates using the STATES data?

Suggestions for Data Analysis:

A.   Make a list of variables from the STATES data and the GSS98 data that relate to this research question.

B.   Determine which variables are independent variables and which variables are dependent variables.

C.   Examine the structure of each of these variables to determine if they are numerical or categorical variables.

D.   Develop a clear hypothesis as to how each independent variable will be related to the dependent variable.

E.   Perform Univariate Analysis
          Means, Medians, Modes, Standard Deviations, Stem and Leaf Plots, Box Plots, Histograms, Pie Charts, Bar Charts.

F.   Perform Bivariate Analysis
          Crosstabulations, Comparison of Means, Correlations, Significance Tests, Box Plots, Bar Charts, Scatter Plots.

G.   Perform Multivariate Analysis
          Linear Regression, Logistic Regression, Significance Tests, Scatter Plots.

Research Project 3: Criminality

Some places have high crime rates and other places have low crime rates. What social factors contribute to this variation of crime from place to place? Do the methods of treating/punishing criminals have an effect on deterring crime? Use the STATES data to examine these issues. Pay particular attention to variation between types of crime in your analysis.

Suggestions for Data Analysis:

A.   Make a list of variables from the STATES data that relate to this research question.

B.   Determine which variables are independent variables and which variables are dependent variables.

C.   Examine the structure of each of these variables to determine if they are numerical or categorical variables.

D.   Develop a clear hypothesis as to how each independent variable will be related to the dependent variable.

E.   Perform Univariate Analysis
                Means, Medians, Modes, Standard Deviations, Stem and Leaf Plots, Box Plots, Histograms, Pie Charts, Bar Charts.

F.   Perform Bivariate Analysis
                Crosstabulations, Comparison of Means, Correlations, Significance Tests, Box Plots, Bar Charts, Scatter Plots.

G.   Perform Multivariate Analysis
                Linear Regression, Logistic Regression, Significance Tests, Scatter Plots.

Research Project 4: Welfare

There is considerable variation in welfare use. One cause for this variation may be that individuals have different expectations of what they are entitled to receive just by living in our society. On the other hand, there may be social structural factors (e.g., unemployment) which either force or lure individuals to use welfare as a means of survival. Use the STATES data to examine which structural factors influence welfare consumption.

Suggestions for Data Analysis:

A.   Make a list of variables from the STATES data which relate to this research question.

B.   Determine which variables are independent variables and which variables are dependent variables.

C.   Examine the structure of each of these variables to determine if they are numerical or categorical variables.

D.   Develop a clear hypothesis as to how each independent variable will be related to the dependent variable.

E.   Perform Univariate Analysis
            Means, Medians, Modes, Standard Deviations, Stem and Leaf Plots, Box Plots, Histograms, Pie Charts, Bar Charts.

F.   Perform Bivariate Analysis
            Crosstabulations, Comparison of Means, Correlations, Significance Tests, Box Plots, Bar Charts, Scatter Plots.

G.   Perform Multivariate Analysis
            Linear Regression, Logistic Regression, Significance Tests, Scatter Plots.

Research Project 5: Sexual Behavior

There is considerable variation in sexual behavior on an individual level, as well as by geographic locale. Using the GSS98 data, determine the social psychological factors that contribute to a permissive attitude toward sexual freedom. Using the STATES data, examine the variation in birth rates to identify social structural factors that also potentially contribute to permissive sexual lifestyles.

Suggestions for Data Analysis:

A.   Make a list of variables from the STATES data and the GSS98 data that relate to this research question.

B.   Determine which variables are independent variables and which variables are dependent variables.

C.   Examine the structure of each of these variables to determine if they are numerical or categorical variables.

D.   Develop a clear hypothesis as to how each independent variable will be related to the dependent variable.

E.   Perform Univariate Analysis
        Means, Medians, Modes, Standard Deviations, Stem and Leaf Plots, Box Plots, Histograms, Pie Charts, Bar Charts.

F.   Perform Bivariate Analysis
        Crosstabulations, Comparison of Means, Correlations, Significance Tests, Box Plots, Bar Charts, Scatter Plots.

G.   Perform Multivariate Analysis
        Linear Regression, Logistic Regression, Significance Tests, Scatter Plots.

Research Project 6: Education

Individuals' educational attainment can be influenced by their personal background and the type of society they live in. Using the GSS98 data, examine the degree to which educational attainment varies by a person's biographical background. Then using the STATES data, examine the degree to which social structural factors influence educational attainment across the United States.

Suggestions for Data Analysis:

A.   Make a list of variables from the STATES data and the GSS98 data that relate to this research question.

B.   Determine which variables are independent variables and which variables are dependent variables.

C.   Examine the structure of each of these variables to determine if they are numerical or categorical variables.

D.   Develop a clear hypothesis as to how each independent variable will be related to the dependent variable.

E.   Perform Univariate Analysis
          Means, Medians, Modes, Standard Deviations, Stem and Leaf Plots, Box Plots, Histograms, Pie Charts, Bar Charts.

F.   Perform Bivariate Analysis
          Crosstabulations, Comparison of Means, Correlations, Significance Tests, Box Plots, Bar Charts, Scatter Plots.

G.   Perform Multivariate Analysis
          Linear Regression, Logistic Regression, Significance Tests, Scatter Plots.

Research Project 7: Your Topic

There are many other variables included in the STATES data set and the GSS98 data set. Can you develop a research question that uses these data to their fullest potential? Ultimately you may need to search for additional data to merge with the STATES data, but don't let this stop you. That is to be expected in social research.

Suggestions for Data Analysis:

A.   Make a list of variables from the STATES data and the GSS98 data that relate to this research question.

B.   Determine which variables are independent variables and which variables are dependent variables.

C.   Examine the structure of each of these variables to determine if they are numerical or categorical variables.

D.   Develop a clear hypothesis as to how each independent variable will be related to the dependent variable.

E.   Perform Univariate Analysis
                Means, Medians, Modes, Standard Deviations, Stem and Leaf Plots, Box Plots, Histograms, Pie Charts, Bar Charts.

F.   Perform Bivariate Analysis
                Crosstabulations, Comparison of Means, Correlations, Significance Tests, Box Plots, Bar Charts, Scatter Plots.

G.   Perform Multivariate Analysis
                Linear Regression, Logistic Regression

APPENDIX 1: STATES.SAV DESCRIPTIVES

Descriptive Statistics

	N	Mean
ARC10 Reported Arrest Rate for Rape in 1998	48	12.4021
ARC12 Reported Arrest Rate for Robbery in 1998	48	39.0563
ARC14 Reported Arrest Rate for Aggravated Assault in 1998	48	157.1708
ARC16 Reported Arrest Rate for Property Crime in 1998	48	749.3979
ARC18 Reported Arrest Rate for Burglary in 1998	48	120.8083
ARC2 Reported Arrest Rate in 1998	48	5876.2438
ARC20 Reported Arrest Rate for Larceny and Theft in 1998	48	565.0917
ARC22 Reported Arrest Rate for Motor Vehicle Theft in 1998	48	56.5542
ARC24 Reported Arrest Rate for Arson in 1998	48	6.9396
ARC26 Reported Arrest Rate for Weapons Violations in 1998	48	68.1646
ARC28 Reported Arrest Rate for Driving Under the Influence in 1998	48	547.7458
ARC30 Reported Arrest Rate for Drug Abuse Violations in 1998	48	546.5312
ARC32 Reported Arrest Rate for Sex Offenses in 1998	48	31.7729
ARC34 Reported Arrest Rate: Prostitution & Commercial Vice, 1998	48	31.1313
ARC36 Reported Arrest Rate: Offens Against Fam. & Children, 1998	47	65.7596
ARC37 % of Crimes Cleared in 1997	47	22.1128
ARC38 % of Violent Crimes Cleared in 1997	47	49.7511
ARC39 % of Murders Cleared in 1997	47	69.4404
ARC4 Reported Arrest Rate for Crime Index Offenses in 1998	48	963.8458
ARC40 % of Rapes Cleared in 1997	47	47.4085
ARC41 % of Robberies Cleared in 1997	47	28.6872
ARC42 % of Aggravated Assaults Cleared in 1997	47	59.3213
ARC43 % of Property Crimes Cleared in 1997	47	18.8809
ARC44 % of Burglaries Cleared in 1997	47	13.8277
ARC45 % of Larcenies and Thefts Cleared in 1997	47	20.7809
ARC46 % of Motor Vehicle Thefts Cleared in 1997	47	17.5234
ARC6 Reported Arrest Rate for Violent Crime in 1998	48	214.4438
ARC8 Reported Arrest Rate for Murder in 1998	48	5.8146
BIH1 Births in 1998	51	77317.1569
BIH15 Births of Low Birthweight as a % of All Births in 1998	51	7.6353
BIH17 % of Births to White Women Low Birthweight 1998	51	6.6373
BIH19 % of Births to Black Women Low Birthweight 1998	43	12.8651
BIH2 Birth Rate per 1000 Pop in 1998	51	14.2098
BIH20 Births to Unmarried Women in 1998	51	25346.6471
BIH21 Births to Unmarried Women as a % of All Births in 1998	51	32.4882
BIH22 Births to Unmarried White Women in 1998	51	16104.5686
BIH23 Births to Unmarried WW as a % of Births to WW 1998	51	25.1216
BIH24 Births to Unmarried Black Women in 1998	50	8415.8000
BIH25 Births to Unmarried Black Women as a % of Births to BW 1998	50	63.4760
BIH26 Births to Teenage Mothers in 1998	51	9677.3922
BIH27 % of Births to Teenage Mothers in 1998	51	12.6431
BIH29 Teenage Birth Rate per 1000 Teenage Women in 1997	51	49.9882
BIH31 Births to White Teenage Mothers in 1997	51	6632.7843
BIH32 % of White Births that were to Teenage Mothers in 1997	51	10.7490
BIH33 Births to Black Teenage Mothers in 1997	51	2520.3725
BIH34 % of Black Births that were to Teenage Mothers in 1997	51	20.7706
BIH35 Pregnancy Rate for 15 to 19 Year Old Women per 1000 in 1996	43	69.0349
BIH38 Teenage Birth Rate per 1000 Teenage Women in 1990	51	57.4686
BIH41 Teenage Birth Rate per 1000 Teenage Women in 1980	51	54.5588
BIH43 Births to Women 35-49 Years Old as a % of All Births 1997	51	12.0510
BIH44 Multiple Birth Rate per 1000 Live Births in 1997	51	27.1941
BIH47 % Births by Vaginal Delivery in 1997	51	80.2608
BIH49 % Births by Cesarean Delivery in 1997	51	20.0275
BIH53 % Mothers Begin Prenatal Care 1st Trimester 1998	51	82.9216
BIH54 % White Mothers Begin Prenatal Care 1st Trimester 1998	51	85.3843
BIH55 % Black Mothers Beginning Prenatal Care 1st trimester 1998	50	73.5260

Descriptive Statistics

	N	Mean
BIH56 % Mothers Receiving Late or No Prenatal Care in 1998	51	3.8392
BIH57 % White Mothers Receiving Late or No Prenatal Care 1997	51	3.0000
BIH58 % Black Mothers Receiving Late or No Prenatal Care 1997	42	7.5024
BIH59 % Births Attended by Midwives in 1997	51	7.1255
BIH61 Reported Legal Abortions per 1000 Live Births in 1996	50	238.7400
BIH62 Reported Legal Abortions per 1000 Women Ages 15 to 44 1996	50	15.0800
BIS359 Fertility Rate per 1000 Women Age 15-44 in 1998	51	64.3333
BIS364 Infant Mortality Rate per 1000 Live Births in 1997	51	7.3765
CAC251 Child Abuse and Neglect per 1000 Pop under 18 in 1997	43	17.3349
CAC253 Physically Abused Children per 1000 Pop under 18 in 1997	43	3.5395
CAC255 Sexually Abused Children per 1000 Pop under 18 in 1997	43	1.6953
CAC257 Emotionally Abused Children per 1000 Pop under 18 in 1997	38	1.2474
CAC259 Neglected Children per 1000 per 1000 Pop under 18 in 1997	43	9.2395
CRC309 Crimes in 1998	51	244620.2745
CRC310 Average Time Between Crimes in 1998	51	6.6298
CRC311 Crimes per Square Mile in 1998	51	19.8216
CRC313 Crime Rate in 1998	51	4532.2333
CRC315 Violent Crimes in 1998	51	30020.4706
CRC319 Violent Crime Rate in 1998	51	490.5000
CRC325 Murders in 1998	51	331.6471
CRC328 Murder Rate in 1998	51	6.3529
CRC330 Murders with Firearms in 1998	47	194.4043
CRC332 % of Murders Involving Firearms in 1998	47	58.3340
CRC344 Rapes in 1998	51	1825.5490
CRC347 Rape Rate in 1998	51	35.4941
CRC350 Robberies in 1998	51	8757.3529
CRC353 Robbery Rate in 1998	51	131.6020
CRC357 % of Robberies Involving Firearms in 1998	50	37.3580
CRC365 Aggravated Assaults in 1998	51	19105.9216
CRC368 Aggravated Assault Rate in 1998	51	317.0588
CRC379 Property Crimes in 1998	51	214599.8039
CRC383 Property Crime Rate in 1998	51	4041.7235
CRC385 Burglaries in 1998	51	45685.2941
CRC388 Burglary Rate in 1998	51	830.8627
CRC390 Larcenies and Thefts in 1998	51	144586.0000
CRC393 Larceny and Theft Rate in 1998	51	2805.0431
CRC395 Motor Vehicle Thefts in 1998	51	24328.5098
CRC398 Motor Vehicle Theft Rate in 1998	51	405.8196
CRC460 Crimes Reported at Universities and Colleges in 1998	40	2458.1250
CRC461 Crimes Reported at Univ&Colleges as % of All Crime 1998	40	1.0250
CRC507 Rate of Hate Crime in 1998	47	3.5915
DIH358 Estimated Rate of New Female Breast Cancer Cases in 2000	51	130.2118
DIH359 % Women 40 and up Who Have Ever Had a Mammogram: 1998	50	84.8440
DIH365 Estimated Rate of New Lung Cancer Cases in 2000	51	60.8824
DIH376 AIDS Rate in 1999	51	14.3686
DIH409 Sexually Transmitted Disease Rate in 1998	51	359.5627
DIH413 Chlamydia Rate in 1998	51	228.8627
DIH415 Gonorrhea Rate in 1998	51	128.0020
DIH417 Syphilis Rate in 1998	51	2.6569
DIS375 Estimated Rate of New Cancer Cases in 2000	51	454.1980
DMC509 Population in 1999	51	5346878.6863
DMC512 Urban Population in 1998	45	4796751.0667
DMC513 Rural Population in 1998	45	634293.3778
DMC514 Population 10 to 17 Years Old in 1998	51	607550.1765
DMC515 Total Area of States in Square Miles in 1999	51	72897.9804
DMS233 % of Land in Metropolitan Areas in 1999	51	30.6333
DMS237 % of Land Owned by the Federal Gvt in 1998	51	15.7667
DMS241 Visitors to State Parks and Recreational Areas in 1998	50	15216598.9000

Descriptive Statistics

	N	Mean
DMS393 Households in 1998	51	1981235.2941
DMS395 Persons per Household in 1998	51	2.5792
DMS400 Average Value of New Housing Units in 1999	51	101063.3137
DMS406 Homeownership Rate per Hundred in 1999	51	68.6373
DMS418 Population in 1998	51	5298980.4510
DMS419 Population in 1997	51	5250658.9608
DMS421 Resident State Population in 1990	51	4878253.4314
DMS423 Resident State Population in 1980	51	4442074.6078
DMS424 Resident State Population in 1970	51	3986274.5098
DMS425 Resident State Population in 1960	51	3516117.6471
DMS426 Resident State Population in 1950	51	2967172.5098
DMS431 Population per Square Mile in 1990	51	358.0039
DMS436 Urban Population in 1990	51	3667715.4314
DMS437 % of Population Urban in 1990	51	68.8039
DMS438 Rural Population in 1990	51	1208948.7451
DMS439 % of Population Rural in 1990	51	31.1961
DMS440 Metropolitan Population in 1996	51	4152666.6667
DMS441 % of Population Living in a Metropolitan Area 1996	51	67.8922
DMS442 Nonmetropolitan Population in 1996	51	1048941.1765
DMS443 % of Population Living in Nonmetropolitan Area 1996	51	32.1078
DMS444 Male Population in 1998	51	2589143.6667
DMS445 Female Population in 1998	51	2710827.3922
DMS447 % of Population White in 1998	51	83.7098
DMS449 % of Population Black in 1998	51	11.1882
DMS451 % of Population Hispanic in 1998	51	6.7098
DMS453 % of Population Asian in 1998	51	3.4255
DMS455 % of Population American Indian in 1998	51	1.6608
DMS466 Median Age in 1998	51	35.3745
DMS475 % of Population 65 Years Old and Older in 1998	51	12.7314
DMS477 % of Population 85 Years Old and Older in 1998	51	1.5294
DMS489 Marriage Rate Per 1000 Pop in 1998	51	9.8804
DMS491 Divorce Rate Per 1000 Pop in 1998	46	4.4087
DMS497 % of Eligible Voters Reported Registered in 1998	49	75.6102
DMS499 % of Eligible Population Reported Voting in 1998	51	38.7196
DMS552 Highway Fatalities in 1998	51	813.1569
DMS553 Highway Fatality Rate Per 100Mill Miles of Travel in 1998	51	1.6482
DMS558 Fatalities in Alcohol-Related Crashes % of All Hwy Fatalities 1998	51	39.1961
DMS567 Annual Miles per Vehicle in 1998	51	12615.4706
DMS90 Veterans in 1999	51	483921.5686
DMS91 Veterans per 1,000 Population 18 and Older in 1999	51	126.9804
DRC122 Male Admissions to Alc&Drug Treatment Programs 1997	48	25587.6875
DRC124 Female Admissions to Alc&Drug Treatment Programs 1997	45	11342.4889
DRC126 White Admissions to Alc&Drug Treatment Programs 1997	45	21873.9556
DRC128 Black Admissions to Alc&Drug Treatment Programs 1997	45	10388.7778
DRC130 Hispanic Admissions to Alc&Drug Treatment Programs 1997	44	3795.3409
DRC133 Per Capita Expend. for State Drug Abuse Services in 1997	48	14.6431
DRC135 Expend. per Alc&Drug Treatment Admission 1997	48	1712.3542
DRC136 Per Capita Expend. for State Drug Abuse Treatment 1997	48	11.5790
DRC138 Per Capita Expend. for State Drug Abuse Prevention 1997	48	1.9246
DRH494 % of Adults Who Abstain from Drinking Alcohol: 1997	51	50.0667
DRH496 Adult Per Capita Beer Consumption in 1997	51	32.6588
DRH498 Adult Per Capita Wine Consumption in 1997	51	2.6176
DRH500 Adult Per Capita Distilled Spirits Consumption 1997	51	1.9471
DRH501 % of Adults Who Are Binge Drinkers: 1997	51	13.6980
DRS389 Alcohol Consumption in 1997	51	9130980.3922
DTH100 Neonatal Death Rate per 1000 Live Births in 1997	51	4.8137
DTH102 White Neonatal Death Rate per 1000 White Live Births in 1997	48	4.0729
DTH104 Black Neonatal Death Rate per 1000 Black Live Births in 1997	33	9.5939

Descriptive Statistics

		N	Mean
DTH107	Death Rate by AIDS in 1997	43	5.9698
DTH110	Estimated Death Rate by Cancer in 2000	51	205.6706
DTH112	Estimated Death Rate by Female Breast Cancer in 2000	51	29.6373
DTH116	Estimated Death Rate by Leukemia in 2000	47	8.6043
DTH120	Estimated Death Rate by Lung Cancer in 2000	51	58.3255
DTH141	Death Rate by Chronic Liver Disease and Cirrhosis in 1997	51	9.0098
DTH165	Death Rate by Injury in 1997	51	60.5294
DTH168	Death Rate by Accidents in 1997	51	38.8255
DTH171	Death Rate by Motor Vehicle Accidents in 1997	51	17.8137
DTH174	Death Rate by Homicide in 1997	49	7.5388
DTH177	Death Rate by Suicide in 1997	51	12.7569
DTH187	Average Annual Death Rate Due to Smoking: 1990-1994	51	347.5490
DTH189	Death Rate from Alcohol-Induced Deaths in 1997	51	6.4667
DTH192	Death Rate from Drug-Induced Deaths in 1997	51	5.5333
DTH195	Occupational Fatalities per 100,000 Workers in 1998	51	5.4941
DTH77	Deaths in 1998	51	45844.5098
DTH78	Death Rate in 1998	51	879.8333
DTH79	Age-Adjusted Death Rate in 1998	50	478.2660
DTH86	Infant Mortality Rate per 1000 Live Births in 1999	50	7.1340
DTH94	White Infant Mortality Rate per 1000 White Live Births in 1997	49	6.1837
DTH96	Black Infant Mortality Rate per 1000 Black Live Births in 1997	36	14.8167
DTS377	Age-Adj Death Rate by Cerebrovascular Diseases in 1997	51	26.2275
DTS379	Age-Adj Death Rate: Chronic Obstr. Pulmonary Disease 1997	51	22.0863
DTS381	Age-Adj Death Rate by Diseases of the Heart in 1997	51	128.0608
DTS383	Age-Adj Death Rate by Suicide in 1997	51	11.9549
DTS385	Age-Adj Death Rate by AIDS in 1997	43	5.5628
DTS387	AIDS Rate in 1999	51	14.3686
ECS101	New Business Incorporations in 1997	51	15665.0392
ECS103	Business Failures in 1997	51	1634.9804
ECS104	Business Failure Rate per 10,000 businesses in 1997	51	78.3529
ECS107	Per Capita Personal Income in 1998	51	25443.6275
ECS110	Median Household Income in 1998	51	37404.2157
ECS111	Per Capita Total Taxes in 1999	51	9698.1373
ECS114	Personal Bankruptcy Rate in 1999	51	463.8627
ECS92	State Cost of Living in 1998	51	.9896
ECS96	Per Capita Gross State Product in 1997	51	30681.2941
EMS159	Average Annual Pay in 1998	51	29840.0784
EMS161	State Minimum Wage Hourly Rates in 2000	44	5.1080
EMS171	Unemployment Rate per Hundred in 1999	51	4.1569
EMS173	% of Women in the Civilian Labor Force 1998	51	61.3980
EMS178	% Nonfarm Employees in Construction 1999	51	5.0745
EMS180	% Nonfarm Employees in Finance, Insurance & RealEst 1999	51	5.5882
EMS182	% Nonfarm Employees in Government 1999	51	17.2745
EMS184	% Nonfarm Employees in Manufacturing 1999	51	13.6216
EMS186	% Nonfarm Employees in Mining 1999	39	.8108
EMS188	% Nonfarm Employees in Service Industries 1999	51	29.3333
EMS190	% Nonfarm Employees in Transport & Public Util 1999	51	5.2588
EMS192	% Nonfarm Employees in Wholesale and Retail 1999	51	23.1451
ENS209	Per Capita Gasoline Used in 1998	51	502.5098
ENS213	Hazard Waste Sites on Natl Priority per 10k SqMi 2000	50	11.6200
ENS214	Pollution Released by Manufacturing Plants in 1997	51	50356224.7255
ENS216	Toxic Waste Sent Out of State in 1997	51	37973755.0980
ENS217	Toxic Waste Received In State in 1997	51	35327064.8431
FIC149	Per Capita State & Local Gvt Expend. for Police 1996	51	154.1373
FIC158	Per Capita State & Local Gvt Expend. for Corrections 1996	51	126.8627
FIC165	Annual Operating Expend. per Inmate in 1996	51	21958.0392
FIC171	Per Capita State & Local Gvt Expend. for Legal 1996	51	77.1253
FIH295	% of Population Covered by Health Insurance in 1998	51	84.9412

Descriptive Statistics

	N	Mean
FIS243 Per Capita Federal Individ Income Tax Revenue in 1997	51	2548.2353
FIS253 Per Capita Federal Gvt Expend. in 1998	51	6262.0784
FIS255 Per Cap Expend. for Fed Gvt Procure Contract Award 1998	51	852.3333
FIS279 Per Capita State & Local Gvt Total Expend. 1996	51	5291.2157
FIS310 State Tax on a Pack of Cigarettes in 2000	51	40.8020
FIS339 % of Population Enrolled in HMO 1999	51	23.9490
FIS342 Per Capita Personal Health Care Expend. in 1993	51	2955.4118
FIS344 Rate of Nonfederal Physicians in 1998	51	269.3137
FIS348 Rate of Community Hospitals in 1998	51	2.4804
HBH502 % of Adults Who Smoke: 1998	51	23.2255
HBH506 % of Adults Overweight: 1998	51	31.9294
HBH507 # of Days Past Month Physical Health was Not Good 1998	51	3.0784
HBH508 Avg # Days in the Past Month Mental Health Not Good 1998	51	2.9549
HBH511 Safety Belt Usage Rate per Hundred in 1999	51	65.0196
HBH512 % of Adults Whose Children Use a Car Safety Seat: 1997	51	94.0196
JCC186 Juvenile Arrest Rate per 100,000 Juv in 1998	48	9287.9292
JCC189 Juvenile Arrest Rate for Crime Index Offenses per 100,000 Juv in 1998	48	2514.4229
JCC192 Juvenile Arrest Rate for Violent Crime per 100,000 Juv in 1998	48	329.1854
JCC195 Juvenile Arrest Rate for Murder per 100,000 Juv in 1998	48	6.7813
JCC198 Juvenile Arrest Rate for Rape per 100,000 Juv in 1998	48	19.5042
JCC201 Juvenile Arrest Rate for Robbery per 100,000 Juv in 1998	48	86.5125
JCC204 Juvenile Arrest Rate for Aggravated Assault per 100,000 Juv in 1998	48	216.3854
JCC207 Juvenile Arrest Rate for Property Crime per 100,000 Juv in 1998	48	2185.2479
JCC210 Juvenile Arrest Rate for Burglary per 100,000 Juv in 1998	48	377.8646
JCC213 Juvenile Arrest Rate for Larceny & Theft per 100,000 Juv in 1998	48	1596.4625
JCC216 Juvenile Arrest Rate Motor Vehicle Theft per 100,000 Juv in 1998	48	179.3875
JCC219 Juvenile Arrest Rate for Arson per 100,000 Juv in 1998	48	32.2625
JCC222 Arrest Rate of Juveniles Weapons Violations per 100,000 Juv in 1998	48	133.3250
JCC225 Juvenile Arrest Rate for DUI per 100,000 Juv in 1998	48	83.8896
JCC228 Juvenile Arrest Rate Drug Abuse Violations per 100,000 Juv in 1998	48	689.2208
JCC231 Arrest Rate of Juveniles for Sex Offenses per 100,000 Juv in 1998	48	48.8521
JCC234 Juvenile Arrest Rate for Prostitution per 100,000 Juv 1998	48	4.1688
JCC237 Juvenile Arrest Rate Offenses Against Families per 100,000 Juv 1998	47	47.1489
JCC239 High School Dropout Rate per Hundred in 1997	38	5.3342
JCC243 Juveniles in Custody per 100,000 Juv in 1997	51	333.4314
JCC244 White Juvenile Custody per 100,000 Juv in 1997	51	195.6471
JCC245 Black Juvenile Custody per 100,000 Juv in 1997	43	1120.5581
LEC275 Full-Time Officers per 100,000 pop 1996	51	24.2157
LEC276 Full-Time Law Enforcement Officers per 1,000 Sq Mi 1996	50	408.0600
LEC278 Full-Time Empl. in Law Enforcmt Agencies per 10,000 1996	51	33.4314
LEC285 % of Female State Gvt Law Enforcement Officers:	49	6.0061
LES67 Full-Time Officers in Law Enforcement Agencies in 1996	51	13010.4902
PFH486 Users of Exercise Equipment in 1998	48	959187.5000
PFH487 Participants in Golf in 1998	48	572416.6667
PFH488 Participants in Running/Jogging in 1998	48	467666.6667
PFH489 Participants in Soccer in 1998	47	279489.3617
PFH490 Participants in Swimming in 1998	48	1212187.5000
PFH491 Participants in Tennis in 1998	47	238595.7447
PFH493 Adult Per Capita Alcohol Consumption in 1997	51	2.6039
PHH418 Physicians in 1998	51	15018.0784
PHH438 % of Population Lacking Access to Primary Care in 1999	51	11.2039
PHH483 Rate of Dentists in 1997	51	52.9020
PHH484 % of Population Lacking Access to Dental Care in 1999	51	5.6980
PRC100 Deaths of State Prisoners by Suicide % of All Prisoners 1997	49	7.2306
PRC104 Rate of Adults on State Probation per 100,000 Adults in 1998	51	1510.7451
PRC106 Rate of Adults on State Parole per 100,000 Adults in 1998	51	243.7059
PRC108 % of All State & loc Gvt Employees in Corrections 1998	51	4.0137
PRC109 State Gvt Employees in Corrections in 1998	50	8894.2200

Descriptive Statistics

	N	Mean
PRC111 State Correctional Officers in 1998	47	4737.3191
PRC114 State Prisoners per Correctional Officer in 1998	42	4.7738
PRC115 Turnover Rate of Correctional Officers in 1998	40	15.3248
PRC47 Prisoners in State Correctional Institutions: Year End 1998	51	23117.2157
PRC50 State Prisoner Incarceration Rate in 1998	51	396.6471
PRC52 State Prison Population as a % of Highest Capacity 1998	50	109.3900
PRC54 Female State Prisoners Incarceration Rate in 1998	51	48.6012
PRC55 % of Females in State Correctional Institutions in 1998	51	6.5059
PRC58 White State Prisoner Incarceration Rate in 1997	51	211.7059
PRC61 Black State Prisoner Incarceration Rate in 1997	51	1676.0196
PRC63 Prisoners Under Sentence of Death in 1998	38	90.3421
PRC72 Prisoners Executed: 1977 to 1998	51	9.8039
PRC91 Death Rate of State Prisoners per 100,000 Inmates in 1997	51	231.8627
PRC94 Deaths of State Prisoners by AIDS per 100,000 Inmates in 1997	50	10.7600
PRC95 State Prisoner AIDS-Related Death Rate per 100,000 Inmates in 1997	50	29.6400
PRC98 % of State Prison Pop. Known to be HIV Positive 1997	47	1.4951
PRC99 Deaths of State Prisoners by Suicide in 1997	49	3.2449
PRS65 Adults on State Parole in 1998	51	12513.7843
PRS66 Adults on State Probation in 1998	51	66359.9804
PRS69 State & loc Gvt Employees in Corrections in 1996	51	12993.2157
PRS71 State & loc Gvt Expend. for Police Protection 1996	51	876135313.7255
PRS73 State & loc Gvt Expend. for Corrections in 1996	51	735492176.4706
PVS338 % of Population Not Covered by Health Insurance 1998	51	15.0588
PVS500 Poverty Rate (%) in 1998	51	12.7333
PVS501 % of Senior Citizens Living in Poverty in 1998	48	10.7167
PVS502 % of Children Living in Poverty in 1998	51	18.0196
PVS503 % of Families Living in Poverty in 1998	51	9.7686
PVS505 Per Capita State/Local Gvt Expend. for Public Welfare Pgms 1996	51	722.4902
PVS506 % of All State/Local Expend. Spent for Public Welfare Pgms 1996	51	15.8255
PVS508 Per Capita Social Security (OASDI) Payments in 1998	51	1376.5294
PVS511 Average Monthly Social Security (OASDI) Payment in 1998	51	700.5863
PVS513 Medicare Enrollees in 1998	51	737621.4118
PVS514 Medicare Payments per Enrollee in 1998	51	5073.9804
PVS515 % of Population Enrolled in Medicare in 1998	51	14.1510
PVS519 Medicaid Cost per Recipient in 1997	50	3824.9600
PVS520 % of Population Receiving Public Aid in 1998	51	4.6235
PVS522 Avg Monthly Soc Sec Supplemental Security Income 1998	51	335.2314
PVS523 Recipients of Temp Assist to Needy Families (TANF) 1999	51	132817.6471
PVS526 Maximum Monthly TANF Benefit for Family of Three in 1999	51	407.7255
PVS529 Average Monthly Food Stamp Benefit per Recipient in 1999	51	71.1776
PVS530 % of Population Receiving Food Stamps in 1999	51	6.8922
PVS533 % of Households Receiving Food Stamps in 1998	51	8.1216
PVS535 WIC Nutrition Program Avrg Mthly Benefit 1999	51	31.7312
PVS537 Participants in National School Lunch Program in 1999	51	519530.6667
PVS538 Avg Payment per Ntnl School Lunch Program Participant 1999	51	183.9804
PVS539 % of Public Elem & Sec Students Eligible for Free Lunch 1998	42	29.6405
REGION4 Census Region 4 Divisions	51	2.6667
REGION9 Census Region 9 Divisions	51	5.1961
SCS122 Enrollment in Public Elem & Sec Schools in 1999	51	907569.6275
SCS125 Pupil-Teacher Ratio in Public Elem & Sec Schools 1999	51	16.1510
SCS127 Average Salary of Teachers in 1999	51	38492.9412
SCS131 % of Population Graduated from High School as of 1998	51	83.9647
SCS133 ACT Average Composite Scores in 1999	51	21.0784
SCS134 Scholastic Assessment Test (SAT) Scores in 1999	51	1065.9804
SCS139 Per Capita State & Local Govt Expend. - Elem & Sec 1996	51	1053.6078
SCS141 Expend. per Pupil in Elem & Sec Schools 1996	51	6341.9804
SCS143 Per Capita State & loc Gvt Expend. for Higher Educ 1996	51	409.3922
SCS145 Average Student Costs at Public Instit of Higher Educ 1996	49	7486.3061

Descriptive Statistics

	N	Mean
SCS146 Average Student Costs at Private Instit of Higher Educ 1996	50	17043.6000
SCS151 % of Population Graduated from College as of 1998	51	24.0176
SCS153 Rate of Public Libraries and Branches per 10,000 Pop in 1996	51	.8716
SCS156 Per Cap State Art Agencies Legislative Appropriations 1999	51	1.1982
SCS158 Enrollment in Head Start Program in 1998	51	14174.3725

APPENDIX 2: GSS98.SAV FILE INFORMATION

Name

ABANY   ABORTION IF WOMAN WANTS FOR ANY REASON
         Please tell me whether or not you think it should be possible for
         a pregnant woman to obtain a legal abortion if...the woman wants
         it for any reason.
         Measurement Level: Nominal
         Missing Values: 9
         Value   Label
            0   NO
            1   YES
            9 M   MISSING

ABDEFECT   STRONG CHANCE OF SERIOUS DEFECT
         Please tell me whether or not you think it should be possible for
         a pregnant woman to obtain a legal abortion if...there is a
         strong chance of a serious defect in the baby.
         Measurement Level: Nominal
         Missing Values: 9
         Value   Label
            0   NO
            1   YES
            9 M   MISSING

ABHLTH   WOMANS HEALTH SERIOUSLY ENDANGERED
         Please tell me whether or not you think it should be possible for
         a pregnant woman to obtain a legal abortion if...the woman's
         health is seriously endangered by the pregnancy.
         Measurement Level: Nominal
         Missing Values: 9
         Value   Label
            0   NO
            1   YES
            9 M   MISSING

ABNOMORE   MARRIED--WANTS NO MORE CHILDREN
         Please tell me whether or not you think it should be possible for
         a pregnant woman to obtain a legal abortion if...she is married
         and does not want any more children.
         Measurement Level: Nominal
         Missing Values: 9
         Value   Label
            0   NO
            1   YES
            9 M   MISSING

ABPOOR   LOW INCOME--CANT AFFORD MORE CHILDREN
          Please tell me whether or not you think it should be possible for
          a pregnant woman to obtain a legal abortion if...the family has a
          very low income and cannot afford any more children.
          Measurement Level: Nominal
          Missing Values: 9
          Value   Label
              0   NO
              1   YES
              9 M MISSING

ABRAPE   PREGNANT AS RESULT OF RAPE
          Please tell me whether or not you think it should be possible for
          a pregnant woman to obtain a legal abortion if...she became
          pregnant as a result of rape.
          Measurement Level: Nominal
          Missing Values: 9
          Value   Label
              0   NO
              1   YES
              9 M MISSING

AGE   AGE OF RESPONDENT
          Measurement Level: Scale
          Missing Values: 98, 99
          Value   Label
             98 M DK
             99 M NA

AGEKDBRN R'S AGE WHEN 1ST CHILD BORN
          Measurement Level: Scale
          Missing Values: 98, 99
          Value   Label
             98 M DK
             99 M MISSING

ATTEND   HOW OFTEN R ATTENDS RELIGIOUS SERVICES
          How often do you attend religious services?
          Measurement Level: Ordinal
          Missing Values: 9
          Value   Label
              0   NEVER
              1   LT ONCE A YEAR
              2   ONCE A YEAR
              3   SEVRL TIMES A YR
              4   ONCE A MONTH
              5   2-3X A MONTH
              6   NRLY EVERY WEEK
              7   EVERY WEEK
              8   MORE THN ONCE WK
              9 M DK,NA

CHILDS   NUMBER OF CHILDREN
          Measurement Level: Scale
          Missing Values: 9
          Value   Label
             8   EIGHT OR MORE
             9 M   NA

CLASS   SUBJECTIVE CLASS IDENTIFICATION
          If you were asked to use one of four names for your social class,
          which would you say you belong in: the lower class, the working
          class, the middle class, or the upper class?
          Measurement Level: Ordinal
          Missing Values: 5 thru 9, 0
          Value   Label
             0 M   NAP
             1   LOWER CLASS
             2   WORKING CLASS
             3   MIDDLE CLASS
             4   UPPER CLASS
             5 M   NO CLASS
             8 M   DK
             9 M   NA

COHORT   YEAR OF BIRTH
          Measurement Level: Scale
          Missing Values: 9999
          Value   Label
          9999.00 M   MISSING

COLATH   ALLOW ANTI-RELIGIONIST TO TEACH
          There are always some people whose ideas are considered bad or
          dangerous by other people. For instance somebody who is against
          all churches and religion...should such a person be allowed to
          teach in a college or university or not?
          Measurement Level: Nominal
          Missing Values: 9
          Value   Label
             4   ALLOWED
             5   NOT ALLOWED
             9 M   MISSING

COLCOM   SHOULD COMMUNIST TEACHER BE FIRED
          Now I would like to ask you some questions about a man who admits
          he is a communist...suppose he is teaching in a college. Should
          he be fired or not?
          Measurement Level: Nominal
          Missing Values: 9
          Value   Label
             4   FIRED
             5   NOT FIRED
             9 M   MISSING

COLHOMO   ALLOW HOMOSEXUAL TO TEACH
           And what about a man who admits that he is homosexual...should
           such a person be allowed to teach in a college or university or
           not?
           Measurement Level: Nominal
           Missing Values: 9
           Value   Label
               4   ALLOWED
               5   NOT ALLOWED
               9 M   MISSING

COLMIL   ALLOW MILITARIST TO TEACH
           Consider a person who advocates doing away with elections and
           letting the military run the country...should such a person be
           allowed to teach in a college or university or not?
           Measurement Level: Nominal
           Missing Values: 9
           Value   Label
               4   ALLOWED
               5   NOT ALLOWED
               9 M   MISSING

COLRAC   ALLOW RACIST TO TEACH
           Or consider a person who believes that Blacks are genetically
           inferior...should such a person be allowed to teach in a college
           or university or not?
           Measurement Level: Nominal
           Missing Values: 9
           Value   Label
               4   ALLOWED
               5   NOT ALLOWED
               9 M   MISSING

CONDOM   USED CONDOM LAST TIME
           The last time you had sex, was a condom used? By "sex" we mean
           vaginal, oral or anal sex.
           Measurement Level: Nominal
           Missing Values: 9
           Value   Label
               0   NOT USED
               1   USED LAST TIME
               9 M   MISSING

DEGREE   RS HIGHEST DEGREE
           Measurement Level: Ordinal
           Missing Values: 7 thru 9
           Value   Label
               0   LT HIGH SCHOOL
               1   HIGH SCHOOL
               2   JUNIOR COLLEGE
               3   BACHELOR
               4   GRADUATE
               7 M   NAP
               8 M   DK
               9 M   NA

DENOM   SPECIFIC DENOMINATION
               Measurement Level: Ordinal
               Missing Values: 0, 98, 99
               Value   Label
                   0 M   NAP
                  10   AM BAPTIST ASSO
                  11   AM BAPT CH IN USA
                  12   NAT BAPT CONV OF AM
                  13   NAT BAPT CONV USA
                  14   SOUTHERN BAPTIST
                  15   OTHER BAPTISTS
                  18   BAPTIST-DK WHICH
                  20   AFR METH EPISCOPAL
                  21   AFR METH EP ZION
                  22   UNITED METHODIST
                  23   OTHER METHODIST
                  28   METHODIST-DK WHICH
                  30   AM LUTHERAN
                  31   LUTH CH IN AMERICA
                  32   LUTHERAN-MO SYNOD
                  33   WI EVAN LUTH SYNOD
                  34   OTHER LUTHERAN
                  35   EVANGELICAL LUTH
                  38   LUTHERAN-DK WHICH
                  40   PRESBYTERIAN C IN US
                  41   UNITED PRES CH IN US
                  42   OTHER PRESBYTERIAN
                  43   PRESBYTERIAN, MERGED
                  48   PRESBYTERIAN-DK WH
                  50   EPISCOPAL
                  60   OTHER
                  70   NO DENOMINATION
                  98 M   DK
                  99 M   NA

DISCAFF   WHITES HURT BY AFF ACTION
               What do you think the chances are these days that a white person
               won't get a job or promotion while an equally qualified black
               person gets one instead. Is this very likely, somewhat likely,
               or not very likely to happen these days?
               Measurement Level: Nominal
               Missing Values: 0, 8, 9
               Value   Label
                   0 M   NAP
                   1   VERY LIKELY
                   2   SOMEWHAT LIKELY
                   3   NOT VERY LIKELY
                   8 M   DON'T KNOW
                   9 M   NA

DIVORCE   EVER BEEN DIVORCED OR SEPARATED
           Have you ever been divorced or legally separated?
           Measurement Level: Nominal
           Missing Values: 9
           Value   Label
              0   NO
              1   YES
              9 M   MISSING

EDUC   HIGHEST YEAR OF SCHOOL COMPLETED
           Measurement Level: Scale
           Missing Values: 97, 98, 99
           Value   Label
             97 M   NAP
             98 M   DK
             99 M   NA

EVPAIDSX   EVER HAVE SEX PAID FOR OR BEING PAID SINCE 18
           Thinking about the time since your 18th birthday, have you ever
           had sex with a person you paid or who paid you for sex?
           Measurement Level: Nominal
           Missing Values: 9
           Value   Label
              0   NO
              1   YES
              9 M   MISSING

EVSTRAY   HAVE SEX OTHER THAN SPOUSE WHILE MARRIED
           Have you ever had sex with someone other than your husband or
           wife while you were married?
           Measurement Level: Nominal
           Missing Values: 9
           Value   Label
              0   NO
              1   YES
              2   NEVER MARRIED
              9 M   MISSING

FEAR   AFRAID TO WALK AT NIGHT IN NEIGHBORHOOD
           Is there any area right around here - that is, within a mile -
           where you would be afraid to walk alone at night?
           Measurement Level: Nominal
           Missing Values: 9
           Value   Label
              0   NO
              1   YES
              9 M   MISSING

FEHELP   WIFE SHOULD HELP HUSBANDS CAREER FIRST
          Now I'm going to read several more statements. As I read each
          one, please tell me whether you strongly agree, agree, disagree,
          or strongly disagree with it. For example, here is the
          statement: it is more important for a wife to help her husband's
          career than to have one herself.
          Measurement Level: Ordinal
          Missing Values: 0, 8, 9
          Value   Label
             0 M   NAP
             1   STRONGLY AGREE
             2   AGREE
             3   DISAGREE
             4   STRONGLY DISAGREE
             8 M   DK
             9 M   NA

FEPRES   VOTE FOR WOMAN PRESIDENT
          If your party nominated a woman for President, would you vote for
          her if she were qualified for the job?
          Measurement Level: Nominal
          Missing Values: 0, 8, 9
          Value   Label
             0 M   NAP
             1   YES
             2   NO
             5   WOULDN'T VOTE
             8 M   DK
             9 M   NA

FEPRESCH PRESCHOOL KIDS SUFFER IF MOTHER WORKS
          Now I'm going to read several more statements. As I read each
          one, please tell me whether you strongly agree, agree, disagree,
          or strongly disagree with it. For example, here is the
          statement: A preschool child is likely to suffer if his or her
          mother works.
          Measurement Level: Ordinal
          Missing Values: 0, 8, 9
          Value   Label
             0 M   NAP
             1   STRONGLY AGREE
             2   AGREE
             3   DISAGREE
             4   STRONGLY DISAGREE
             8 M   DK
             9 M   NA

FEWORK   SHOULD WOMEN WORK
   Do you approve or disapprove of a married woman earning money in business or industry if she has a husband capable of supporting her?
   Measurement Level: Nominal
   Missing Values: 0, 8, 9
   Value   Label
      0 M   NAP
      1   APPROVE
      2   DISAPPROVE
      8 M   DK
      9 M   NA

GETAHEAD   OPINION OF HOW PEOPLE GET AHEAD
   Some people say that people get ahead by their own hard work: others say that lucky breaks or help from other people are more important. Which do you think is more important?
   Measurement Level: Nominal
   Missing Values: 0, 8, 9
   Value   Label
      0 M   NAP
      1   HARD WORK
      2   BOTH EQUALLY
      3   LUCK OR HELP
      4   OTHER
      8 M   DK
      9 M   NA

GRASS   SHOULD MARIJUANA BE MADE LEGAL
   Do you think marijuana should be made legal or not?
   Measurement Level: Nominal
   Missing Values: 0, 8, 9
   Value   Label
      0 M   NAP
      1   LEGAL
      2   NOT LEGAL
      8 M   DK
      9 M   NA

HAPMAR   HAPPINESS OF MARRIAGE
   Taking things all together, how would you describe your marriage? Would you say that your marriage is very happy, pretty happy, or not too happy?
   Measurement Level: Ordinal
   Missing Values: 0, 8, 9
   Value   Label
      0 M   NAP
      1   VERY HAPPY
      2   PRETTY HAPPY
      3   NOT TOO HAPPY
      8 M   DK
      9 M   NA

HAPPY
: GENERAL HAPPINESS
Taken all together, how would you say things are these days—would you say that you are very happy, pretty happy, or not too happy?
Measurement Level: Ordinal
Missing Values: 0, 8, 9

Value		Label
0	M	NAP
1		VERY HAPPY
2		PRETTY HAPPY
3		NOT TOO HAPPY
8	M	DK
9	M	NA

HOMOSEX
: HOMOSEXUAL SEX RELATIONS
What about sexual relations between two adults of the same sex - do you think it is always wrong, almost always wrong, wrong only sometimes, or not wrong at all?
Measurement Level: Ordinal
Missing Values: 0, 8, 9

Value		Label
0	M	NAP
1		ALWAYS WRONG
2		ALMST ALWAYS WRONG
3		SOMETIMES WRONG
4		NOT WRONG AT ALL
5		OTHER
8	M	DK
9	M	NA

HRS2
: NUMBER OF HOURS USUALLY WORK A WEEK
How many hours a week do you usually work, at all jobs?
Measurement Level: Scale
Missing Values: 98, 99

Value		Label
98	M	DK
99	M	NA

INCOME
: TOTAL FAMILY INCOME
Measurement Level: Ordinal
Missing Values: 0, 98, 99

Value		Label
0	M	NAP
1		LT $1000
2		$1000 TO 2999
3		$3000 TO 3999
4		$4000 TO 4999
5		$5000 TO 5999
6		$6000 TO 6999
7		$7000 TO 7999
8		$8000 TO 9999
9		$10000 - 14999
10		$15000 - 19999
11		$20000 - 24999
12		$25000 OR MORE
13		REFUSED
98	M	DK
99	M	NA

```
INCOME98   TOTAL FAMILY INCOME
           Measurement Level: Ordinal
           Missing Values: 0, 98, 99
           Value     Label
               0 M   NAP
               1     UNDER $1000
               2     $1000 to 2999
               3     $3000 to 3999
               4     $4000 to 4999
               5     $5000 to 5999
               6     $6000 to 6999
               7     $7000 to 7999
               8     $8000 to 9999
               9     $10000 to 12499
              10     $12500 to 14999
              11     $15000 to 17499
              12     $17500 to 19999
              13     $20000 to 22499
              14     $22500 to 24999
              15     $25000 to 29999
              16     $30000 to 34999
              17     $35000 to 39999
              18     $40000 to 49999
              19     $50000 to 59999
              20     $60000 to 74999
              21     $75000 to $89999
              22     $90000 - $109999
              23     $110000 or over
              24 M   REFUSED
              98 M   DK
              99 M   NA


LETDIE1    ALLOW INCURABLE PATIENTS TO DIE
              When a person has a disease that cannot be cured, do you think
              doctors should be allowed by law to end the patient's life by
              some painless means if the patient and the family request it?
           Measurement Level: Nominal
           Missing Values: 9
           Value     Label
               0     NO
               1     YES
               9 M   MISSING


MARITAL    MARITAL STATUS
              What is your current marital status?
           Measurement Level: Nominal
           Missing Values: 9
           Value     Label
               1     MARRIED
               2     WIDOWED
               3     DIVORCED
               4     SEPARATED
               5     NEVER MARRIED
               9 M   NA
```

MATESEX   WAS 1 OF RS PARTNERS SPOUSE OR REGULAR
           (Of the sexual partners you had in the last 12 months) was one of
           the partners your husband or wife or regular sexual partner?
           Measurement Level: Nominal
           Missing Values: 9
           Value   Label
               0   NO
               1   YES
               9 M MISSING

NEWS   HOW OFTEN DOES R READ NEWSPAPER
           How often do you read the newpaper - every day, a few times a
           week, once a week, less than once a week, or never?
           Measurement Level: Ordinal
           Missing Values: 0, 8, 9
           Value   Label
               0 M NAP
               1   EVERYDAY
               2   FEW TIMES A WEEK
               3   ONCE A WEEK
               4   LESS THAN ONCE WK
               5   NEVER
               8 M DK
               9 M NA

NUMMEN   NUMBER OF MALE SEX PARTNERS SINCE 18
           Now thinking about the time since your 18th birthday (including
           the past 12 months) how many male partners have you had sex with?
           Measurement Level: Scale
           Missing Values: 990 thru 999
           Value   Label
           989.00   989 OR HIGHER
           990.00 M   DASH OR SLASH
           991.00 M   SOME,1+
           992.00 M   X
           993.00 M   GARBLED TEXT
           994.00 M   SEVERAL
           995.00 M   MANY,LOTS
           996.00 M   N A
           997.00 M   REFUSED
           998.00 M   DK
           999.00 M   NA

NUMWOMEN   NUMBER OF FEMALE SEX PARTNERS SINCE 18
            Now thinking about the time since your 18th birthday (including
            the past 12 months) how many female partners have you had sex
            with?
            Measurement Level: Scale
            Missing Values: 990 thru 999
            Value   Label
            989.00   989 OR HIGHER
            990.00 M DASH OR SLASH
            991.00 M SOME,1+
            992.00 M X
            993.00 M GARBLED TEXT
            994.00 M SEVERAL
            995.00 M MANY,LOTS
            996.00 M NA
            997.00 M REFUSED
            998.00 M DK
            999.00 M NA

OWNGUN   HAVE GUN IN HOME
            Do you happen to have in your home any guns or revolvers?
            Measurement Level: Nominal
            Missing Values: 3 thru 9, 0
            Value   Label
              0 M NAP
              1   YES
              2   NO
              3 M REFUSED
              8 M DK
              9 M NA

PARSOL   RS LIVING STANDARD COMPARED TO PARENTS
            Compared to your parents when they were the age you are now, do
            you think your own standard of living now is much better,
            somewhat better, about the same, somewhat worse, or much worse
            than theirs was?
            Measurement Level: Ordinal
            Missing Values: 0, 8, 9
            Value   Label
              0 M NAP
              1   MUCH BETTER
              2   SOMEWHAT BETTER
              3   ABOUT THE SAME
              4   SOMEWHAT WORSE
              5   MUCH WORSE
              8 M DK
              9 M NA

PARTNERS   HOW MANY SEX PARTNERS R HAD IN LAST YEAR
                How many sex partners have you had in the last 12 months?
            Measurement Level: Scale
            Missing Values: 98, 99
            Value   Label
                0   NO PARTNERS
                1   1 PARTNER
                2   2 PARTNERS
                3   3 PARTNERS
                4   4 PARTNERS
                5   5-10 PARTNERS
                6   11-20 PARTNERS
                7   21-100 PARTNERS
                8   MORE THAN 100 PARTNERS
                9   1 OR MORE, DK #
               95   SEVERAL
               98 M   DK
               99 M   NA

POLVIEWS   THINK OF SELF AS LIBERAL OR CONSERVATIVE
                We hear a lot of talk these days about liberals and
                conservatives. I'm going to show you a seven point scale on
                which the political views that people might hold are arranged
                from extremely liberal--point 1--to extremely conservative--point
                7. Where would you place yourself on this scale?
            Measurement Level: Ordinal
            Missing Values: 0, 8, 9
            Value   Label
                0 M   NAP
                1   EXTREMELY LIBERAL
                2   LIBERAL
                3   SLIGHTLY LIBERAL
                4   MODERATE
                5   SLGHTLY CONSERVATIVE
                6   CONSERVATIVE
                7   EXTREMELY CONSERVATIVE
                8 M   DK
                9 M   NA

PRAY   HOW OFTEN DOES R PRAY
                How often do you pray?
            Measurement Level: Ordinal
            Missing Values: 0, 8, 9
            Value   Label
                0 M   NAP
                1   SEVERAL TIMES A DAY
                2   ONCE A DAY
                3   SEVERAL TIMES A WEEK
                4   ONCE A WEEK
                5   LT ONCE A WEEK
                6   NEVER
                8 M   DK
                9 M   NA

RACDIF1   DIFFERENCES DUE TO DISCRIMINATION
           On average Blacks have worse jobs, income, and housing than white
           people. Do you think these differences are mainly due to
           discrimination?
           Measurement Level: Nominal
           Missing Values: 9
           Value   Label
               0   NO
               1   YES
               9 M MISSING

RACDIF2   DIFFERENCES DUE TO INBORN DISABILITY
           On average Blacks have worse jobs, income, and housing than white
           people. Do you think these differences are mainly because Blacks
           have less inborn ability to learn?
           Measurement Level: Nominal
           Missing Values: 9
           Value   Label
               0   NO
               1   YES
               9 M MISSING

RACDIF3   DIFFERENCES DUE TO LACK OF EDUCATION
           On average Blacks have worse jobs, income, and housing than white
           people. Do you think these differences are mainly because most
           Blacks don't have the chance for education that it takes to rise
           out of poverty?
           Measurement Level: Nominal
           Missing Values: 9
           Value   Label
               0   NO
               1   YES
               9 M MISSING

RACDIF4   DIFFERENCES DUE TO LACK OF WILL
           On average Blacks have worse jobs, income, and housing than white
           people. Do you think these differences are mainly because most
           Blacks just don't have the motivation or will power to pull
           themselves up out of poverty?
           Measurement Level: Nominal
           Missing Values: 9
           Value   Label
               0   NO
               1   YES
               9 M MISSING

RACE   RACE OF RESPONDENT
           What race do you consider yourself?
           Measurement Level: Nominal
           Missing Values: 0, 8, 9
           Value   Label
               1   WHITE
               2   BLACK
               3   OTHER

RACWORK   RACIAL MAKEUP OF WORKPLACE
    Are the people who work where you work all white, mostly white, about half and half, mostly black, or all black?
Measurement Level: Nominal
Missing Values: 0, 8, 9

Value		Label
0	M	NAP
1		ALL WHITE
2		MOSTLY WHITE
3		HALF WHITE-BLACK
4		MOSTLY BLACK
5		ALL BLACK
6		WORKS ALONE
8	M	DON'T WORK
9	M	NA

RELIG   RS RELIGIOUS PREFERENCE
    What is your religious preference? Is it Protestant, Catholic, Jewish, some other religion, or no religion?
Measurement Level: Nominal
Missing Values: 0, 98, 99

Value		Label
0	M	NAP
1		Protestant
2		Catholic
3		Jewish
4		None
5		OTHER (SPECIFY)
6		BUDDHISM
7		HINDUISM
8		OTHER EASTERN
9		MOSLEM/ISLAM
10		Orthodox-christian
11		Christian
12		NATIVE AMERICAN
13		INTER-NONDENOMINATIONAL
98	M	DK
99	M	NA

RICHWORK   IF RICH, CONTINUE OR STOP WORKING
    If you were to get enough money to live as comfortably as you would like for the rest of your life, would you continue to work or would you stop working?
Measurement Level: Nominal
Missing Values: 0, 8, 9

Value		Label
0	M	NAP
1		CONTINUE WORKING
2		STOP WORKING
8	M	DK
9	M	NA

RIFLE   RIFLE IN HOME
               Do you happen to own a rifle?
            Measurement Level: Nominal
            Missing Values: 0, 8, 9
            Value   Label
               0 M   NAP
               1   YES
               2   NO
               3   REFUSED
               8 M   DK
               9 M   NA

SEI   RESPONDENT SOCIOECONOMIC INDEX
            Measurement Level: Scale

SEX   RESPONDENTS SEX
            Measurement Level: Nominal
            Value   Label
               1   MALE
               2   FEMALE

SEXEDUC   SEX EDUCATION IN PUBLIC SCHOOLS
               Would you be for or against sex education in the public schools?
            Measurement Level: Nominal
            Missing Values: 0, 8, 9
            Value   Label
               0 M   NAP
               1   FAVOR
               2   OPPOSE
               3   DEPENDS
               8 M   DK
               9 M   NA

SEXFREQ   FREQUENCY OF SEX DURING LAST YEAR
               About how ofen did you have sex during the last 12 months?
            Measurement Level: Ordinal
            Missing Values: 8, 9
            Value   Label
               0   NOT AT ALL
               1   ONCE OR TWICE
               2   ONCE A MONTH
               3   2-3 TIMES A MONTH
               4   WEEKLY
               5   2-3 PER WEEK
               6   4+ PER WEEK
               8 M   DK
               9 M   NA

SEXSEX5   SEX OF SEX PARTNERS LAST FIVE YEARS
> Have your sex partners in the last five years been...

Measurement Level: Nominal
Missing Values: 0, 8, 9

Value		Label
0	M	NAP
1		EXCLUSIVELY MALE
2		BOTH MALE AND FEMALE
3		EXCLUSIVELY FEMALE
8	M	DK
9	M	NA

SOCBAR   SPEND EVENING AT BAR
> Would you use this card and tell me which answer comes closest to how often you do the following things...go to a bar or tavern?

Measurement Level: Ordinal
Missing Values: 8, 9

Value		Label
1		ALMOST DAILY
2		SEV TIMES A WEEK
3		SEV TIMES A MNTH
4		ONCE A MONTH
5		SEV TIMES A YEAR
6		ONCE A YEAR
7		NEVER
8	M	DK
9	M	NA

SPANKING   FAVOR SPANKING TO DISCIPLINE CHILD
> Do you strongly agree, agree, disagree, or strongly disagree that it is sometimes necessary to discipline a child with a good, hard spanking?

Measurement Level: Ordinal
Missing Values: 0, 8, 9

Value		Label
0	M	NAP
1		STRONGLY AGREE
2		AGREE
3		DISAGREE
4		STRONGLY DISAGREE
8	M	DK
9	M	NA

SUICIDE1   SUICIDE IF INCURABLE DISEASE
> Do you think a person has the right to end his or her own life if this person...has an incurable disease?

Measurement Level: Nominal
Missing Values: 9

Value		Label
0		NO
1		YES
9	M	MISSING

SUICIDE2   SUICIDE IF BANKRUPT
           Do you think a person has the right to end his or her own life if
           this person...has gone bankrupt?
           Measurement Level: Nominal
           Missing Values: 9
           Value   Label
               0   NO
               1   YES
               9 M   MISSING

SUICIDE3   SUICIDE IF DISHONORED FAMILY
           Do you think a person has the right to end his or her own life if
           this person...has dishonored his or her family?
           Measurement Level: Nominal
           Missing Values: 9
           Value   Label
               0   NO
               1   YES
               9 M   MISSING

SUICIDE4   SUICIDE IF TIRED OF LIVING
           Do you think a person has the right to end his or her own life if
           this person...is tired of living and is ready to die?
           Measurement Level: Nominal
           Missing Values: 9
           Value   Label
               0   NO
               1   YES
               9 M   MISSING

TIMEFAM   TIME R WOULD SPEND ON FAMILY
           Suppose you could change the way you spend your time, spending
           more on some things and less on others. Which of these things on
           the following list would you like to spend more time on, which
           would you like to spend less time on, and which would you like to
           spend the same amount of time as now?...time with your family.
           Measurement Level: Ordinal
           Missing Values: 8, 9
           Value   Label
               0   NO ISSP
               1   SPEND MUCH MORE
               2   SPEND A BIT MORE
               3   SPEND SAME
               4   SPEND A BIT LESS
               5   SPEND MUCH LESS
               8 M   CAN'T CHOOSE
               9 M   NA

TIMEFRND   TIME R WOULD SPEND ON FRIENDS
           Suppose you could change the way you spend your time, spending
           more on some things and less on others. Which of these things on
           the following list would you like to spend more time on, which
           would you like to spend less time on, and which would you like to
           spend the same amount of time as now?...time with your friends.
           Measurement Level: Ordinal
           Missing Values: 8, 9
           Value   Label
             0   NO ISSP
             1   SPEND MUCH MORE
             2   SPEND A BIT MORE
             3   SPEND SAME
             4   SPEND A BIT LESS
             5   SPEND MUCH LESS
             8 M   CAN'T CHOOSE
             9 M   NA

TIMELEIS   TIME R WOULD SPEND ON LEISURE
           Suppose you could change the way you spend your time, spending
           more on some things and less on others. Which of these things on
           the following list would you like to spend more time on, which
           would you like to spend less time on, and which would you like to
           spend the same amount of time as now?...time in leisure
           activities.
           Measurement Level: Ordinal
           Missing Values: 8, 9
           Value   Label
             0   NO ISSP
             1   SPEND MUCH MORE
             2   SPEND A BIT MORE
             3   SPEND SAME
             4   SPEND A BIT LESS
             5   SPEND MUCH LESS
             8 M   CAN'T CHOOSE
             9 M   NA

TIMEPDWK   TIME R WOULD SPEND ON PAID WORK
           Suppose you could change the way you spend your time, spending
           more on some things and less on others. Which of these things on
           the following list would you like to spend more time on, which
           would you like to spend less time on, and which would you like to
           spend the same amount of time as now?...time in a paid job.
           Measurement Level: Ordinal
           Missing Values: 8, 9
           Value   Label
             0   NO ISSP
             1   SPEND MUCH MORE
             2   SPEND A BIT MORE
             3   SPEND SAME
             4   SPEND A BIT LESS
             5   SPEND MUCH LESS
             8 M   CAN'T CHOOSE
             9 M   NA

TVHOURS   HOURS PER DAY WATCHING TV
           On the average day, about how many hours do you personally watch
           television?
           Measurement Level: Scale
           Missing Values: 98, 99
           Value   Label
              98 M DK
              99 M NA

WANTJOB1   WHICH JOB WOULD YOU PREFER
           Measurement Level: Nominal
           Missing Values: 0, 9
           Value   Label
               0 M NAP
               1   A FULL-TIME JOB
               2   A PART-TIME JOB
               3   JOB LESS THAN 10 HRS/WK
               4   NO PAID JOB
               9 M NA

WRKENJOY   ENJOY JOB EVEN IF $ NOT NEEDED
           Thinking of work in general, please circle one number for each
           statement below to show how much you agree or disagree with
           each...I would enjoy having a paying job even if I did not need
           that money.
           Measurement Level: Ordinal
           Missing Values: 8, 9
           Value   Label
               0   NO ISSP
               1   STRONGLY AGREE
               2   AGREE
               3   NEITHER
               4   DISAGREE
               5   STRONGLY DISAGREE
               8 M CAN'T CHOOSE
               9 M NA

XHAUSTN   HOW OFTEN DOES WORK EXHAUST R
           How often do you come home from work exhausted?
           Measurement Level: Ordinal
           Missing Values: 8, 9
           Value   Label
               0   NO ISSP
               1   ALWAYS
               2   OFTEN
               3   SOMETIMES
               4   HARDLY EVER
               5   NEVER
               8 M CAN'T CHOOSE
               9 M NA

```
ZODIAC      RESPONDENTS ASTROLOGICAL SIGN
            Measurement Level: Nominal
            Missing Values: 98, 99
            Value     Label
                0     NAP
                1     ARIES
                2     TAURUS
                3     GEMINI
                4     CANCER
                5     LEO
                6     VIRGO
                7     LIBRA
                8     SCORPIO
                9     SAGITTARIUS
               10     CAPRICORN
               11     AQUARIUS
               12     PISCES
               98 M   DK
               99 M   NA
```

APPENDIX 3: VARIABLE LABEL ABBREVIATIONS

Abbreviation	Text
%	Percent
Adj	Adjusted
Admits	Admissions
Alc&Drug	Alcohol and drug
Avg	Average
Avrg	Average
BW	Black Women
Cap	Capita
DK	Don't Know
Dvision	Division
Ed	Education
Educ	Education
Elem&Sec	Elementary and Secondary
Expend	Expenditures
Gvt	Government
Highe	Higher Education
Individ	Individual
Instit	Institution
Juv	Juvenile
NA	No answer
NAP	Not applicable
Natnl	National
Pop	Population
Public	Public Welfare
RealEst	Real Estate
Rt	Rate
SqMi	Square Mile
Univ	University
Univ&Colleges	Universities and Colleges
Util	Utilities
Vic	Victims
Wel	Welfare
WW	WhiteWomen

Permissions

Variables in the STATES.SAV data are used by permission from Kathleen O'Leary Morgan and Scott Morgan (2000) *State Rankings 2000*, *Crime State Rankings 2000, and Health Care State Rankings 2000*, Morgan Quitno, Lawrence, Kansas.

Variables in the GSS98.SAV data are used by permission from the *Roper Center for Public Opinion Research*, Storrs, Ct. and the National Opinion Research Center at the University of Chicago, Chicago, IL.

Index

25th percentile 51
75th percentile 51

Abstract 182, 183-184
Adjusted R-Square 141
Alpha Coefficient 79
Alternative Hypothesis 88, 98, 113-114
Analysis Syntax Files 77
Anova 113-123
    Assumptions 119-120, 123
        Independence Assumption
        119, 123
        Normality Assumption 120,
        123
    One-way Analysis of Variance 113-
    120
    Post-hoc Tests 113, 118-119, 123
Association 8, 87-90, 91, 102, 121-122, 123,
131-135, 142, 147
    Negative Association 8
    Positive Association 8

B 135-136, 141-142
Bar Chart 39, 57-59, 95-96, 102, 113, 115-
116
Binary Variable 159-160, 172
Box Plot 40, 51-53, 58-59, 113, 115, 117,
123

Case 3, 21-24, 40, 42, 45-46, 48-49
    Adding Cases 28
    Sorting Cases 28-29, 42
Case Summaries 40, 42, 47, 70-73
Categorical Variable 22, 53-59, 68, 87,
90-91, 95-96, 113, 123, 146, 157-159,
161,167, 169
Causality 7-8, 147
Chart Editor 44, 56-58, 95, 101, 116, 138
Chi Square Test 94-95
Class 55, 57
Cleaning Data 73
Coefficient 135-137
    Unstandardized Coefficient 135-136

Also see Linear Regression, Logistic
    Regression
Collinearity 145-146
Conclusion 182, 188
Contingency Cleaning 73
Continuous Variable 22
Control Variable 132, 139, 158
Correlation 87, 96-111, 133-135, 146
    Also see Pearson's Correlation
    Coefficient
Count Variable 22
Cross Tabulations (Crosstabs) 87, 91-95
Curvilinear Relationship 99

Data 2-3
    Missing Data 27, 54-55, 57, 70,
    79, 95, 161, 167
    Also see Data Set
Data Cleaning 42, 73
Data Editor Window 19-30, 77
Data Set 2
    Defining 22-27
    Importing 28
    Loading 22, 29, 40
    Merging 28-29
    Saving 27
Data View Spreadsheet 23, 27
Date Variable Type 25
Datum 2-3
Deductive Approach 6
Degrees of Freedom 145
Dependent Variable 7-8, 49, 93, 101,
131-133, 134-145, 146-147, 157-161, 166
Deterministic Relationship 7
Distribution 39, 40-59
    Bell-shaped Distribution 46, 50-51,
    120, 132-133
    Bimodal Distribution 46
    Negatively Skewed Distribution 46
    Positively Skewed Distribution 46
Dummy Variables 146-147, 148, 157-158,
166-167

Ecological Fallacy 99-100

Empirical 1-2, 186, 191
Evaluation Report 182
Executive Summary 183-184
Experimental Studies 9
Exploratory Data Analysis 6-7
External Validity 188

Findings Section 187-188
Five Number Summary 51-52
Frequency Distribution Table 53-55
    Cumulative Percent 54
    Percent 54
    Valid Percent 54

General Social Survey data (GSS98) 2-3, 53, 213-233
Generalization 188
Graphing 55, 87, 102, 115-116, 137-138, 141-143, 161, 164-166, 170-171
    Also see Bar Chart, Box Plot, Histogram, Pie Chart, Stem and Leaf Plot, Scatter Plot
Goodness of Fit 166
Grounded Theory 6

Histogram 39, 42-44, 46, 55, 57, 58, 74-75, 120, 132, 144-145
Hypothesis 6-7, 139-141, 145, 187, 191-192
    Also see Null Hypothesis, Alternative Hypothesis

Independent Samples T Test 121-122,123
Independent Variable 7-8, 93, 101, 131-137, 139-146, 146, 148, 157-158, 161-163
Index 67, 78-79
Indicator 3, 78-79, 186, 191
Inductive Approach 6
Intercept 135
Interquartile Range (IQR) 51-52
Introduction 182, 185

Linear Regression 131-148
    Adjusted R-Square 141
    Assumptions 132-133,143-145
        Constant Variance 143

    Normality of Residuals 143-145
    B 135-136, 141-142
    Coefficients 135-137, 140-141, 146-147, 148
    Collinearity 145-146
    Constant 135-136
    Degrees of Freedom 145
    Dummy Variables 146-147, 148
    Graphing 137-138, 141-143
    Intercept 135
    Multiple Regression 139-143
    Regression Line 134, 138, 141-144, 148
    R-Square 135, 141, 148
Linear Relationship 96-97, 135, 164
Literature Review 5, 182, 185-186
Log-odds 158-163, 164, 169, 171
Logistic Regression 157-172
    Assumptions 159
    Coefficients 157, 158-172
    Dummy Variables 157-158, 166-167
    Graphing 161, 164-166, 170-171
    Odds 158-160, 161-163, 168-170
    Odds Ratio 161-163, 168-169

Maximum 51
Mean 49-51, 58, 79, 113-123, 141-142, 143, 162, 169-171
Measures of Central Tendency 47-49
Median 49-52, 57, 119
Menu Bar 19, 21
Merging Data 27-28
Methods Section 179-180
Minimum 50
Missing Data 26, 53-54, 67-68, 75
Mode 47, 57
Model Chi Square 163
Multiple Linear Regression 138-143
    Also see Linear Regression
Multivariate Analysis 131-146, 155, 163-168, 184
Mutually Exclusive 157

Nominal Variable 21, 25, 157
Nonspuriousness 7-8

Also see Spurious Relationship
Normality 121, 124, 142-143
Null Hypothesis 86-89, 91, 94-95, 115-116
Numerical Variable 21, 88, 93-99, 115-124, 132, 142, 156-157, 158

Observation 1-2, 40-42, 44, 46-48, 85-86, 117, 121, 142
Odds 156-160, 164-166, 168
       Also see Logistic Regression
Odds Ratio 158-159, 165, 168
       Also see Logistic Regression
One-way Analysis of Variance 115-121, 122
       Also see Anova
Ordinal Variable 21, 25, 158
Outlier 46-47, 49-51, 68, 145
Output Window 29

Paired-Samples T Test 122-123, 124
Pearson's Correlation Coefficient 93-95
       Also see Correlation
Pie Chart 54-55, 57
Possible Code Cleaning 69-70
Post-hoc Tests 115, 119-120, 124
Preparation Syntax Files 74
Printing Data 59
Probabilistic Relationship 6
Probability 86-87, 95, 134, 155-163, 166

Range 50
Rate 69
Recoding Variables 53, 65-68, 76, 93, 115, 156-157, 163-164
Reference Section 181
Regression Line 133, 135-138, 140, 142-143, 146
Reliability 1, 3, 76, 179
Research Question 4-5, 6, 8, 26, 65, 69, 116, 175-181, 183
Research Report 175-182
Residuals 142-143, 146
R-Square 134, 135, 140, 146, 163

Sample Size 87-89, 116-117, 124, 179-180
Scatter Plots 100-102, 133-134, 138, 142-144, 166, 171

Sigmoidal Relationship 161-163
Significance Level 88-90, 95, 102, 115, 118, 121-122, 133, 162
Significance Tests 87-90, 94-95, 99, 102, 115, 134, 139-140, 148, 161, 182, 187-188
Spread 39, 49-52, 57, 116, 118, 183
Spurious Relationship 7-8, 88, 131-132, 145-146, 179
S-shaped Relationship 161
Standard Deviation 49-50, 57, 116-117
STATES Data 2, 30, 193-199
Stem and Leaf Plot 44-45, 57
Syntax Commands 21
Syntax Files 65, 73-75, 76
       Analysis Syntax Files 74
       Notes in Syntax Files 74
       Pasting Computations 76
       Preparation Syntax Files 77-78

Theory 4, 6, 7, 193
Thin Cells 92
Time Order 8-9, 147
Title 56, 58, 95, 182, 183
Tool Bar 21
T Test 113, 121-123
       Independent Samples T Test 121
       Paired-Samples T Test 122-123
Tukey Test 118-119

U-Shaped Relationship 120
Univariate Analysis 39-57, 131, 145, 191
Unstandardized Coefficient 135

Validity 1, 4, 79, 188, 192
Value Label 25
Value Neutral 2
Variable Label 24-25, 30-32, 41, 69-72, 77-79, 165-167, 170
Variable View Spreadsheet 23-26, 70
Variable 3, 21-22, 67-80
       Adding Variables 27-28
       Alphabetizing Variables 40-41
       Binary Variable 157, 159-161, 172
       Categorical Variable 22, 53-59, 68, 87, 90-91, 95-96, 113, 123, 146, 157-159, 161, 167, 169

Computing Variables 71-75
Continuous Variable 22
Control Variable 132, 139, 158
Count Variable 22
Defining Variables 22-27
Deleting Variables 27-28
Dependent Variable 7-8, 49, 93, 101,
131-133, 134-145, 146-147,
157-161, 166
Independent Variable 7-8, 93, 101,

131-137, 139-146,148, 157-158,
161-163
Nominal Variable 22, 26, 161
Numerical Variable 22, 26, 40-52,
55, 67-68, 87, 96-101, 113-123, 143,
157
Ordinal Variable 22, 26, 161
Recoding Variables 55, 67-71, 80,
96, 113, 159,166-167